Charles George Harper

The Portsmouth Road and it's Tributaries

Today and in Days of Old

Charles George Harper

The Portsmouth Road and it's Tributaries
Today and in Days of Old

ISBN/EAN: 9783744678414

Printed in Europe, USA, Canada, Australia, Japan

Cover: Foto ©ninafisch / pixelio.de

More available books at **www.hansebooks.com**

WORKS BY THE SAME AUTHOR.

ENGLISH PEN ARTISTS OF TO-DAY: Examples of their work, with some Criticisms and Appreciations. Super royal 4to, £3 3s. net.

THE BRIGHTON ROAD: Old Times and New on a Classic Highway. With 95 Illustrations by the Author and from old prints. Demy 8vo, 16s.

FROM PADDINGTON TO PENZANCE: The Record of a Summer Tramp. With 105 Illustrations by the Author. Demy 8vo, 16s.

A PRACTICAL HANDBOOK OF DRAWING FOR MODERN METHODS OF REPRODUCTION. Illustrated by the Author and others. Demy 8vo, 7s. 6d.

THE MARCHES OF WALES: Notes and Impressions on the Welsh Borders, from the Severn Sea to the Sands o' Dee. With 115 Illustrations by the Author and from old-time portraits. Demy 8vo, 16s.

REVOLTED WOMAN: Past, Present, and to Come. Illustrated by the Author and from old-time portraits. Demy 8vo, 5s. net.

THE DOVER ROAD: Annals of an Ancient Turnpike. With 100 Illustrations by the Author and from other sources. Demy 8vo. [*In the Press.*

"Till, voe is me, so lubberly,
The cornin came and prissed me."

From a painting by George Morland.

THE PORTSMOUTH ROAD AND ITS TRIBUTARIES: TO-DAY AND IN DAYS OF OLD.

By CHARLES G. HARPER,

AUTHOR OF

The Brighton Road,
The Marches of Wales,
Drawing for Reproduction,
&c., &c., &c.

Illustrated by the Author, and from Old-time Prints and Pictures.

LONDON: CHAPMAN & HALL LIMITED
1895
(All Rights Reserved.)

To HENRY REICHARDT, Esq.

My dear Reichardt,

Here is the result of two years' hard work for your perusal; the outcome of delving amid musty, dusty files of by-gone newspapers; of research among forgotten books, and pamphlets curious and controversial; of country jaunts along this old road both for pleasure's sake and for taking the notes and sketches that go towards making up the story of this old highway.

You will appreciate, more than most, the difficulties of contriving a well-ordered narrative of times so clean forgotten as those of old-road travel, and better still will you perceive the largeness of the task of transmuting the notes and sketches of this undertaking into paper and print. Hence this dedication.

Yours, &c.,
CHARLES G. HARPER.

Preface

THERE has been of late years a remarkable and widespread revival of interest in the old coach-roads of England; a revival chiefly owing to the modern amateur's enthusiasm for coaching; partly due to the healthy sport and pastime of cycling, that brings so many afield from populous cities who would otherwise grow stunted in body and dull of brain; and in degree owing to the contemplative spirit that takes delight in scenes of by-gone commerce and activity, prosaic enough to the most of them that lived in the Coaching Age, but now become hallowed by mere lapse of years and the supersession of horse-flesh by steam-power.

The Story of the Roads belongs now to History, and History is, to your thoughtful man, quite as interesting as the best of novels. Sixty years ago the Story of the Roads was brought to an end, and at that time (so unheeded is the romance of every-day life) it seemed a story of the most commonplace type, not worthy the telling. But we have gained what was of necessity denied our fathers and grand-fathers in this matter—the charm of Historical Perspective, that lends a saving grace to experiences of the most ordinary description, and to happenings the most untoward. Our forebears travelled the roads from necessity, and saw nothing save unromantic discomforts in their journeyings to and fro. We who read the records of their times are apt to lament their passing, and to wish the leisured life and not a few of the usages of our grandfathers back again. The wish is vain, but natural, for it is a characteristic of every succeeding generation to look back lovingly on times past, and in the retrospect to see in roseate colours what was dull and neutral-tinted to folk who lived their lives in those by-gone days.

If we only could pierce to the thought of æons past, perhaps we should find the men of the Stone Age regretting the times of the Arboreal Ancestor, and should discover that distant relative, while swinging by his prehensile tail from the branches of some forest tree, lamenting the careless, irresponsible life of his remote forebear, the Primitive Pre-atomic Globule.

However that may be, certain it is that when our day is done, when Steam shall have been dethroned and natural forces of which we know nothing have revolutionized the lives of our descendants, those heirs of all the ages will look back regretfully upon this Era of ours, and wistfully meditate upon the romantic life we led towards the end of the nineteenth century!

The glamour of old-time travel has appealed to me equally with others of my time, and has led me to explore the old coach-roads and their records. Work of this kind is a pleasure, and the programme I have mapped out of treating all the classic roads of England in this wise, is, though long and difficult, not (to quote a horsey phrase suitable to this subject) all "collar work."

CHARLES G. HARPER.

35, CONNAUGHT STREET, HYDE PARK,
   LONDON, *April* 1895.

LIST of ILLUSTRATIONS

SEPARATE PLATES

		PAGE
1. THE PRESS GANG. *By George Morland.* Frontispiece.		
2. OLD "ELEPHANT AND CASTLE," 1824		22
3. "ELEPHANT AND CASTLE," 1826		30
4. ADMIRAL BYNG		48
5. A STRANGE SIGHT SOME TIME HENCE		52
6. THE SHOOTING OF ADMIRAL BYNG		56
7. WILLIAM PITT		74
8. THE RECRUITING SERGEANT		90
9. ROAD AND RAIL: DITTON MARSH, NIGHT		94
10. THE "NEW TIMES" GUILDFORD COACH		98
11. THE "TALLY-HO" HAMPTON COURT AND DORKING COACH		104
12. MICKLEHAM CHURCH		108
13. BROCKHAM BRIDGE		114
14. ESHER PLACE		120
15. LORD CLIVE		124
16. PRINCESS CHARLOTTE OF WALES		128
17. THE "ANCHOR," RIPLEY		142
18. GUILDHALL, GUILDFORD		148
19. CASTLE ARCH		152
20. AN INN YARD, 1747. *After Hogarth*		162
21. THE "RED ROVER" GUILDFORD AND SOUTHAMPTON COACH		166

		PAGE
22.	ST. CATHERINE'S CHAPEL. *After J. M. W. Turner* .	170
23.	MARY TOFTS . .	178
24.	NEW GODALMING STATION . .	184
25.	THE DEVIL'S PUNCH BOWL . . .	194
26.	HINDHEAD. *After J. M. W. Turner* .	198
27.	TYNDALL'S HOUSE .	208
28.	SAMUEL PEPYS .	236
29.	JOHN WILKES	240
30.	SAILORS CAROUSING. *From a Sketch by Rowlandson* .	252
31.	THE "FLYING BULL" INN . .	268
32.	PETERSFIELD MARKET-PLACE .	278
33.	THE "COACH AND HORSES" INN	298
34.	CATHERINGTON CHURCH	320
35.	AN EXTRAORDINARY SCENE ON THE PORTSMOUTH ROAD. *By Rowlandson* . . .	330
36.	THE SAILOR'S RETURN	334
37.	TRUE BLUE; OR BRITAIN'S JOLLY TARS PAID OFF AT PORTSMOUTH, 1797. *By Isaac Cruikshank* . .	338
38.	THE LIBERTY OF THE SUBJECT, 1782. *By James Gillray* . . .	346

ILLUSTRATIONS IN TEXT

	PAGE
The Revellers	12
Edward Gibbon	19
"Dog and Duck" Tavern	28
Sign of the "Dog and Duck"	29
Jonas Hanway	43
"If the shades of those antagonists foregather"	44
The First Umbrella	46
The "Green Man," Putney Heath	70
The Windmill, Wimbledon Common	74
Mr. Walter Shoolbred	97
Boots at the "Bear"	102
The "Bear," Esher	103
Burford Bridge	111
The "White Horse," Dorking	112
The Road to Dorking	113
Castle Mill	117
Cobham Churchyard	137
Pain's Hill	139
Fame up-to-Date	142
Herbert Liddell Cortis	146
Market-House, Godalming	176
Charterhouse Relics	189
Gowser Jug	190
Wesley	191
Bust of Nelson	192
Tombstone, Thursley	204
Thursley Church	205

	PAGE
Sun-dial, Thursley	206
"Considering Cap"	223
Milland Chapel	260
"The Wakes," Selborne	261
Badge of the Selborne Society	267
The "Flying Bull" Sign	271
The "Jolly Drovers"	272
"Shaved with Trouble and Cold Water"	284
Edward Gibbon	288
Windy Weather	304
Benighted	319
Dancing Sailor	361

THE ROAD TO PORTSMOUTH

	Miles
Stone's End, Borough, to—	
Newington	¼
Vauxhall	1½
Battersea Rise	4
Wandsworth (cross River Wandle)	5½
Tibbet's Corner, Putney Heath	7¾
"Robin Hood," Kingston Vale	9
Norbiton Church	11¼
Kingston Market-place	12
Thames Ditton	13¾
Esher	16
Cobham Street (cross River Mole)	19½
Wisley Common	20¼
Ripley	23½
Guildford (cross River Wey)	29½
St. Catherine's Hill	30½
Peasmarsh Common (cross River Wey)	31¼
Godalming	34
Milford	35¾
Moushill and Witley Commons	36¼
Hammer Ponds	38½
Hindhead (Gibbet Hill)	41¼
Cold Ash Hill and "Seven Thorns" Inn	44¼
Liphook ("Royal Anchor")	46¾
Milland Common	47½
Rake	50¼

	Miles
Sheet Bridge (cross River Rother)	$53\frac{3}{4}$
Petersfield	55
"Coach and Horses"	59
Horndean	$62\frac{1}{2}$
Waterlooville and White Lane End	$65\frac{1}{2}$
Purbrook (cross Purbrook stream)	$66\frac{1}{2}$
Cosham	$68\frac{1}{4}$
Hilsea	$69\frac{1}{2}$
North End	$70\frac{3}{4}$
Landport	$71\frac{1}{2}$
Portsmouth Town	72
Portsmouth, Victoria Pier	73

THE START.

I

THE Portsmouth Road is measured (or was measured when road-travel was the only way of travelling on *terra firma*, and coaches the chiefest machines of progression) from the Stone's End, Borough. It went by Vauxhall to Wandsworth, Putney Heath, Kingston-on-Thames, Guildford, and Petersfield; and thence came presently into Portsmouth through the Forest of Bere and past the frowning battlements of Porchester. The distance was, according to Cary,— that invaluable guide, philosopher, and friend of our grandfathers,—seventy-one miles, seven furlongs; and our forebears who prayerfully entrusted their bodies to the dangers of the roads and resigned their souls to Providence, were hurried along this route at the break-neck speed of something under eight miles an hour, with their hearts in their mouths and their money in their boots for fear of the highwaymen who infested the roads, from London suburbs to the gates of Portsmouth Citadel.

"Cary's Itinerary" for 1821 gives nine hours as the speediest journey performed in that year by what was then considered the meteoric and previously unheard-of swiftness of the "Rocket," which, in that new and most fashionable era of mail and stage-coach travelling, had deserted the grimy and decidedly unfashionable precincts of the Borough and the "Elephant and Castle," for modish Piccadilly. So imagine the "Rocket" (do you not perceive the subtle allusion to speed in that title?) starting from the "White Bear," Piccadilly, which stood where the "Criterion" now soars into the clouds—any morning at nine o'clock, to the flourishes of the guard's "yard of tin," and to the admiration of a motley crowd of 'prentice-boys; Corinthians, still hazy in their ideas and unsteady on their legs from debauches and card-playing in the night-houses of the Haymarket round the corner; and of a frowzy, importunate knot of Jew pedlars, and hawkers of all manner of useful and useless things which might, to a vivid imagination, seem useful on a journey by coach. Away, with crack of whip, tinful, rather than tuneful, fanfare, performed by scarlet-coated, purple-faced guard, and with merry rattle of harness, to Putney, where, upon the Heath, the coach joined the

> "... old road, the high-road,
> The road that's always new,"

thus to paraphrase the poet.

They were jolly coach-loads that fared along the roads in coaching days, and, truly, all their jollity was needed, for unearthly hours, insufficient protection from inclement weather, and the tolerable certainty of falling in with thieves on their way, were experiences and contingencies that, one might imagine, could scarce fail of depressing the most buoyant spirits. But our forebears were composed of less delicate nerves and tougher thews and sinews than ourselves. Possibly they had not our veneer of refinement; they certainly possessed a most happy ignorance of science and art; of microbes, and all the recondite ailments that perplex us moderns, they knew nothing; they did all their work by that glorious rule, the rule of thumb; and for their food, they lived on roast beef and home-brewed ale, and damned kickshaws, new-fangled notions, gentility, and a hundred other innovations whole-heartedly, like so many Cobbetts. And Cobbett, in very truth, is the pattern and exemplar of the old-time Englishman, who cursed tea, paper money, "gentlemen" farmers, and innumerable things that, innovations then, have long since been cast aside as old-fashioned and out of date.

The Englishman of the days of road-travel was a much more robust person than the Englishman of railway times. He had to be! The weaklings were all killed off by the rigours of the undeniably harder winters than we experience to-day, and by the rough-and-ready conditions of existence that made for the survival of the strongest constitutions. Luxurious times and easier conditions of life breed their own peculiar ills, and the Englishman of a hundred years ago was a very fine animal indeed, who knew little of nerves, and, altogether, compared greatly to his own advantage with his neuralgia-stricken descendants of to-day.

Still, our ancestors saw nothing of the romance of their times. That has been left for us to discover, and that glamour in which we see their age is one afforded only by the lapse of time.

No : coaching days had their romance, more obvious perhaps to ourselves than to those who lived in the times of road-travel; but most certainly they had their own peculiar discomforts which we who are hurled at express speed in luxurious Pullman cars, or in the more exclusive and less sociable " first," to our destination would never endure were railways abolished and the coaching era come again. I should imagine that three-fourths of us would remain at home.

Here are some of the coaching miseries experienced by one who travelled before steam had taken the place of good horseflesh, and, sooth to say, there is not much in the nature of romantic glamour attaching to them :—

Misery number one. Although your place has been contingently secured some days before, and although you have risen with the lark, yet you see the ponderous vehicle arrive full. And this, not unlikely, more than once.

2. At the end of a stage, beholding the four panting, reeking, foaming animals which have dragged you

twelve miles, and the stiff, galled, scraggy relay, crawling and limping out of the yard.

3. Being politely requested, at the foot of a tremendous hill, to ease the horses. Mackintoshes, vulcanized india-rubber, gutta-percha, and gossamer dust-coats unknown then.

4. An outside passenger, resolving to endure no longer "the pelting of the pitiless storm," takes refuge, to your consternation, inside; together with his dripping hat, saturated cloak, and soaked umbrella.

5. Set down with a promiscuous party to a meal bearing no resemblance to that of a good hotel, excepting in the charge; and no time allowed in which to enjoy it.

6. Closely packed in a box, "cabin'd, cribb'd, confin'd, bound in," with *five* companions morally or physically obnoxious, for two or three comfortless days and nights.

7. During a halt overhearing the coarse language of the ostlers and the tipplers of the roadside pot-house: and besieged with beggars exposing their horrible mutilations.

8. Roused from your fitful nocturnal slumber by the horn or bugle; the lashing and cracking of whips; the noisy arrivals at turnpike gates, or by a search for parcels (which, after all, are not there) under your seat: to say nothing of solicitous drivers who pester you with their entirely uncalled-for attentions.

9. Discovering, at a diverging-point in your journey, that the "Tally-ho" coach runs only every other day or so, or that it has been finally stopped.

10. Clambering from the wheel by various iron

projections to your elevated seat, fearful, all the while, of breaking your precious neck.

11. After threading the narrowest streets of an ancient town, entering the inn-yard by a low archway, at the imminent risk of decapitation.

12. Seeing the luggage piled "Olympus high," so as to occasion an alarming oscillation.

13. Having the reins and whip placed in your unpractised hands while coachee indulges in a glass and chat.

14. To be, when dangling at the edge of a seat, overcome with drowsiness.

15. Exposed to piercing draughts, owing to a refractory glass; or, *vice versâ*, being in a minority, you are compelled, for the sake of ventilation, to thrust your umbrella accidentally through a pane.

16. At various seasons, suffocated with dust and broiled by a powerful sun; or crouching under an umbrella in a drenching rain—or petrified with cold —torn by fierce winds—struggling through snow— or wending your way through perilous floods.

17. Perceiving that a young squire is receiving an initiatory lesson into the art of driving; or that a jibbing horse, or a race with an opposition coach, is endangering your existence.

18. Losing the enjoyment, or employment, of much precious time, not only on the road, but also from subsequent fatigue.

19. Interrupted by your two rough-coated, big-buttoned, many-caped friends, the coachman and guard, who hope you will remember them before the termination of your hurried meal. Although

the gratuity has been frequently calculated in anticipation, you fail in making the mutual reminiscences agreeable.

Clearly this was no *laudator temporis acti*.

II

But there are two sides to every medal, and it would be quite as easy to draw up an equally long and convincing list of the joys of coaching. It was not always raining or snowing when you wished to go a journey. Highwaymen were always too many, but they did not lurk in every lane; and the coach was not overturned on every journey, nor, even when a coach *did* upset, were the spilled passengers killed and injured with the revolting circumstance and hideous complexity of a railway accident. On a trip by coach, it was possible to see something of the country and to fill one's lungs with fresh air, instead of coal-smoke and sulphur—and so forth, *ad infinitum!*

The Augustan age of coaching,—by which I mean the period when George IV. was king,—was celebrated for the number of gentlemen-drivers who ran smart coaches upon the principal roads from London. Many of them mounted the box-seat for the sake of sport alone: others, who had run through their property and come to grief after the manner of the time, became drivers of necessity. They could fulfil no other useful occupation, for at that day professionalism was confined only to the Ring, and although professors

of the Noble Art of Self-Defence were admired and
(in a sense) envied, they were not gentlemen, judge
them by what standard you please. What was a
poor Corinthian to do? To beg he would have been
ashamed, to dig would have humiliated him no less;
the only way to earn a living and yet retain the
respect of his fellows, was to become a stage-coach-
man. He had practically no alternative. Not yet
had the manly sports of cricket and football produced
their professionals; lawn-tennis and cycling were not
dreamed of, and the professional riders, the "makers'
amateurs," subsidized heavily from Coventry, were a
degraded class yet to be evolved by the young nineteenth century. So coachmen the young Randoms
and Rake-hells of the times became, and let us do
them the justice to admit that when they possessed
handles to their names, they had the wit and right
feeling to see that those accidents of their birth gave
them no licence to assume "side" in the calling they
had chosen for the love of sport or from the spur
of necessity. If they were proud by nature, they
pocketed their pride. They drove their best, took
their fares, and pocketed their tips with the most
ordinary members of the coaching fraternity, and
they were a jolly band. Such were Sir St. Vincent
Cotton; Stevenson of the "Brighton Age," a gradu-
ate he of Trinity College, Cambridge; and Captain
Tyrwhitt Jones.

St. Vincent Cotton, known familiarly to his contemporaries as "Vinny," was one who drove a coach
for a livelihood, and was not ashamed to own it.
He became reduced, as a consequence of his own

folly, from an income of five thousand a year to nothing; but he took Fortune's frowns with all the nonchalance of a true sportsman, and was to all appearance as light-hearted when he drove for a weekly wage as when he handled the reins upon his own drag.

"One day," says one who knew him, "an old friend booked a place and got up on the box-seat beside him, and a jolly five hours they had behind one of the finest teams in England. When they came to their journey's end, the friend was rather put to it as to what he ought to do; but he frankly put out his hand to shake hands, and offered him a sovereign. 'No, no,' said the coachman. 'Put that in your pocket, and give me the half-crown you give to another coachman; and always come by me, and tell all your friends and my old friends to do the same. A sovereign might be all very well for once, but if you think that necessary for to-day you would not like to feel it necessary the many times in the year you run down this way. Half-a-crown is the trade price. Stick to that, and let us have many a merry meeting and talk of old times.'"

"What was right," says our author, "he took as a matter of course in his business, as I can testify by what happened between him and two of my young brothers. They had to go to school at the town to which their old friend the new coachman drove. Of course they would go by him whom they had known all their little lives. They booked their places and paid their money, and were proud to sit behind their friend with such a splendid team.

"The Baronet chaffed and had fun with the boys, as he was always hail-fellow-well-met with every one, old and young, all the way down; and at the end, when he shook hands and did not see them prepare to give him anything, he said, as they were turning away, 'Now, you young chaps, hasn't your father given you anything for the coachman?'

"'Yes,' they said, looking sheepish, 'he gave us two shillings each, but we didn't know what to do: we daren't give it to you.'

"'Oh,' said he, 'it's all right. You hand it over to me and come back with me next holidays, and bring me a coach-full of your fellows. Good-bye.'"

"I drive for a livelihood," said the Baronet to a friend. "Jones, Worcester, and Stevenson have their liveried servants behind, who pack the baggage and take all short fares and pocket all the fees. That's all very well for them. I do all myself, and the more civil I am (particularly to the old ladies) the larger fees I get." And with that he stowed away a trunk in the boot, and turning down the steps, handed into the coach, with the greatest care and civility, a fat old woman, saying as he remounted the box, "There, that will bring me something like a fee."

The Baronet made three hundred a year out of this coach, and got his sport out of it for nothing.

III

THE "Rocket," and the other fashionable West-end coaches of the Regency and George IV.'s reign, scorning the plebeian starting-point of the "Elephant and Castle," whence the second and third-rate coaches, the "rumble-tumbles" and the stage-wagons set out, took their departure from the old City inns, and, calling at the Piccadilly hostelries on their way, crossed the Thames at Putney, even as Captain Hargreaves' modern Portsmouth "Rocket" did in the notable coaching revival some years since, and as Mr. Shoolbred's Guildford coach, the "New Times," does now.

Here they paid their tolls at the old bridge—eighteenpence a time—and laboriously toiled up the long hill that leads to Putney Heath, not without some narrow escapes of the "outsiders" from having their heads brought into sudden and violent contact with the archway of the old toll-house that—though by no means picturesque in itself—was so strange and curious an object in its position, straddling across the roadway.

What Londoner worthy the name does not regret the old crazy, timbered bridge that connected Fulham with Putney? Granted that it was inconveniently narrow, and humped in unexpected places, like a dromedary; conceded that its many and mazy piers obstructed navigation and hindered the tides; allowing every objection against it, old Putney Bridge was infinitely more interesting than the present one of stone that sits so low in the water and offends the eye with its matter-of-fact regularity, proclaiming fat contracts and the unsympathetic baldness of outline characteristic of the engineer's most admired efforts.

Perhaps an artist sees beauty where less privileged people discover only ugliness; how else shall I account for the singular preference of the guide-book, in which I read that "the ugly wooden bridge was replaced in 1886 by an elegant granite structure"?

Old Putney Bridge could never have been anything else than picturesque, from the date of its opening,

THE REVELLERS.

in 1729, to its final demolition twelve years ago: the new bridge will never be less than ugly and formal, and an eyesore in the broad reach that was spanned so finely by the old timber structure for over a hundred and fifty years. The toll for one person walking across the bridge was but a halfpenny, but it frequently happened in the old days that people had not even that small coin to pay their passage, and in such cases it was the recognized custom for the tollman to take their hats for security. The old gatekeepers of Putney Bridge were provided with impressive-looking gowns and wore something the appearance of beadles. Also they were provided with stout staves, which frequently came in useful during the rows which were continually occurring upon the occasions when wayfarers had their hats snatched off. "Your halfpenny or your hat" was an offensive cry, and, together with the scuffles with strayed revellers, left little peace to the guardians of the bridge.

Everything is altered here since the old coaching-days; everything, that is to say, but the course of the river and the trim churches of Fulham and Putney, whose towers rise in rivalry from either shore. And Putney church-tower is altogether dwarfed by the huge public-house that stands opposite: a flaunting insult scarcely less flagrant than the shame put upon the House of God by Cromwell and his fellows who sate in council of war in the chancel, and discussed battles and schemed strife and bloodshed over the table sacred to the Lord's Communion. Putney has suffered from its nearness to London. Where, until ten years ago, old mansions and equally old shops lined its steep High Street, there are now only rows of pretentious frontages occupied by up-to-date butchers and bakers and candlestick-makers; by drapers, milliners, and "stores" of the suburban, or five miles radius, variety. Gone is "Fairfax House," most impressive and dignified of suburban mansions, dating from the time of James I., and sometime the headquarters of the "Army of God and the Parliament"; gone, too, is Gibbon's birthplace, and the very church is partly rebuilt—although *that* is a crime of which our forebears of 1836 are guilty. It is guilt, you will allow, who stand on the bridge and look down upon the mean exterior brick walls of the nave, worse still by comparison with the rough, weathered stones of the old tower. Every part of the church was rebuilt then, except that tower, and though the Perpendicular nave-arcade was set up again, it has been scraped and painted to a newness that seems quite of a piece with other "improvements." All the monuments, too, were moved into fresh places when the general post of that sixty-years-old "restoration" was in progress. The dainty chantry of that notable native of Putney, Bishop West, who died in 1533, was removed from the south aisle to the chancel, and the ornate monument to Richard Lussher placed in the tower, as one enters the church from the street.

Richard Lussher was not a remarkable man, or if he was the memory of his extraordinary qualities has not been handed down to us. But if he was not remarkable, his epitaph is, as you shall judge :—

"Memoriae Sacrum.

"Here lyeth ye body of Ric: Lussher of Puttney in ye Cõnty of Surey, Esq : who married Mary, ye second daughter of George Scott of Staplefoord, tanner, in ye Cõnty of Essex, Esq : he departed y^s lyfe ye 27th of September, An^o 1618. Aetatis sue 30.

> "What tounge can speake ye Vertues of y^s Creature?
> Whose body fayre, whose soule of rarer feature;
> He livd a Saynt, he dyed an holy wight,
> In Heaven on earth a Joyfull heavy sight.
> Body, Soule united, agreed in one.
> Lyke strings well tuned in an unison,
> No discord harsh y^s navell could untye.
> 'Twas Heauen ye earth y^s musick did envye;
> Wherefore may well be sayd he lived well,
> & being dead, ye World his vertues tell."

Some scornful commentator has called this doggerel; but I would that all doggerel were as interesting.

We have already heard of one Cromwell at Putney, but another of the same name, Thomas Cromwell,—almost as great a figure in the history of England as "His Highness" the Protector,—was born here, a good deal over a hundred years before warty-faced Oliver came and set his men in array against the King's forces from Oxford. Thomas was the son of a blacksmith whose forge stood somewhere in the neighbourhood of the Wandsworth Road, on a site now lost; but though of such humble origin he rose to be a successor of Wolsey, that romantic figure whom we shall meet lower down the road, at Esher, who himself was of equally lowly birth, being but the son of a butcher. But while Wolsey,—that "butcher's dogge," as some jealous contemporary called him,—rendered much service to the Church, Cromwell, like his namesake, had a genius for destruction, and became a veritable *malleus ecclesia*. He it was who, unscrupulous and servile in attendance upon the King's freaks, unctuous in flatteries of that Royal paragon of vanity, sought and obtained the Chancellorship of England, by suggesting that Henry should solve all his difficulties with Rome by establishing a national Church of which he should be head. No surer way of rising to the kingly favour could have been devised. Henry listened to his adviser and took his advice, and Thomas Cromwell rose immediately to the highest pinnacle of power, a lofty altitude which in those times often turned men giddy and lost them their heads, in no figurative sense. None so bitter and implacable towards an old faith than those who, having once held it, have from one reason or another embraced new views; and Cromwell was no exception from this rule. He was most zealous and industrious in the work of disestablishing the religious houses, and the most rapacious in securing a goodly share of the spoils. He was a terror to the homeless monks and religious brethren whom his untiring industry had sent to beg their bread upon the roads, and "fierce laws, fiercely executed—an unflinching resolution which neither danger could daunt nor saintly virtue move to mercy— a long list of solemn tragedies weigh upon his memory."

But these topmost platforms were craggy places in Henry VIII.'s time, and the occupants of such dizzy heights fell frequently with a crash that was all the greater from the depth of their fall. Wolsey had been more than usually fortunate in his disgrace, for he was ill, and died from natural causes. When his immediate successor, Sir Thomas More, fell, his life was taken upon Tower Green. "*Decollat,*" says a contemporary document, with a grim succinctness, "*in castrum Londin: vulgo turris appellatur.*" Indeed, this was the common end of all them that walked arm-in-arm with the King, and could have at one time boasted his friendship in the historic phrase, "*Ego et Rex meus.*" Why, the boast was a sure augury of disaster. Wolsey found it so, and so also did More; and now Cromwell was to follow More to the block. That his head fell amid protestations of his belief in the Catholic faith is a singular comment upon the conduct of his life, which was chiefly passed in violent persecutions of its ministers.

Another famous man was born at Putney: Edward Gibbon, the historian. Him also we shall meet at another part of the road, but we may halt awhile to hear some personal gossip at Putney, although it would be vain to seek his birthplace to-day.

He says, in his posthumously-published "Memoirs of My Life and Writings": "I was born at Putney, the 27th of April, O.S., in the year one thousand seven hundred and twenty-seven; the first child of the marriage of Edward Gibbon, Esq., and of Judith Porten. My lot might have been that of a slave, a savage, or a peasant; nor can I reflect without pleasure on the bounty of Nature, which cast my birth in a free and civilized country, in an age of science and philosophy, in a family of honourable rank, and decently endowed with the gifts of fortune. From my birth I have enjoyed the rights of primogeniture; but I was succeeded by five brothers and one sister, all of whom were snatched away in their infancy. My five brothers, whose names may be found in the parish register of Putney, I shall not pretend to lament. . . . In my ninth year," he continues, " in a lucid interval of comparative health, my father adopted the convenient and customary mode of English education; and I was sent to Kingston-upon-Thames, to a school of about seventy boys, which was kept by a Doctor Wooddeson and his assistants. Every time I have since passed over Putney Common, I have always noticed the spot where my mother, as we drove along in the coach, admonished me that I was now going into the world, and must learn to think and act for myself."

At that time of writing he had "not forgotten how often in the year '46 I was reviled and buffetted for the sins of my Tory ancestors." At length, "by the common methods of discipline, at the expence of many tears and some blood, I purchased the knowledge of the Latin syntax; and, not long since, I was possessed of the dirty volumes of Phædrus and Cornelius Nepos, which I painfully construed and darkly understood."

Gibbon's "Miscellaneous Works," published after his death, are prefaced by a silhouette portrait, cut in 1794 by a Mrs. Brown, and reproduced here. Lord Sheffield, who edited the volume, remarks that "the extraordinary talents of this lady have furnished as complete a likeness of Mr. Gibbon, as to person, face, and manner, as can be conceived; yet it was done in his absence." By this counterfeit presentment we see that the author of the "Decline and Fall of the Roman Empire" was possessed of a singular personality, curiously out of keeping with his stately and majestic periods.

This is how Gibbon's personal appearance struck

one of his contemporaries—that brilliant Irishman, Malone:—

"Independent of his literary merit, as a companion Gibbon was uncommonly agreeable. He had an immense fund of anecdote and of erudition of various kinds, both ancient and modern, and had acquired such a facility and elegance of talk that I had always great pleasure in listening to him. The manner and voice, though they were peculiar, and I believe artificial at first, did not at all offend, for they had become so appropriated as to appear natural. His indolence and inattention and ignorance about his own state are scarce credible. He had for five-and-twenty years a hydrocele, and the swelling at length was so large that he quite straddled in his walk; yet he never sought for any advice or mentioned it to his most intimate friend, Lord Sheffield, and two or three days before he died very gravely asked Lord Spencer and him whether they had perceived his malady. The answer could only be, 'Had we eyes?' He thought, he said, when he was at Althorp last Christmas, the ladies looked a little oddly. The fact is that poor Gibbon, strange as it may seem, imagined himself

EDWARD GIBBON.

well-looking, and his first motion in a mixed company of ladies and gentlemen was to the fireplace, against which he planted his back, and then, taking out his snuff-box, began to hold forth. In his late unhappy situation it was not easy for the ladies to find out where they could direct their eyes with safety, for in addition to the hydrocele it appeared after his death that he had a rupture, and it was perfectly a miracle how he had lived for some time past, his stomach being entirely out of its natural position."

For other memories of Gibbon we must wait until we reach his ancestral acres of Buriton, near Petersfield, and meanwhile, we have come to the hill-brow, where the new route and the old meet, and the Portsmouth Road definitely begins.

There are many other memories at Putney; too many, in fact, to linger over, if we wish to come betimes to the dockyard town that is our destination.

So no more than a mention of Theodore Hook, who lived in a little house on the Fulham side of Putney Bridge, which was visited by Barham (dear, genial Tom Ingoldsby!) while rowing up the Thames one fine day. Hook was absent, and Barham wrote some impromptu verses in the hall, beginning—

> "Why, gadzooks! here's Theodore Hook's,
> Who's the author of so many humorous books!"

But the author of those books was the author also of many practical jokes, of which the Berners Street Hoax is still the undisputed classic. But that monumental piece of foolery is not more laughable than the jape he put upon the Putney inn-keeper

(I think he was the landlord of the old "White Lion").

He called one day at that house and ordered an excellent dinner, with wine and all manner of delicacies for one, and having finished his meal and made himself particularly agreeable to the host (who by some singular chance did not know his guest), he suddenly asked him if he would like to know how to be able to draw both old and mild ale from the same barrel. Of course he would! "Then," said Hook, "I'll show you, if you will take me down to your cellar, and will promise never to divulge the secret." The landlord promised. "Then," said the guest, "bring a gimlet with you, and we'll proceed to work." When they had reached the cellar the landlord pointed out a barrel of mild ale, and the stranger bored a hole in one side with the gimlet. "Now, landlord," said he, "put your finger over the hole while I bore the other side." The second hole having been bored, it was stopped, in the same way, by the landlord's finger. "And now," said the stranger, "where's a glass? Didn't you bring one?" "No," said mine host. "But you'll find one up-stairs," replied the guest. "Yes; but I can't leave the barrel, or all the ale will run away," rejoined the landlord. "No matter," exclaimed the stranger, "I'll go for you," and ran up the cellar steps for one. Meanwhile, the landlord waited patiently, embracing the barrel, for five minutes—ten minutes—a quarter of an hour, and then began to shout for the other to make haste, as he was getting the cramp. His shouts at length brought—not the stranger—but his own wife. "Well, where's the glass? where's the gentleman?" said he. "What, the gentleman who came down here with you?" "Yes." "Oh, he went off a quarter of an hour ago. What a pleasant-spoken gent——" "What!" cried the landlord, aghast, "what did he say?" "Why," said his spouse, after considering a moment, "he said you had been letting him into the mysteries of the cellar." "Letting *him* in," yelled the landlord, in a rage, "letting *him* in! Why, confound it, woman, he let *me* in—he's never paid for the dinner, wine, or anything."

When Hook subsequently called upon the landlord and settled his bill, it is said that he and his victim had a good laugh over the affair, but if that tale is true, that landlord must have been a very forgiving man.

IV

LET us now turn our attention to the original route to Portsmouth; the road between the Stone's End, Borough, and Wandsworth. I warrant we shall find it much more interesting than going from the West-end coach-offices with the fashionables; for they were more varied crowds that assembled round the old "Elephant and Castle" than were any of the coach-loads from the "Cross Keys," Cheapside, or from that other old inn of coaching memories, the "Golden Cross," Charing Cross.

Every one journeyed from the "Elephant and Castle" in the old stage-coach days, before the mails were introduced, and this well-known house early became

OLD "ELEPHANT AND CASTLE," 1824.

famous. It was about 1670 that the first inn bearing this sign was erected here, on a piece of waste ground that, although situated so near the borders of busy Southwark, had been, up to the time of Cromwell and the era of the Commonwealth, quite an unconsidered and worthless plot of ground, at one period the practising-ground for archers,—hence the neighbouring title of Newington Butts,—but then barren of everything but the potsherds and general refuse of neighbouring London. In 1658, some one, willing to be generous at inconsiderable cost, gave this Place of Desolation towards the maintenance of the poor of Newington; and it is to be hoped that the poor derived much benefit from the gift. I am, however, not very sure that they found their condition much improved by such generosity. Fifteen years later, things wore a different complexion, for when we hear of the gift being confirmed in 1673, and that the premises of the "Elephant and Castle" inn were but recently built, the prospects of the poor seem to be improving in some slight degree. Documents of this period put the rent of this piece of waste at £5 *per annum!* and this amount had only risen to £8 10*s*. in the space of a hundred years. But so rapidly did the value of land now rise, that in 1776 a lease was granted at the yearly rent of £100; and fourteen years later a renewal was effected for twenty-one years at £190.

The poor of Newington should have been in excellent case by this time, unless, indeed, their numbers increased with the times. And certainly the neighbourhood had now grown by prodigious leaps and bounds, and Newington Butts had now become a busy coaching centre. How rapidly the value of land had increased about this time may be judged from the results of the auction held upon the expiration of the lease in 1811. The whole of the estate was put up for auction in four lots, and a certain Jane Fisher became tenant of "the house called the 'Elephant and Castle,' used as a public-house," for a term of thirty-one years, at the enormously increased rent of £405, and an immediate outlay of £1200. The whole estate realized £623 a year. As shown by a return of charities, printed for the House of Commons in 1868, the "Elephant and Castle" Charity, including fourteen houses and an investment in Government stock, yielded at that time an annual income of £1453 10s. 0d.

The two old views of the "Elephant and Castle" reproduced here, show the relative importance of the place at different periods. The first was in existence until 1824, and the larger house was built two years later. A dreadful relic of the barbarous practice by which suicides were buried in the highways, at the crossing of the roads, was discovered, some few years since, under the roadway opposite the "Elephant and Castle," during the progress of some alterations in the paving. The mutilated skeleton of a girl was found, which had apparently been in that place for considerably over a hundred years. Local gossips at once rushed to the conclusion that this had been some undiscovered murder, but the registers of St. George's Church, Southwark, probably afford a clue to the mystery. The significant entry occurs—

"1666: Abigall Smith, poisoned herself: buried in the highway neere the Fishmongers' Almshouses."

No one has come forward to explain the reason of this particular sign being selected. "Y^t is call'd ye Elephaunt and Castell," says an old writer, "and this is ye cognizaunce of ye Cotelers, as appeareth likewise off ye Bell Savage by Lud Gate;" but this was never the property of the Cutlers' Company, while the site of "Belle Sauvage" is still theirs, and is marked by an old carved stone, bearing the initials "J. A.," with a jocular-looking elephant pawing the ground and carrying a castle.

When the first "Elephant and Castle" was built on this site, the land to the westward as far as Lambeth and Kennington was quite rustic, and remained almost entirely open until the end of last century. Lambeth and Kennington were both villages, difficult of access except by water, and this tract of ground, now covered with the crowded houses of an old suburb, was known as St. George's Fields. It was low and flat, and was traversed by broad ditches, generally full of stagnant water. Roman and British remains have been found here, and it seems likely that some prehistoric fighting was performed on this site, but as all this took place a very long while before the Portsmouth Road was thought of, I shall not propose to go back to the days of Ostorius Scapula or of Boadicea to determine the facts. Instead, I will pass over the centuries until the times of King James I., when there stood in the midst of St. George's Fields, and on the site of Bethlehem Hospital, a disreputable tavern known as the "Dog and Duck," at which no good young man of that period who held his reputation dear would have been seen for worlds.

There still remains, let into the boundary-wall of "Bedlam," the old stone sign of the "Dog and Duck," divided into two compartments; one showing a dog holding what is intended for a duck in his mouth, while the other bears the badge of the Bridge House Estate, pointing to the fact that the property

"DOG AND DUCK" TAVERN.

belonged to that corporation. Duck-hunting was the chiefest amusement here, and was carried on before a company the very reverse of select in the grounds attached to the tavern, where a lake and rustic arbours preceded the establishment of Rosherville.

At later periods St. George's Fields were the scene of "Wilkes and Liberty" riots, and of the lively proceedings of Lord George Gordon's "No Popery" enthusiasts. It is by a singular irony that upon the very spot where forty thousand rabid

Protestants assembled in 1780 to wreak their vengeance upon the Catholics of London, there stands to-day the Roman Catholic cathedral of St. George.

This event brings us to the threshold of the coaching era, for in 1784, four years after the Gordon Riots, mail-coaches were introduced, and the roads were set in order. Years before, when only the slow stages were running, a journey from London to

SIGN OF THE "DOG AND DUCK."

Portsmouth occupied fourteen hours, *if the roads were good!* Nothing is said of the time consumed on the way in the other contingency; but we may pluck a phrase from a public announcement towards the end of the seventeenth century that seems to hint at dangers and problematical arrivals. "Ye 'Portsmouth Machine' sets out from ye Elephant and Castell, and arrives presently *by the Grace of*

God. . . ." In those days men did well to trust to grace, considering the condition of the roads; but in more recent times coach-proprietors put their trust in their cattle and McAdam, and dropped the piety.

A fine crowd of coaches left town daily in the '20's. The "Portsmouth Regulator" left at eight a.m., and reached Portsmouth at five o'clock in the afternoon; the "Royal Mail" started from the "Angel," by St. Clement's, Strand, at a quarter-past seven every evening, calling at the "George and Gate," Gracechurch Street, at eight, and arriving at the "George," Portsmouth, at ten minutes past six the following morning; the "Rocket" left the "Belle Sauvage," Ludgate Hill, every morning at half-past eight, calling at the "White Bear," Piccadilly, at nine, and arriving (quite the speediest coach of this road) at the "Fountain," Portsmouth, at half-past five, just in time for tea; while the "Light Post" coach took quite two hours longer on the journey, leaving London at eight in the morning, and only reaching its destination in time for a late dinner at seven p.m.

The "Night Post" coach, travelling all night, from seven o'clock to half-past seven the next morning, took an intolerable time; the "Hero," which started from the "Spread Eagle," Gracechurch Street, at eight a.m., did better, bringing weary passengers to their destination in ten hours; and the "Portsmouth Telegraph" flew between the "Golden Cross," Charing Cross, and the "Blue Posts," Portsmouth, in nine hours and a half.

"ELEPHANT AND CASTLE," 1826.

V

MANY were the travellers in olden times upon the Portsmouth Road, from Kings and Queens—who, indeed, did not "travel," but "progressed"—to Ambassadors, nobles, Admirals of the Red, the White, the Blue, and sailor-men of every degree. The admirals went, of course, in their own coaches, the captains more frequently in public conveyances, and the common ruck of sailors went, I fear, either on foot, or in the rumble-tumble attached to the hinder part of the slower stages; or even in the stage-wagons, which took the best part of three days to do the distance between the "Elephant and Castle" and Portsmouth Hard. If they had been paid off at Portsmouth and came eventually to London, they would doubtless have walked, and with no very steady step at that, for the furies of Gosport and the red-visaged trolls of Portsea took excellent good care that Jack should be fooled to the top of his bent, and that having been done, there would be little left either for coach journeys or indeed anything else, save a few shillings for that indispensable sailor's drink, rum. So, however Jack might go *down* to Portsmouth, it is tolerably certain that he in many cases either tramped to London on his return from a cruise, or else was carried in one of those lumbering stage-wagons that, drawn by eight horses, crawled over these seventy-three miles with all the airy grace and tripping step of the tortoise. He lay, with one or two companions, upon the noisome straw of the interior, alternately swigging at the rum-bottle which when all else had failed him was his remaining stay, and singing, with husky and uncertain voice, seafaring chanties or patriotic songs, salty of the sea, of the type of the "Saucy Arethusa" or "Hearts of Oak." He was a nauseous creature, full of animal and ardent spirits, redolent of rum, and radiant of strange and most objectionable oaths. He had, perhaps, been impressed into the Navy against his will; had seen, and felt, hard knocks, and expected—nay, hoped—to see and feel more yet, and, whatever might come to him, he did his very best to enjoy the fleeting hour, careless of the morrow. He was frankly Pagan, and fatalist to a degree, but he and his like won our battles by sea and made England mistress of the waves, and so we should contrive all our might to blink his many faults, and apply a telescope of the most powerful kind to a consideration of his sterling virtues of bull-dog courage and cheerfulness under the misfortunes which he brought upon himself.

Marryat gives us in "Peter Simple" a vivid and convincing picture of the sailor going to Portsmouth to rejoin his ship. He must have witnessed many such scenes on his journeys to and from the great naval station, and it is very likely that this incident of the novel was drawn from actual observation.

Peter is setting out for Portsmouth for the first time, and everything is new to him. He starts of course from the time-honoured starting-point of the Portsmouth coaches, the historic "Elephant and Castle"; now, alas! nothing but a huge ordinary "public," where a grimy railway-station and tinkling tram-cars have taken the place of the old stage-coaches.

"Before eight," says Peter, "I had arrived at the 'Elephant and Castle,' where we stopped for a quarter of an hour. I was looking at the painting representing this animal with a castle on its back; and assuming that of Alnwick, which I had seen, as a fair estimate of the size and weight of that which he carried, was attempting to enlarge my ideas so as to comprehend the stupendous bulk of the elephant, when I observed a crowd assembled at the corner; and asking a gentleman who sat by me in a plaid cloak whether there was not something very uncommon to attract so many people, he replied, 'Not very, for it is only a drunken sailor.'

"I rose from my seat, which was on the hinder part of the coach, that I might see him, for it was a new sight to me, and excited my curiosity; when, to my astonishment, he staggered from the crowd, and swore that he'd go to Portsmouth. He climbed up by the wheel of the coach and sat down by me. I believe that I stared at him very much, for he said to me—

"'What are you gaping at, you young sculping? Do you want to catch flies? or did you never see a chap half-seas-over before?'

"I replied, 'that I had never been to sea in my life, but that I was going.'

"'Well then, you're like a young bear, all your sorrows to come—that's all, my hearty,' replied he. 'When you get on board, you'll find monkey's allowance—more kicks than halfpence. I say, you pewter-carrier, bring us another pint of ale.'

"The waiter of the inn, who was attending the coach, brought out the ale, half of which the sailor drank, and the other half threw into the waiter's face, telling him 'that was his allowance. And now,' said he, 'what's to pay?' The waiter, who looked very angry, but appeared too much afraid of the sailor to say anything, answered fourpence: and the sailor pulled out a handful of bank-notes, mixed up with gold, silver, and coppers, and was picking out the money to pay for his beer, when the coachman, who was impatient, drove off.

"'There's cut and run,' cried the sailor, thrusting all the money into his breeches pocket. 'That's what you'll learn to do, my joker, before you have been two cruises to sea.'

"In the meantime the gentleman in the plaid cloak, who was seated by me, smoked his cigar without saying a word. I commenced a conversation with him relative to my profession, and asked him whether it was not very difficult to learn.

"'Larn,' cried the sailor, interrupting us, 'no; it may be difficult for such chaps as me before the mast to larn, but you, I presume, is a reefer, and they a'n't got much to larn, 'cause why, they pipeclays their weekly accounts, and walks up and down with their hands in their pockets. You must larn to chaw baccy, drink grog, and call the cat a beggar, and then you knows all a midshipman's expected to know now-a-days. Ar'n't I right, sir?' said the sailor, appealing to the gentleman in a plaid cloak. 'I axes you, because I see you're a sailor by the cut of your jib. Beg pardon, sir,' continued he, touching his hat, 'hope no offence.'

"'I am afraid that you have nearly hit the mark, my good fellow,' replied the gentleman.

"The drunken fellow then entered into conversation with him, stating that he had been paid off from the 'Audacious' at Portsmouth, and had come up to London to spend his money with his messmates; but that yesterday he had discovered that a Jew at Portsmouth had sold him a seal as gold for fifteen shillings, which proved to be copper, and that he was going back to Portsmouth to give the Jew a couple of black eyes for his rascality, and that when he had done that he was to return to his messmates, who had promised to drink success to the expedition at the 'Cock and Bottle,' St. Martin's Lane, until he should return.

"The gentleman in the plaid cloak commended him very much for his resolution: for he said, 'that although the journey to and from Portsmouth would cost twice the value of a gold seal, yet that in the end it might be worth a *Jew's eye*.' What he meant I did not comprehend.

"Whenever the coach stopped, the sailor called for more ale, and always threw the remainder which he could not drink into the face of the man who brought it out for him, just as the coach was starting off, and then tossed the pewter pot on the ground for him to pick up. He became more tipsy every stage, and the last from Portsmouth, when he pulled out his money he could find no silver, so he handed down a note, and desired the waiter to change it. The waiter crumpled it up and put it into his pocket, and then returned the sailor the change for a one-pound note: but the gentleman in the plaid had observed that it was a five-pound note which the sailor had given, and insisted upon the waiter producing it, and giving the proper change. The sailor took his money, which the waiter handed to him, begging pardon for the mistake, although he coloured up very much at being detected. 'I really beg your pardon,' said he again, 'it was quite a mistake,' whereupon the sailor threw the pewter pot at the waiter, saying, 'I really beg your pardon too,'—and with such force, that it flattened upon the man's head, who fell senseless on the road. The coachman drove off, and I never heard whether the man was killed or not."

"Liberty" Wilkes was a frequent traveller on this road, as also was Samuel Pepys before him; but as I have a full and particular account of them both later on in these pages, at the "Anchor" at Liphook—a house which they frequently patronized,—we may pass on to others who were called this way on business or on pleasure bent. And the business of one very notorious character of the seventeenth century was a most serious affair: nothing, in short, less than murder, red-handed, sudden, and terrible.

John Felton's is one of the most lurid and outstanding figures among the travellers upon the Portsmouth Road. For private and public reasons he conceived he had a right to rid the world of the gay and debonair "Steenie," George Villiers, Duke of Buckingham. Felton at this time was a man of thirty-two, poor and neglected. He was an officer in the army who had chanced, by his surly nature, to offend his superior, one Sir Henry Hungate, a friend of the Duke's, and who effectually prevented his obtaining a command. Felton retired from the service with the rank of lieutenant, disgusted and vindictive at having juniors promoted over his head. Arrears of pay, amounting, according to his own statement, to £80 were withheld from him, and no amount of entreaty could induce the authorities to make payment. Ideas of revenge took possession of him while in London, staying with his mother in an alley-way off Fleet Street. The famous Remonstrance of the Commons presented to the King convinced Felton that to deprive Buckingham of existence was to serve the best interests of the nation, and to this end he determined to set out for Portsmouth, where the Duke lay, directing the expedition for the relief of La Rochelle. He first desired the prayers of the clergy and congregation of St. Bride's for himself, as one wretched and disturbed in mind, and, buying a tenpenny knife at a cutler's upon Tower Hill, he set out, Tuesday, August 19, 1628, upon the road, first sewing the sheath of the knife in the lining of his right-hand pocket, so that with his right hand (the other was maimed) he could draw it without trouble. He also transcribed the opinion of a contemporary polemical writer, that "that man is cowardly and base, and deserveth not the name of a gentleman or soldier, who is not willing to sacrifice his life for his God, his King, and his country," and pinned the paper, together with a statement of his own grievances, upon his hat. He did not arrive at Portsmouth until the next Saturday, having ridden upon horseback so far as his slender funds would carry him, and walking the rest of the way.

Buckingham was staying at a Portsmouth inn—the "Spotted Dog," in High Street—long since demolished. Access to him was easy, among the number who waited upon his favours, and so Felton experienced no difficulty in approaching within easy striking distance. The Duke had left his dressing-room to proceed to his carriage on a visit to the King at Porchester, when, in the hall of the inn, Colonel Friar, one of his intimates, whispered a word in his ear. He turned to listen, and was instantly stabbed by Felton, receiving a deep wound in the left breast; the knife sticking in his heart. Exclaiming "Villain!" he plucked it out, staggered backwards, and falling against a table, was caught in the arms of his attendants, dying almost immediately. No one saw the blow struck, and the cry was raised that it was the work of a Frenchman; but Felton, who had coolly walked from the room, returned, and with equal composure declared himself to be the man. Thus died the gay and profligate Buckingham, in the thirty-seventh year of his age. Surrounded by his friends, his Duchess in an upper room, he was struck down as surely as though his assailant had met him solitary and alone.

Within the space of a few minutes from his falling dead and the removal of his body into an adjoining room, the place was deserted. The very horror of the sudden deed left no room for curiosity. The house, awhile before filled with servants and sycophants, was left in silence.

Many were found to admire and extol Felton and his deed. "God bless thee, little David," said the country folk, crowding to shake his hand as he was conveyed back to London for his trial. "Excellent Felton!" said many decent people in London; and tried to prevent the only possible ending to his career. That end came at Tyburn, where, we are told, "he testified much repentance, and so took his death very stoutly and patiently. He was very long a-dying. His body is gone to Portsmouth, there to be hanged in chains."

VI

AMONG the memorable passengers along the Portsmouth Road in other days who have left any record of their journeys is "that strenuous and painful preacher," the Rev. John Wesley, D.D. On the fifth day of October, 1753, he left the "humane, loving people" of Cowes, "and crossed over to Portsmouth." Here he "found another kind of people" from the complaisant inhabitants of the Isle of Wight. They had, unlike the Cowes people, none of the milk of human kindness in their breasts, or if they possessed any, it had all curdled, for they had "disputed themselves out of the power, and well-nigh the form of religion," as Wesley remarks in his "Journals." So, after the third day among these backsliders and curdled Christians, he shook the dust of Portsmouth (if there was any to shake in October) off his shoes, and departed, riding on horseback to "Godalmin."

We do not meet with him on this road for another eighteen years, when he seems to have found the Portsmouth folk more receptive, for now "the people in general here are more noble than most in the south of England." Curiously enough, on another fifth of October (1771), he " set out at two " from Portsmouth. This was, apparently, two o'clock in the morning, for " about ten, some of our London friends met me at Cobham, with whom I took a walk in the neighbouring gardens "—he refers, doubtless, to the gardens of Pain's Hill, and is speaking of ten o'clock in the morning of the same day; for no one, after a ride of fifty miles, would take walks in gardens at ten o'clock of an October night—" inexpressibly pleasant, through the variety of hills and dales and the admirable contrivance of the whole ; and now, after spending all his life in bringing it to perfection, the grey-headed owner advertises it to be sold ! Is there anything," he asks, "under the sun that can satisfy a spirit made for God ?" This query is no doubt a very correct and moral one, but it seems somewhat cryptic.

Another traveller of a very singular character was Jonas Hanway, who, coming up to town from Portsmouth in 1756, wrote a book purporting to be "A Journal of an Eight Days' Journey from Portsmouth to Kingston-on-Thames." This is a title which, on the first blush, rouses interest in the breast of the historian, for such a book must needs (he doubts not) contain much valuable information relating to this road and old-time travelling upon it. Judge then of his surprise and disgust when, upon a perusal of those ineffable pages, the inquirer into old times and other manners than our own discovers that the author of that book has simply enshrined his not particularly luminous remarks upon things in general in two

volumes of leaded type, and that in all the weary
length of that work, cast in the form of letters addressed to "a Lady," no word appears relating to
roads or travel. Vague discourses upon uninteresting
abstractions make up the tale of his pages, together
with an incredibly stupid "Essay on Tea, considered

JONAS HANWAY.

as pernicious to Health, obstructing Industry, and
Impoverishing the Nation."

The disappointed reader, baulked of his side-lights
on manners and customs upon the road, reflects with
pardonable satisfaction that this book was the occasion of an attack by Doctor Johnson upon Hanway

and his "Essay on Tea." It was not to be supposed
that the Doctor, that sturdy tea-drinker, could silently
pass over such an onslaught upon his favourite beverage. No; he reviewed the work in the "Literary
Magazine," and certainly the author is made to cut
a sorry figure. Johnson at the outset let it be understood that one who described tea as "that noxious
herb" could expect but little consideration from a

"IF THE SHADES OF THOSE ANTAGONISTS FOREGATHER."

"hardened and shameless tea-drinker" like himself,
who had "for twenty years diluted his meals with
only the infusion of this fascinating plant; whose
kettle has scarcely time to cool; who with tea amuses
the evening, with tea solaces the midnight, and with
tea welcomes the morning."

No; Hanway was not successful in his crusade
against tea. As a merchant whose business had
called him from England into Persia and Russia, he

had attracted much attention; for in those days Persia was almost an unknown country to Englishmen, and Russia itself unfamiliar. His first printed work—an historical account of British trade in those regions—was therefore the means of gaining him a certain literary success, which attended none of the seventy other works of which he was the author. Boswell, indeed, goes so far as to say that " he acquired some reputation by travelling abroad, and lost it all by travelling at home;" and Johnson, to whom Hanway addressed an indignant letter, complaining of that unkind review, regarded with contempt one who spoke so ill of the drink upon which he produced so much solid work.

Johnson's defence of tea is vindicated by results; and if the shades of those antagonists foregather somewhere up beyond the clouds, then Ursa Major, over a ghostly dish of his most admired beverage, may point to the astonishing and lasting vogue of the tea-leaf as the best argument in favour of his preference.

Hanway was more successful as Champion of the Umbrella. He was, with a singular courage, the first person to carry an umbrella in the streets of London at a time when the unfurling of what is now become an indispensable article of every-day use was regarded as effeminate, and was greeted with ironical cheers or the savage shouts of hackmen, " Frenchman, Frenchman, why don't you take a coach!" Those drivers of public conveyances saw their livelihood slipping away when folk walked about in the rain, sheltered by the immense structure the umbrella was upon its first introduction: a heavy affair of cane ribs and oiled cloth, with a handle like a broomstick. In fact, the ordinary

THE FIRST UMBRELLA.

umbrella of that time no more resembled the dainty silk affair of modern use than an omnibus resembles a stage-coach of last century. Hanway defended his use of the umbrella by saying he was in delicate health after his return from Persia. Imagine the parallel case of an invalid carrying a heavy modern carriage umbrella, and then you have some sort of an idea of the tax Hanway's *parapluie* must have been upon his strength.

For the rest, Jonas Hanway was a philanthropist who did good in the sight of all men, and was rejoiced beyond measure to find his benevolence famous. He was, in short, one of the earliest among professional philanthropists, and to such good works as the founding of the Marine Society, and a share in the establishment of the Foundling Hospital, he added agitations against the custom of giving vails to servants, schemes for the protection of youthful chimney-sweeps, and campaigns against midnight routs and evening assemblies. Carlyle calls him a dull, worthy man; and he seems to have been, more than aught else, a County Councillor of the Puritan variety, spawned out of all due time. He died, in fact, in 1786, rather more than a hundred years before County Councils were established, and was buried in Westminster Abbey. He was a meddlesome man, without humour, who dealt with a provoking seriousness with trivial things, and was the forerunner and *beau ideal* of all earnest " Progressives."

The year after Jonas Hanway travelled on this road, noting down an infinite deal of nothing with great unction and a portentous gravity, there went down from London to Portsmouth a melancholy cavalcade, bearing a brave man to a cruel, shameful, and unjust death on the quarter-deck of the man-o'-war " Monarque," in Portsmouth Harbour.

Admiral Byng was sent to Portsmouth to be tried by court-martial; and at every stage of his progress there came and clamoured round his guards noisy crowds of people of every rank, who reviled him for a traitor and a coward, and thirsted for his blood in a practical way that only furious and prejudiced crowds could show. Their feeling was intense, and had been wrought to this pitch by the emissaries of a weak but vindictive Government, which sought to cloak its disastrous parsimony and the ill fortunes of war by erecting Byng into a sort of lightning-conductor which should effectually divert the bolts of a popular storm from incapable ministers. And these efforts of Government were, for a time, completely successful. The nation was brought to believe Byng a poltroon of a particularly despicable kind; and the crowds that assembled in the streets of the country towns through which the discredited Admiral was led to his fate were with difficulty prevented from anticipating the duty of the firing-party that on March 14, 1757, woke the echoes of Gosport and Portsmouth with their murderous volley.

Admiral Byng was himself the son of an admiral, who was created Viscount Torrington for his distinguished services. Some of the innumerable caricaturists who earned a blackguardly living by attacking a man who had few friends and powerful enemies, fixed upon his honourable birth as an additional means of wounding him; and thus there exists a rare print entitled "B-ng in Horrors; or T-rr-ngt-n's Ghost," which shows the shade of the father as he

ADMIRAL BYNG.

> Darts through the Caverns of the Ship
> Where *Britain's Coward rides*,"

appearing to his son as he lies captive on board the "Monarque," and reproaching him in a set of verses from which the above lines are an elegant extract.

Other caricatures of the period more justly include ministers in their satire. One is reproduced here, chiefly with the object of showing the pleasing roadside humour of hanging criminals in chains. By this illustration the native ferocity of the eighteenth-century caricaturists is glaringly exemplified. The figure marked *A* is intended for Admiral Lord Anson, *B* is meant for Byng, and *C* represents the Duke of Newcastle, the Prime Minister of the Administration that detached an insufficient force for service in the Mediterranean. The fox who looks up with satisfaction at the dangling bodies is of course intended for Charles James Fox, whose resignation produced the fall of the ministry. The other figures explain themselves by the aid of the labels issuing from their mouths.

And what was Byng's crime, that his countrymen should have hated him with this ferocious ardour? The worst that can be said of him is that he probably felt disgusted with a Government which sent him on an important mission with an utterly inadequate force. His previous career had not been without distinction, and that he was an incapable commander had never before been hinted. He doubtless on this occasion felt aggrieved at the inadequacy of a squadron of ten ships, poorly manned, and altogether ill-found, which he was given to oppose the formidable French armament then fitting at Toulon for the reduction of Minorca, and possibly for a descent upon our own coasts in the event of its first object being attained.

When Byng reached Gibraltar with his wallowing ships and wretched crews, he received intelligence of the French having already landed on the island, and laying siege to Port St. Philip. His duty was to set sail and oppose the enemy's fleet, and thus, if possible, cut off the retreat of their forces already engaged on the island. He had been promised a force from the garrison of Gibraltar, but upon his asking for the men the Governor refused to obey his instructions, alleging that the position of affairs would not allow of his sparing a single man from the Rock. So Byng sailed without his expected reinforcement, and arrived off Minorca too late for any communication to be made with the English Governor, who was still holding the enemy at bay. For as he came in sight of land the French squadron appeared, and the battle that became imminent was fought on the following day.

Byng attacked the enemy's ships vigorously: the French remained upon the defensive, and the superior weight of their guns told so heavily against the English ships that they were thrown into confusion, and several narrowly escaped capture. The Admiral sheered off and held a council of war, whose deliberations resulted four days later in a retreat to Gibraltar, leaving Minorca to its fate. Deprived of outside aid the English garrison capitulated, and Byng's errand had thus failed. He was sent home under arrest, and confined in a room

A STRANGE SIGHT SOME TIME HENCE.

of Greenwich Hospital until the court-martial that was now demanded could be formed.

The action at sea had taken place on May 20, 1756, but the court-martial only assembled at Portsmouth on December 28, and it took a whole month's constant attendance to hear the matter out. The court found Byng guilty of negligence in not having done his utmost in the endeavour to relieve Minorca. It expressly acquitted him of cowardice and disaffection, but condemned him to death under the provisions of the Articles of War, at the same time recommending him to mercy.

But no mercy was to be expected of King, Government, or country, inflamed with rage at a French success, and all efforts, whether at Court or in Parliament, were fruitless. The execution was fixed for March 14, and Byng's demeanour thenceforward was equally unaffected and undaunted. He met his death with a calmness of demeanour and a fortitude of spirit that proved him to be no coward of that ignoble type which fears pain or dissolution as the greatest and most awful of evils. His personal friends were solicitous to avoid anything that might give him unnecessary pain, and one of them, a few days before the end, inventing a pitiful ruse, said to him, " Which of us is tallest ? " " Why this ceremony ? " asked the Admiral. " I know well what it means ; let the man come and measure me for my coffin."

At the appointed hour of noon he walked forth of his cabin with a firm step, and gazed calmly upon the waters of Portsmouth Harbour, alive with boats full of people who had come to see a fellow-creature die.

He refused at first to allow his face to be covered, lest he might be suspected of fear, but upon some officers around him representing that his looks might confuse the soldiers of the firing-party and distract their aim, he agreed to be blindfolded; and thus, kneeling upon the deck, and holding a handkerchief in his hand, he awaited the final disposition of the firing-party that was to send him out of the world by the aid of powder and ball, discharged at the range of half-a-dozen paces. At the pre-arranged signal of his dropping the handkerchief, the soldiers fired, and the scapegoat fell dead, his breast riddled with a dozen bullets.

The execution of Byng was (to adopt Fouché's comment upon the murder of the Duc d'Enghien) worse than a crime; it was a blunder. The ministry fell, and the populace, who had before his death regarded Byng with a consuming hatred, now looked upon him as a martyr. The cynical Voltaire, who had unavailingly exerted himself to save the condemned man (and had thereby demonstrated that your cynic is at most but superficially currish), resumed his cynicism in that mordant passage of "Candide" which will never die so long as the history of the British Fleet is read : "*Dans ce pays-ci,*" he wrote, "*il est bon de tuer de temps en temps un Amiral pour encourager les autres!*"

VII

ONE of the earliest records we have of Portsmouth Road travellers is that which relates to three sixteenth-century inspectors of ordnance:

THE SHOOTING OF ADMIRAL BYNG.

"July 20th, 1532—Paid to X pofer Morys, gonner, Cornelys Johnson, the Maister Smythe, and Henry Johnson for their costs in ryding to Portismouthe to viewe the King's ordenaunce there, by the space of X dayes at Xs' the daye—V li."

So runs the record. But the business of most of them that fared this way whose faring has been preserved was of a very doleful character. I except, of course, royal personages, who, as previously noted in these pages, "progressed," and did nothing so plebeian as to "travel." Monmouth, who, though of royal birth, had failed to achieve a throne in his ill-fated rebellion of 1685, "travelled," "unfriended, melancholy, slow," on that fatal journey from Ringwood to London in a carriage guarded by a strong body of troops and militia-men. Poor fellow! the once gay and handsome Duke of Monmouth, the prettiest fellow and courtliest gallant of a courtly age, was conveyed, a prematurely grey and broken man, to his death, the due reward, it is true, of rebellion, but none the less pathetic. The mournful *cortège* halted a night on the road at Guildford, where, in a room over the great entrance-gateway of Abbot's Hospital, the prisoners—the wretched Monmouth and the undaunted Lord Grey—were lodged, until daylight should come again and their road to execution be resumed.

A more lightsome tour must have been that undertaken by the four Indian kings who, in 1710, came to pay their devoirs to Queen Anne, and journeyed up to London, much to the wonderment of the country-folk, to whose lurid imaginations their copper-coloured countenances represented everything that was evil. Twenty years later seven chiefs of the

Cherokees came this way, on a mission to the English Court; but the first pedestrian of whom we have any account who walked the whole distance between London and Portsmouth was a Mr. John Carter, who, having witnessed the proclamation of George I. in London on August 1, 1714, in succession to Queen Anne, set forth immediately for Portsmouth on foot. It is an emphatic comment upon contemporary social conditions to note that when Carter reached Portsmouth, on August 3, he was the first to bring the news. His zeal might conceivably have been attended with serious consequences had the Jacobites been more active; but as it was, Gibson, the Governor of Portsmouth, an ardent adherent of the Stuarts, threatened the newsmonger with imprisonment for what he was pleased to term " a false and seditious report."

A journey quite in keeping with the sombre history of this road was that by which the body of General Wolfe, the victor of Quebec, was brought to London. The remains of the General were landed at Portsmouth on Sunday, November 17, 1759, and were escorted by the garrison to the outskirts of the town. He was buried at Greenwich on the night of the 20th.

For the rest the history of travel upon the Portsmouth Road in olden times is chiefly made up of accounts of felons condemned to death for crimes ranging from petty larceny to high treason. The halo of a questionable kind of romance has perpetuated the enormities of the greater malefactors, but the sordid histories of the sheep-stealers and cattle-lifters, the miserable footpads, and contemptible minor sneaks and rogues who suffered death and were gibbeted with great profusion and publicity by the wayside, are clean forgotten.

Modern times of road travel, that range from the reign of George IV. to the beginning of the Railway Era, are chiefly filled with stories of the Allied Sovereigns, who ate and drank a great deal too much on their way down to Portsmouth to celebrate the Peace of 1814; of the Duke of Wellington, who followed them in a carriage drawn by eight horses, and ate sparingly and drank little; and of all sorts of naval and military bigwigs and left-handed descendants of Royalty who held fat offices in army or navy, and lorded it grandly over meaner, but more legitimate, mortals. No literary or artistic annals belong to this time, saving only the well-known scenes in "Nicholas Nickleby."

It was on the Portsmouth Road that Nicholas Nickleby and Smike met that redoubtable *impresario*, Mr. Vincent Crummles. Nicholas, it may be remembered, had fallen upon evil times. His capital "did not exceed, by more than a few halfpence, the sum of twenty shillings," and so he and Smike were compelled to foot it from London.

"'Now listen to me, Smike,' said Nicholas, as they trudged with stout hearts onwards. 'We are bound for Portsmouth.'

"Smike nodded his head and smiled, but expressed no other emotion; for whether they had been bound for Portsmouth or Port Royal would have been alike to him, so they had been bound together.

"'I don't know much of these matters,' resumed Nicholas; 'but Portsmouth is a seaport town, and if no other employment is to be obtained, I should think we might get on board some ship. I am young and active, and could be useful in many ways. So could you.' . . . .

"'Do we go all the way to-day?' asked Smike, after a short silence.

"'That would be too severe a trial, even for your willing legs,' said Nicholas, with a good-humoured smile. 'No. Godalming is some thirty and odd miles from London—as I found from a map I borrowed—and I purpose to rest there. We must push on again to-morrow, for we are not rich enough to loiter.' . . . .

"To Godalming they came at last, and here they bargained for two humble beds, and slept soundly. In the morning they were astir: though not quite so early as the sun: and again afoot; if not with all the freshness of yesterday, still, with enough of hope and spirit to bear them cheerily on.

"It was a harder day's journey than that they had already performed, for there were long and weary hills to climb; and in journeys, as in life, it is a great deal easier to go down hill than up. However, they kept on, with unabated perseverance, and the hill has not yet lifted its face to heaven that perseverance will not gain the summit of at last.

"They walked upon the rim of the Devil's Punch Bowl; and Smike listened with greedy interest as Nicholas read the inscription upon the stone which, reared upon that wild spot, tells of a foul and treacherous murder committed there by night. The grass on which they stood had once been dyed with gore; and the blood of the murdered man had run down, drop by drop, into the hollow which gives the place its name. 'The Devil's Bowl,' thought Nicholas, as he looked into the void, 'never held fitter liquor than that!'"

VIII

AND now, having disposed of this batch of travellers, let us ourselves proceed, through Kennington and past Battersea Rise, to Wandsworth. There is, doubtless, much to be said of Kennington, seeing that its name is supposed to derive from *Köningtun,* or "the King's town," but that is no affair of ours; and while its history is much too remote for inclusion in these pages, its present-day appearance does not invite us to linger. But with Wandsworth the case is very different.

Wandsworth is set down at the mouth of a little river whose confluence with the greater Thames determined the precise locality of the first village established on what were, in the far-off days of Wandlesworth, the sedgy banks of the little Wandle. This stream, taking its source from Croydon, "flows ten miles and turns forty mills," and is in our own times perhaps the most despitefully-used river within the London area.

For, at the very beginning of its brief career, the Wandle now rises from a brick culvert beneath a railway embankment, where once its source bubbled up freely in the light of day; and, flowing through

Beddington and Carshalton, comes through Mitcham and Earlsfield to its outlet at Wandsworth, a muddy river, defiled with sewage and the refuse of factories and mills whose produce ranges from linoleum and snuff, to paper, copper, and chemicals of every noxious variety.

There would have been no Wandsworth, either in fact or in name, had there been no Wandle, for the water-power that brought prosperity to the mills also provided a natural outlet for the manufacturers; and so there early grew up a series of wharves by the river's mouth that have done a great quantity of business at any period during these last two hundred years. Aubrey, indeed, says that in his time there were many factories here, and that here were made "brass plates for kettles, skellets, and frying-pans, by Dutchmen, who kept it a mystery." Many of these old Dutchmen's places of business lasted until comparatively recent years, and were known as the "Frying Pan Houses." The greater part, however, of old Wandsworth is gone. Gone, too, is the hamlet of Garratt, whose mock elections of a Mayor caused such convivial excitement a century ago. But a few old houses of a Dutch style of architecture still remain to show what manner of place this was before it had become suburban and its spacious old architecture destroyed to make way for the interminable back streets where City clerkdom dwells in houselets composed of slack-baked bricks built on ash-heaps, "comprising" four cupboards, miscalled "rooms," with what the estate-agent magniloquently terms "the usual domestic offices."

Here and there in the High Street and on Wandsworth Plain stand these remains of Old Wandsworth, and they give a distinct *cachet* to "the village." But the fury of the dabblers in bricks and mortar continues unabated, and they will not last long. One of the oldest houses here was destroyed some years back, and on its site stands a new police-station. This was the well-known "Sword House," which took its name, not from the making of swords, but from a *chevaux de frise* of claymores, of which, up to the beginning of the present reign, some few vestiges were left. The story goes that the occupant of the house was a retired officer of the army who had taken part in the defeat of the Scotch rebels at Culloden, and had collected a number of claymores for the protection of his house at Wandsworth, at that time a secluded place round whose outskirts hung a number of footpads. He defended the outer walls of his residence with these weapons, but they gradually disappeared, being stolen, one by one, by timid and peaceable wayfarers as some sort of protection against the gentry who rendered the suburbs dangerous o' nights.

But if these purlieus were infested by a rascally crew who rendered all the outlying districts notorious for violence and robbery, Wandsworth can at least boast one conspicuously good man. This was that Alderman Henry. Smith whose tomb and effigy are so conspicuous in the parish church. The Alderman was one of the greatest benefactors of the seventeenth century, and left his large estate in trust for the purchase of lands " for setting the poor

F

people a-worke," and in bequests to parishes in Surrey. Henry Smith was a native of Wandsworth, an Alderman of the City of London, and a silversmith. He died in 1627; but in 1620, having neither wife nor children, made a disposition of his property, reserving for himself only sufficient for his personal needs. It is said that every parish in the county of Surrey benefits by his charity, with the sole exception of Mitcham, which owes this unenviable distinction to his having been whipped through its bounds as a common beggar. But how or why came so wealthy and well-considered a man as this respected Alderman of London City to be whipped as a rogue and vagabond? It is an old story which professes to explain this, and it is a story to which so respectable a gentleman as John Evelyn, the diarist, lends his authority, in Aubrey's "Surrey." It is, however, entirely apocryphal. According, then, to John Evelyn, the benefactor was known as "Dog Smith," and was a beggar who wandered through the country accompanied by his dog, and received alms in money and in kind. By this means was his vast fortune supposed to have been amassed. But this tale is too grotesque for belief, put beside the well-known facts of his membership of the Silversmiths' Company, and of his friendship with the Earls of Essex and Dorset, who were also two of the executors of his will. The story of Mitcham may be dismissed when it is learned that the parishes of Surrey certainly owed their bequests to Henry Smith, but that the incidence of them was at the discretion of the trustees.

IX

The parish of Wandsworth extends up to Putney Heath, to which we come up-hill past the singularly-named "Tibbets' Corner." Research has failed to discover who or what was Tibbets, after whom or which the Corner was named; but a familiarity with the old-time character of the neighbourhood suggests that "Tibbets" is merely a corruption of "Gibbets," which were at one time the chiefest features of the landscape in these parts.

Putney Heath was the scene of the notorious Jerry Abershawe's exploits in highway robbery. Where Veitch's nurseries now stand, at the corner of Stag Lane, in Putney Bottom, just before you come to the Beverley Brook, formerly stood the "Bald-faced Stag," or "Half-way House," at one time a notorious house of call for this youthful but daring desperado, who with numerous lesser lights infested the neighbourhood, in the latter half of last century, lurking in the remotenesses of Coombe Wood, and plundering unhappy wayfarers.

There is a story told of this lawless and picturesque figure to the effect that on a dark and inclement night of November, after having stopped every passenger along the road, he was suddenly taken ill and compelled to retire to the shelter of this public-house, standing lonely upon the roadside. His comrades—" pals," he would, doubtless, have called them—sent for a doctor, and a Dr. William Roots attended. He was bled, and the doctor was about to return home, when his patient, with a great appearance of earnestness, said, "You had better, sir, have some one to go back with you, as it is a very dark and lonesome journey." This, however, the doctor declined, remarking that "he had not the least fear, even should he meet with Abershawe

THE "GREEN MAN," PUTNEY HEATH.

himself," little thinking to whom he was speaking. This story was a favourite with Abershawe: it afforded him a reliable criterion of his unholy prowess.

Louis Jeremiah Avershawe—to give him his proper name—was born in 1773, and ended his career with a hempen cravat round his neck on August 3, 1795. He was tried at Croydon Assizes, on July 30, for the murder of David Price, an officer sent to apprehend him in Southwark, whom he had shot; wounding at the same time another officer with a second pistol. A flaw in the indictment acquitted him on the first count, but he was convicted on the charge of feloniously shooting at one Barnaby Taylor. With all his crimes, he was no coward, for, as a contemporary account of his trial says, "When Mr. Baron Penryn put on the black cap, the prisoner, regardless of his sad situation, at the same time put on his own hat, observing the judge with contemptuous looks while he was passing the awful sentence of the law."

He was executed on Kennington Common. Arriving at the gallows, he kicked off his boots and died unshod, to disprove the letter, if not the spirit, of an old warning of his mother's, that he was a bad lad and would die in his shoes. His body was subsequently hanged in chains in Putney Bottom, the scene of his exploits; and the satisfaction with which the passers-by beheld his tattered skeleton, swinging in its iron cage from the gibbet, may well be imagined; although it was not unlikely that, before they had reached the streets of Kingston, or the High Street of Putney, some surviving member of the malefactor's fraternity would exact his unauthorized tolls.

Imagine how palpitating with incertitude the breasts of eighteenth-century travellers must have been when once the oil-lit streets of the towns were left behind. The stage-coach passengers sat glum and nervous,—each suspecting his fellow,—with their money in their boots, their watches in the lining of their hats, and other light valuables secreted in unlikely parts of their persons, in the fond hope that the fine fellow, mounted on a mettlesome horse, and bristling with weapons, who would presently bring the coach to a stop in some gloomy bend of the road, might be either too unpractised or in too great a hurry to think of those very obvious hiding-places. Rarely, at one time, did the mails or the stages escape the highwayman's unwelcome attentions, for, during a lengthy period, the wide, unenclosed waste lands in the neighbourhood of London were the nocturnal resorts of all who desired to better their fortunes at the expense of whoever happened to be travelling upon these lonely roads after nightfall. All the ruined gamesters and unconventional or reckless ne'er-do-wells who could manage to buy, hire, or steal a horse, took to the exciting occupation of highway robbery. This diversion promised at once to be remunerative, and satisfying to the Englishman's sporting instincts, and if the end of it was identical with a rope's end and a morning dance upon nothing, why, the sportsman was unlucky,—and so an end. For although death was the penalty for highway robbery, yet the pursuit of it does not seem to have been looked upon as so very disgraceful; and the bold gentlemen (!) who, well-armed and not ill-horsed, lurked upon Putney Heath or Barnes Common, or any other of the many wildernesses that surrounded London in the midst of last century, were accounted somewhat romantic, even by the contemporaries whose pockets they occasionally lightened.

Believe me, these rascals who hung by the dark

roadside, and, disguised in black crêpe or velvet masks, cried hoarsely in the ears of travellers, "Stand and deliver!" were not the social pariahs they would be to-day, could they revisit their suburban haunts. These fellows robbed the mails " with the utmost regularity and dispatch," and despoiled every one who was not sufficiently well armed to withstand them, without distinction of class or sex. " Purses," says one, who recounts his memories of these times, " rings, watches, snuff-boxes, passed from their owners to the attentive highwayman, almost as soon as the muzzle of his pistol obtruded through the window"; and when at last the poor fellow was lagged, and languished in the stone jug of Newgate, the ladies whom he had relieved, with much politeness, of their money and jewels came and condoled with him, and flaunted their handkerchiefs out of window as he passed one fatal morning to Tyburn in a tumbril, seated on his coffin, with the chaplain beside him, preaching of kingdom-come.

Jerry Abershawe was a hero of this stamp, only he did not make his last appearance on so fashionable a stage as Tyburn. Croydon was the scene of his trial, and Wandsworth, as we have seen, was the place of his taking off.

Two other highwaymen — William Brown and Joseph Witlock — who were both hanged at Tyburn in 1773, for house-breaking, haunted the neighbourhood of Putney Heath and Kingston, and robbed solitary pedestrians or children. They were not of the fine flower of their profession, as one may judge from the evidence given at their trial, by which it appeared that they laid in wait for topers in wayside taverns, and robbed them upon their coming out in a more or less helpless state. Two convivial fellows whom they had seen carousing in the "Green Man" they waited for, and having tied their hands behind their backs, relieved them of some twenty guineas, together with such small

THE WINDMILL, WIMBLEDON COMMON.

odds and ends as knives and tobacco-boxes. A little way further on, upon this occasion, they chanced upon a baker's boy, and disdaining not even the merest trifles, they "persuaded" him to hand over a few halfpence and a silver buckle he was carrying in a bag.

But Putney Heath and the adjoining Wimbledon Common were not notorious only for highwaymen and footpads: they were the favourite meeting-grounds of belligerent gentlemen with an exaggerated and altogether mistaken idea of honour, who faced one another armed with swords or pistols, and fought duels at an early hour of the morning, when courage was apt to be insufficiently warmed. Their notions of honour and "satisfaction" were, possibly, somewhat ridiculous, but it seems to me that a man who would get up at an unearthly hour of the morning, perhaps in the coldest of weather, to shoot at a fellow-creature, or to be shot at by him,—to be run through the body with a rapier, or else to run his opponent through some vital part,—must have been either singularly courageous or peculiarly vindictive.

To either (or both) of these categories, then, must have belonged my Lord Chandos and Colonel Compton, who were among the earliest to be " out " upon this spot. The affair took place in 1652, and was fought with swords, the Colonel being run through the body in a trice. In later times one of the most extraordinary duels of the eighteenth century took place on Wimbledon Common, between the Duke of York and Colonel Lennox, afterwards Duke of Richmond and Viceroy of Ireland. It seems that the Duke of York, with his brother the Prince of Wales (afterwards George IV.), was insulted one night at Vauxhall by two gentlemen and a lady, all three masked, whose identity, although shrewdly suspected, could not be certainly ascertained at the time. They were, as a matter of fact, Lady Charlotte Lennox, who had some grievance against the Prince, and her two brothers, the Duke of Grafton and Lieutenant-Colonel Lennox. Now, the latter being

Lieutenant-Colonel of the Coldstream Guards, of which regiment the Duke of York was full Colonel, was thus in a position of considerable delicacy when his commanding officer took the first opportunity that offered of putting an affront upon him on parade; for if he challenged and killed a Royal Duke in a duel, the severest penalties would no doubt be inflicted upon him,[1] but if, on the other hand, he pocketed the insult, his "honour" was indelibly stained. Colonel Lennox took what he thought the best course, and challenged the Duke of York to a hostile meeting, which duly came off in a dell near where that well-known landmark, the Wimbledon Common windmill, now stands. The seconds were Lord Rawdon and the Earl of Winchilsea, and the weapons chosen were pistols. On the word "Fire!" being given, only the Colonel's pistol was discharged: the Duke not having pulled the trigger, and the Colonel not being desirous of another shot, honour was declared to have been satisfied; the only damage done, according to a contemporary account, being the loss of a curl from his Royal Highness's head. An historian of the duello, however, throws unkind doubts upon this story, and insinuates that the seconds, mindful no less of their own safety than that of the Duke of York, took very good care that the pistols were primed without bullets.

In 1798 Mr. Pitt and Mr. George Tierney, M.P. for Southwark, had a bloodless set-to, and two other

---

[1] It is due, though, to the memory of the Duke of York to state that *he* was content to be regarded in this affair as an ordinary private gentleman.

WILLIAM PITT.

political antagonists — Lord Castlereagh and the jocular George Canning—fought, without a scratch, in 1809. In the same year Lord Paget and Captain Cadogan had a "hostile meeting" here, and exchanged shots without effect, the cause being, not politics this time, but that much more fruitful origin of discord—a woman. Lord Paget, himself a married man, had eloped with Lady Charlotte Wellesley, the wife of his friend Henry Wellesley, and the lady's brother (one would have thought the injured husband should have given battle) decided to avenge the outraged honour of his family. So, as related, the combatants faced one another and fired. The Captain's bullet went wide: my lord's pistol merely flashed, and he, with a spark of right feeling, declined to shoot again at a man whose family he had wronged. Mr. Henry Wellesley, though apparently pusillanimous, was a more formidable, if less romantic, antagonist. That gentleman brought an action for *crim. con.* against Lord Paget, and salved his wounded feelings effectually with a verdict carrying damages to the tune of £20,000.

One of the very few serious encounters that took place here happened to be also the last. This was the duel between General Lorenzo Moore and Mr. Miles Stapylton, fought with pistols on February 13, 1832. The General wounded the civilian, who was seen to fall to the ground by the passengers in the Godalming coach, which happened to be passing at the time. Some of them came to his assistance, conveyed him off in a carriage, and desired the General to consider himself under arrest. General

Moore was ignominiously marched off by a police-constable (so unromantic had the times grown!), and was charged at Kingston. His antagonist, however, becoming better, the man of war was released on bail, and no more was ever heard of the affair.

Mr. Pitt, "the Great Commoner," who fought here without a scratch, was, if not upon his "native heath" (for he was born at Hayes, in Kent), at least within sight of his home. In fact, he practically went forth to do battle at the very gates of Bowling Green House, where he lived—and died, broken-hearted at Napoleon's successes, in later years. The house still stands, altered, 'tis true, but not rebuilt; and the trees that shade its lawn and make beautiful its rearward gardens have in their ranks some that grew here when Pitt was resident under this roof. To call him "master" here were to use the wrong expression, for the private conduct, and the incomings and out-goings of this great man, who made continental alliances and whose political ascendancy set vast armies in motion all over Europe, were very fully ordered by his eccentric and imperious niece, Lady Hester Stanhope, who kept his bachelor household, acted as a secretary, and filled by her own appointment the post of candid friend and adviser. If Pitt endured uncomplainingly all this frank criticism under his own roof-tree, the fact says much for the natural sweetness of his temper; if he followed the advice of his volatile and irresponsible niece, then he must have been weak-minded indeed. But the things that she did and said, and he endured, are written by Lady Hester herself, and no less reliable witness could be cited than she of her uncle's domestic life.

The " Telegraph " inn, that stands so short a distance from Bowling Green House, marks the site of one of the old Admiralty telegraph-towers that were placed in a line between London and Portsmouth, and whence signals were transmitted by semaphores before the introduction of the electric telegraph. Here it was that the anxious politicians gathered while Pitt lay a-dying up the road in January 1806, in his forty-seventh year, struck down by an attack of gout brought on by news of Austerlitz. He received the " heavy news " while at Bath, sent in haste by courier; and shortly afterwards he journeyed home to Putney, whence he was never fated to go, only to his grave. It was on January 12 that he arrived at Bowling Green House, and the first thing that met his gaze when he entered was the map of Europe, hanging in the hall. The sight of it struck the dying man like the thrust of a dagger, for of what use were political divisions and boundaries, now that Napoleon was master? " Roll up that map," he exclaimed; " it will not be wanted these ten years !" On January 23 he was dead, and his last words, " My country, how I leave my country !" show the mental agonies of his passing.

Thus died the greatest statesman of the eighteenth century, and the most precocious in our annals. His opponents held it truth that he died of port wine; his colleagues and his admirers of our own times say his wounded patriotism dealt him the fatal blow; and this last, with some modification, seems the correct view. Port he drank in prodigious quantities : in his childhood it saved his life, and it probably enabled a weakly constitution to hold out for forty-seven years. But save for the coloration of his face, which in later days had a port-wine complexion, his appearance showed nothing of the *viveur*. He was tall, angular, and emaciated, and his features were cast in a most irregular mould. His nose was long and tip-tilted, his face thin and spare, and his upper lip, according to George III. (who certainly should have been an excellent judge of obstinacy, seeing that he was perhaps the most self-willed and unreasonable man of his time), was "d——d long and obstinate." But Pitt's unprepossessing and even mean appearance was redeemed by the fire and brilliancy of his eyes, and the dignity and lofty bearing he assumed in public transfigured the awkward figure that was so severely commented upon in private life.

X

From here, where Pitt died, it is a long and gentle descent to Kingston Vale and the Robin Hood Gate. As you go down, the eye ranges over the hills of Surrey, blue in the distance, and the picturesquely-broken waste of Wimbledon Common appears in the foreground, now all innocent of the bustle and turmoil, the business and the pleasure of the Wimbledon Meeting. Alas! for the days, and still more alas! for the nights, of Wimbledon Camp.

At the foot of the hill, going down from the Heath

to Kingston, there used to stand, beside the road, a mounting-block for assisting horsemen in alighting from or mounting their horses. On it was carved the name of Thomas Nuthall, Surveyor of Rochampton, 1654, with the curious jingle :—

"From London towne to Portse downe
They say 'tis miles three score."

This has disappeared, like many another quaint roadside relic, and there comes now nothing but evidence of suburban activity until Kingston is reached, save indeed the ruined Chapel of St. Mary Magdalene, now a school-house, beside the footpath.

Kingston-on-Thames is still provincial in appearance, though now the centre of a great growth of modern suburbs. Here we are eleven miles from the Borough, and at the end of the first stage out of London in the old days of the mail-coaches. Modern drags, like the "Rocket" Portsmouth coach of some years back, changed at the "Robin Hood," in Kingston Vale, but the coachmen of coaching times made longer stages.

The story of Kingston is a great deal too long for me to dwell upon in these pages, which are not intended for a topographical dictionary. I am, indeed, not at all sure but that a book might not be written upon this old town, both to the advantage of the writer and the inhabitants of this truly royal borough; and here is the suggestion, generously offered to any one who wishes a subject!

Kingston-upon-Thames is so explicitly named in order to distinguish it from the many other Kingstons which loyalty or snobbery (please to take your choice) has created all over England. There is a Kingston near Portsmouth, and the town of Hull was always known as Kingston-upon-Hull until conveniency and democracy conspired together (much, I should imagine, to the delight of Citizen Carnegie, the Almighty Millionaire and Astounding Autocrat of Homestead) to dock it of two-thirds of its name. But the list of Kingstons is too long for this place, and so you are referred to the "Gazetteer" for the rest, while I proceed to delve amid antiquarian matter in respect of the kings whose coronations took place here.

It seems, then, that before their Saxon majesties had conferred this undying distinction upon the town it was (or what little there was of it) called Moreford, from the ford by which Julius Cæsar and his hosts crossed the Thames ; if, indeed, they did not cross at quite a different place, as some antiquaries contend, called Coway Stakes, by Shepperton. When ninth-century Unification prevailed, and the Heptarchy was knocked into a cocked hat, Egbert (only the late Mr. Freeman would have preferred to call him " Ecgbehrt") held a great council here; but that first great Bretwalda was crowned elsewhere, and the Kingston coronations begin in A.D. 900 with Edward the Elder, who sat upon a big stone in the market-place and received his crown amid the acclamations of the people and the confoundedly rough horse-play of the chiefs, who bore him aloft upon a buckler, and (I assure you it was so) tossed him vigorously in the air until the new king became sick and silly, and was devoutly thankful that a Coronation came only once in a lifetime!

I trouble you with these details merely because the stone upon which these kings received their crowns is still in existence in the market-place, enclosed by and mounted on a modern seven-sided pedestal, upon whose every face is carved the name of one of those Seven Kings, fearfully and wonderfully spelled, to the amazement of .the thousands of cyclists who pass by and darkly remember to have heard of Edward the Elder and his successors. When they come and read of Eadweard and similar perversions, they go away, more than ever determined to forget all about the pre-Norman monarchs and to confine their attention to those nineteenth-century bounders, the idols of their little purview—I name the " Makers' Amateurs."

But this Anglo-Saxon line of kings, from Edward the Elder to Edmund the Martyr and Ethelred, is a great deal more interesting than the professional cyclist. True, you cannot well lay a wager about Athelstan or Edred, who have been dead a considerable time, something, in fact, a little under a thousand years,—and they never played things low down for " records " or took sordid cheques or shared in " gate-money "; but they are still interesting, and made things so lively in their days that some of their doings have been handed down through ten centuries —and *that* is a kind of " record " in itself!

The Saxons managed to defeat the Danes here in some great battle, half mythical, half historic, and the old Shrovetide game of football that used to be indulged in, within the town, is supposed to have been derived from the (certainly unchivalric) way in which the townsfolk of that dim era indulged in the sport of kicking the decapitated head of the Danish leader about their streets.

However that may have been, here was the chosen spot of Saxon coronation, and here stands the stone within a modern iron railing which is fondly believed to be of Saxon character. This stone is supposed to have been one of thirteen, originally forming a Druidical circle, and invested with a sacred character, if not a godlike power. Indeed, the connection between sacred stones and coronation stones is very close, for at one time kings were heirs of the gods, and not only pretended to Divine right, but were actually regarded as themselves divine. People, however, shed this last superstition, and began to disregard sacred stones at a comparatively early date, and the other twelve deities or sacred objects of Kingston soon disappeared, for when the townsfolk set about rebuilding their original wooden houses with more enduring materials, they quickly broke up the gods and built walls of their fragments.

Kingston has ever been a place of importance, and its castle (than which no other stronghold in England has so utterly passed away and vanished, even its site being a mere matter of conjecture) was several times captured and recaptured by opposing hosts in the Middle Ages. In later times Kingston became celebrated much in the same way as Yankee Boston leaped into fame; for it was here that the first armed force assembled in the Civil War between Charles I. and his Parliament. Colonel Lunsford and other Royalist officers attempted to seize for the King the store of arms in the town, intending to proceed afterwards to Portsmouth, to hold that fortress in the Royal cause. The King was at that time at Hampton Court. But Lunsford's enterprise failed, for the Parliament got wind of it and speedily arrested him. By a singular coincidence, Kingston was also the scene of one of the last stands of the Royalists, for, in July 1648, a body of some six hundred men was assembled here under the commands of Lord Holland, the second Duke of Buckingham, and his brother, Lord Francis Villiers.

They set out for Carisbrooke, with the object of releasing the King, who was imprisoned there, but a superior force met them at Reigate, and in the last skirmish that followed their retreat to Kingston, Lord Francis Villiers was slain, in a road between the town and Surbiton Common, at a spot long marked by the tree against whose trunk he stood and fought single-handed a hopeless fight against six Roundheads.

"Here," says Aubrey, the historian of Surrey, "was slain the beautiful Francis Villiers, at an elm in the hedge of the east side of the lane; where, his horse being killed under him, he turned his back to the elm, and fought most valiantly with half-a-dozen. The enemy, coming on the other side of the hedge, pushed off his helmet and killed him, July 7, 1648, about six or seven o'clock in the afternoon. On the elm, cut down in 1680, was cut an ill-shaped V for Villiers, in memory of him."

Indeed, Kingston has always been a loyal town, and its people High Tories of a kind that warms my heart towards them when I think of their bravery. Not resting content with appearing in arms against the Parliament, they petitioned in behalf of their King, thereby incurring considerable danger of being "remembered" in no kindly wise by my lords and commons of Puritan sympathies. Their High Toryism and hatred of modernity have been seen in recent times by their objection to having their Corporation reformed, and even in the persecution of cyclists has their bias been shown; but centuries ago these traits took a much less pleasing shape: the whipping and despiteful using of beggars, the ducking of scolds and the plentiful hangings of petty criminals; although, to be sure, there were some kindly souls in the town, as evidenced by the entries given in the parish registers of alms bestowed instead of scourgings, and we have here no such record of brutality as Godalming registers afford. Kingston, being on a well-worn road and itself a considerable place, was in receipt of much custom from wayfarers of every class, travelling to the sea. Here came sea-salts, men-of-war, personages of the highest station, and Dick, Tom, and ragged Harry. The fine old inns that Kingston boasted afford proof of the amount of custom the town enjoyed. Of these, alas! only the "Castle" is left, and that well-known house, going back to Elizabethan times, is cut up into separate tenements.

The travellers who "put up" here must have made a goodly crowd, and were, doubtless, the source of much prosperity to this ancient borough,

"A praty town, by Tamise ripe."

Another kind of mediæval wayfarers (who took away what others brought) were those who went from place to place, collecting alms for the relief of their distresses. These beggars were "briefed" or authorized by the Ecclesiastical Courts to collect alms and solicit aid at any church they might think fit, even at great distances away from their homes.

Thus the country was, before the passing of the Poor Laws, infested with certificated beggars and tramps who, coming with pitiful tales of robbery, disease, and spoliation, worked upon the charitable feelings of country churchwardens, who listened to the woeful tales of mendicants both native and from over sea, and relieved them with a few pence and a "God be with you," passing them over to the next parish, where the process would be repeated. The roads leading to and from the sea-board would be particularly favoured by these unfortunates, and the Portsmouth Road, in especial, must have witnessed at times quite a procession of dolorous alms-seekers telling of sad mishaps on land and sea in foreign climes. Some of the items given in this way are recorded in old parish registers and churchwardens' accounts. Here are some significant extracts from Kingston-upon-Thames records:—

"June 25, 1570. Sonday was her Ihō Jinkin by pattin wch was robbid on the sea by Spanyards.

"February 1571.

"10 Sonday was her a man for his Father who was robbed on the Sey by Lycence from my Lord Admirall."

Here we are not to assume, from the absence of punctuation, that this unfortunate man was robbed by licence from the Admiral, but that this was a variety of licence from the ecclesiastical kind—a kind of secular recommendation to all and sundry, subscribed by the man's commanding officer.

"10 Item was here the proctor of Kingsland beside Knightbrig.

"24 Sonday was here ij weman the mother and dowghter owte of Ireland she called Elynor Salve to gather upon the deathe of her howsbande a gentlman slayne amongst the wylde Iryshe being Captain of Gallyglasses and gathered xviij*d*.

"May 26 Item her was a man from Dorkinge whose howse was brent.

"August 20 Item the proctor of Kingsland was here the Sonday being the 20 of August. In the same day was here ij men being robbid on the Seye."

This licensed mendicancy was finally suppressed by the Act of Parliament, passed in the thirty-ninth year of Queen Elizabeth's reign, " For the Suppressing of Rogues, Vagabonds, and Sturdy Beggars." It begins by setting forth in detail all those who were considered to come under these designations. These were :— "Persons calling themselves scholars, going about begging; all idle persons going about in any country either begging or using any subtil craft or unlawful games or plays, or feigning knowledge in physionomy or palmestry; patent-gatherers; common players of interludes, other than players belonging to any Baron of the Realm; juglers, tinkers, pedlers, and petty chapmen; and generally all wandering persons using, loytering, and refusing to work for reasonable wages, or pretending to be Egyptians. These are to be taken, adjudged, and deemed rogues, vagabonds, and sturdy beggars, and on apprehension to be, by appointment of any justice of the peace, &c.,

being assisted therein with the advice of the minister and one other of the parish, stripped naked, from the middle upward, and openly whipped until his or her body be bloody; and then sent from parish to parish to his or her last residence, and in default of going there within a time limited, to be eftsoons taken and whipped again."

This statute was continued and altered in subsequent reigns, and not repealed until the twelfth year of Queen Anne.

There is an entry in Godalming parish registers, on this very road, which shows that this was no disregarded law. On April 26, 1658, the Godalming authorities seem to have inflicted a peculiarly brutal scourging:—

"Here was taken a vagrant"—says this yellow page, stained with time and grotesque with crabbed writing and singular spelling—"one Mary Parker, Widow, with a Child; and she was wipped according to law, about the age of Thirty years, proper of personage; and she was to goo to the place of her birth, that is, in Grauesend in Kent, and she is limitted to iiij days, and to be caried from Tithing to Tything tell she comes to the end of the s^d jerney."

Oh, those "good old times"!

Other singular entries occur at Kingston. In 1570, for instance, we read that, on October 9—

"Thursday at nyght rose a great winde and rayne that the Temps rosse so hye that they myght row w^t bott^s owte of the Temps a gret waye in to the market place and upon a sodayne."

Two years later, a new cucking-stool was made at the expense of the parish. It cost £1 3s. 4d., and seems to have been freely used. The cucking-stool was a contrivance for the punishment of shrewish women who made such ill use of their tongues as to disturb their neighbours as well as their own families. Wherever there happened to be a pond or watercourse in a parish a post was set up in it; across this post was placed a transverse beam turning on a swivel, with a chair at one end of it, in which when the offender was comfortably placed, that end was turned to the water and let down into it as many times as the occasion was supposed to require.

This new cucking-stool had not long been made when it was brought into use, for, as the registers say—

"1572, August. On Tewsday being the xix day of this monthe of August —— Downing wyfe to —— Downinge gravemaker of this parysshe she was sett on a new cukking stolle made of a grett hythe and so browght a bowte the markett place to Temes brydge and ther had iij Duckinges over hed and eres because she was a common scolde and fyghter."

During the next month the registers give the information that, September 8—

"This day in this towne was kept the Sessions of gayle Delyverye and her was hangyd vj persons and seventeene taken for roges and vagabonds and whippid abowte the market place and brent in the ears."

I think these extracts are sufficient to give a portraiture of the place in olden times. For the Kingston of that remote date it were well not to seek: it has gone with the snows of yester-year and the fallen leaves of autumns past. There hangs to-day, in the Kingston Public Library, an old drawing by a former Secretary of the Royal Academy, which,

THE RECRUITING SERGEANT

although as a drawing it is as bad as may well be, has become, since the old market-place was rebuilt, very valuable as a piece of documentary evidence, showing what Kingston was like in olden times. This is negative praise, but, even so, it is praise to which little of the handiwork of by-past Secretaries of the Royal Academy can attain; for it has ever been the practice of that distinguished body to confer the salaried posts at their disposal upon those of their numerous members who could neither draw nor paint. This old drawing shows dimly what manner of place Kingston was until well on into the last century: the old timbered houses and the projecting signs of the crazy inns making a brave show.

I should suppose it was at Kingston that John Collett conceived the idea of his picture of "The Recruiting Sergeant," reproduced here; for the wagon that stands in the road is labelled "Portsmouth Common Stage Waggon," and the sign of the "Three Jolly Butchers" is clearly a reminiscence of the "Jolly Butchers" at Clattern Bridge.

The recruiting sergeant was a scarcely less familiar figure on the road than the stage-coach a hundred years ago, and a figure, too, that has ever been seized upon by painters and writers alike for sentimental reasons. Has he not been made notorious as "Sergeant Kite," the unscrupulous ruffian who inveigled the country yokel into drink and the acceptance of the King's shilling at the roadside inn? Evidently the painter of this picture was a sentimentalist who regarded the recruiting sergeant in the worst light. The composition and the figures are alike theatrical and conventional. The weeping sweetheart is a figure borrowed from the stage, and so are the two other prominent actors, the Sergeant and the Recruit. The other figures are interesting. In the wagon a fellow is in the act of kissing a girl, while an old woman belabours him about the head. Two children are fearfully feeling the edge of a halberd in the foreground, while a distressed dame—possibly the Recruit's mother—is being comforted by some women friends.

At Kingston we had better take Mr. Shoolbred's "New Times" coach to Guildford. That is to say, if we can find a seat; for this popular drive is patronized so extensively that booking is brisk throughout the coaching season. At eleven o'clock punctually, on every week-day forenoon in the heyday of the year, the "New Times" starts from the "Berkeley" Hotel, Piccadilly. The fame of this sole survivor of the Guildford coaches is of no mere mushroom growth, for it is now over twenty years since Mr. Walter Shoolbred first drove his own teams over this road, so that to-day he is become an institution. Time was (and that but a few years since) when a Portsmouth coach was the delight of the road; but Captain Hargreaves' "Rocket" no longer enlivens the way, and, below Guildford, the Portsmouth Road is unexploited. To-day we fare no farther behind our four-in-hand than Mr. Shoolbred can take us, and he has the route entirely to himself.

It is but rarely that this "well-appointed coach"—to speak after the manner of advertisements—leaves London without a full load or an admiring crowd of onlookers to witness its departure, and you feel yourself

ROAD AND RAIL: DITTON MARSH, NIGHT.

(wrongly, it may well be) an essential part of the performance, as, perched on the box-seat beside the driver, you are driven through the thronging traffic of a May morning in Piccadilly. Not until the streets of London are left behind us do the clean-limbed

MR. WALTER SHOOLBRED.

chestnuts of our team have the opportunity of showing their paces; but Kingston Vale is done smartly, and Kingston itself reached at 12.8. Presently we are out upon Ditton Marsh, flat and broad and sombre, and we bowl along here at a fine round pace until we reach the foot of the ascent where, outside a roadside public-house—the "Orleans Arms"—stands a huge stone post, a century old, carved with the names and distances of many towns and villages, and known as the "White Lady" milestone.

Away to the right lies Thames Ditton, beloved of Theodore Hook and a certain "lazy minstrel," well known to fame in these days, Mr. Ashby Sterry. There also lived at Ditton, during the early part of this present century, that eminent lawyer, Sir Edward Sugden, afterwards Lord St. Leonards, and Lord Chancellor of England. His career was an example of the rise of worth, for he was the son of a hairdresser in Duke Street, Piccadilly, and won his way by the sole aid of his own bright intellect. But, on the other hand, he remains the most dreadful example of the man who draws his own will, and thus gives rise to wasteful litigation with his testamentary incoherencies. He was also the victim of a particularly odious witticism while living here. It shall be recounted, to the perpetual infamy and dishonour of the man who uttered it. Theodore Hook and Croker were on one occasion the guests of Sir Edward Sugden at Boyle Farm. They were admiring a very beautiful vase that stood in the hall, and Sir Edward told them it was a copy of the celebrated Warwick vase. "Yes," said Croker, "it is extremely handsome; but don't you think a facsimile of the Barberini vase would have been more appropriate to the place?" I do not remember to have heard if Sugden kicked his unmannerly guest: if he did *not*, I regret the omission.

On the way to Esher, up the hillside, the coach passes the entrance-gates of Sandown Park, that most

THE "NEW TIMES" GUILDFORD COACH.

fashionable of race-courses, opened in 1870, and ever since then the "ladies' race-course" *par excellence*. Those ornamental iron gates that face the road have a history: they came from Baron Albert Grant's mansion, Kensington House, that stood where now Kensington Court faces the Gardens and the old Palace.

At Esher we make our second change, at that old-fashioned hostelry the "Bear," and are shown those religiously preserved boots worn by the post-boy who drove Philippe Egalité to Claremont in 1848, when escaping "the red fool-fury of the Seine," then at flood-tide. These are boots indeed, and more resemble the huge jack-boots in which Marlborough's soldiers won Ramilies and Malplaquet, than nineteenth-century foot-gear. The "Bear" is one of the finest of the old inns that ornament this old road, and its stables, large enough, as the proprietor says, to hold a hundred horses, are a sight to see.

Esher is a pleasant village, prettily rural, with a humble old church behind that old coaching inn the "Bear," and a newer church, not at all humble, across the way. Nearly all the monuments have been removed to the new building; the most notable among them an elaborate memorial to Richard Drake, Equerry to Queen Elizabeth, and father of the famous Sir Francis Drake, who caused it to be placed in the old church. Some minor literary lights, too, are buried here, among them Samuel Warren, Q.C., Recorder of Hull and Master in Lunacy, who was born in 1807. This literary character and legal luminary (of no great brilliancy, indeed) lived until 1877, when his feeble flicker was finally dowsed in death. The injunction "de mortuis" is kindly, but I cannot refrain from remarking here that I have seen this shining light of law and letters characterized

BOOTS AT THE "BEAR."

in print as a "pompous ass." What else but pompous could he possibly have been after his remarkable training, first for a degree in medicine, and, secondly, for the bar? Such a career as this would be sufficient to turn any man of average intelligence and more than average conceit into a third-rate Johnson—such a man, in fact, as Warren became. Add to these advantages (or disadvantages, you are free to choose your epithet) that of an author successful more by hitting the bull's-eye of public taste than by intrinsic

THE "BEAR," ESHER.

merit, and you will wonder the less at his self-sufficient mental attitude.

Warren was the author of such one-time extremely popular works as "Ten Thousand a Year" and the "Diary of a Late Physician": applauded to the echo in their day—a day that is done. He is additionally famous, however, on another and very different count. His vanity was monumental, and he possessed a prig's delight in recounting details of the social functions to which he was used to be invited by the notabilities of his day.

A good anecdote survives of this unpleasing trait in Warren's character. Let us howk it up again, and send it forth with a new lease of life.

Warren, it would seem, was narrating to Douglas Jerrold,[1] with much oily circumstantiality, the splendid details of one of the dinners to which he had been bidden in the mansions of the great. He constantly referred to the unusual fact of no fish having been served at one of these feasts, and asked Jerrold what explanation he thought could be offered of so strange an omission. The reply was worthy of that wounding and blackguardly wit for which Jerrold was so notorious; a form of ill-natured satire that seems never to have brought him the sound thrashing he so richly deserved.

"Perhaps they ate it all up-stairs," said he.

XI

AND now, before we proceed further along the Portsmouth Road, we must "change here" for Dorking, a coach-route greatly favoured of late years, both by Mr. Rumney's "Tally-ho" coach, and Mr. E. Brown's "Perseverance," by way of a relief from their accustomed haunts, to St. Albans and elsewhere. The "Perseverance" (which, alas! no longer perseveres) left Northumberland Avenue at eleven

---

[1] Edmund Yates says it was Sergeant Murphy, the eminent lawyer, and not Jerrold. See his "Recollections."

THE "TALLY-HO" HAMPTON COURT AND DORKING COACH.

a.m., and came down the old route until Surbiton was passed, when it turned off by way of Hook and Telegraph Hill, by Prince's Coverts to Leatherhead, and so into Dorking.

Mr. Rumney's "Wonder"—bah! what do I say? —I *should* say that gentleman's "Tally-ho" ran to Dorking in 1892, what time the "Perseverance" also ran thither, and a fine seven-and-sixpenny ride it was, there and back. By "there and back" I do not name the route between London and the old Surrey town. Oh no; Mr. Rumney's was quite an original idea. He gave Londoners the benefit of a country drive throughout, and ran between the sweet rurality of Hampton Court and Dorking. At 11.10 every morning he started from the "Mitre" Hotel, and so, across Hampton Bridge, to Ditton and Claremont, and thence to Dorking, where, at the "White Horse"——

But I anticipate, as the Early Victorian novelists were wont to say. I will quote an account of the journey that appeared in one of the weekly papers at the time, and have the less hesitation in quoting therefrom, because I wrote the article myself, and if a man may not quote himself, who, in Heaven's name, *may* he quote?

"Every week-day of this spring-time the 'Tally-ho' leaves the 'Mitre,' at Hampton Court, for Dorking. At eleven o'clock everything is in readiness save the driver, who puts in a staid and majestic appearance on the box only at the last moment. All around are ostlers and stablemen and men who, although they have nothing whatever to do with the coach, and do not even intend to go by it, are yet drawn here to admire the horses and to surreptitiously pat them after the manner of all Englishmen, who, even if they know nought of the noble animal's 'points,' at least love to see good horse-flesh. Vigorous blasts from 'yards of tin' arouse alarums and excursions, and bring faces to the hotel-windows, reminding one, together with the gold-laced red coat of the guard, of the true coaching age, so eloquently written of by that mighty historian of the road, C. J. Apperley, whom men called 'Nimrod.'

"The appointments and the horse-flesh that go to make a first-rate modern turn-out are luxurious beyond anything that 'Nimrod' could have seen, splendid as were some of the crack coaches of his day. Were he here now, he could but acknowledge our superiority in this respect; but we can imagine his critical faculties centred upon what he would have called the 'tooling' of the drag, and his disappointment, not in the workmanship of the driver, but in the excellence of the highways of to-day, which give a coachman no opportunities of showing how resourceful he could be with his wrist, nor how scientific with his 'springing' of his team. Let us compassionate the critic whose well-trained faculties are thus wasted!

"But it is full time we were off. A final flourish of the horn, and away we go, our coach making for the heart of Surrey. 'Southward o'er Surrey's pleasant hills,' as Tom Ingoldsby says, we go, to Leatherhead, beside Drayton's 'mousling Mole'; and so, with a clatter and a cheery rattle of the harness, past Mickle-

MICKLEHAM CHURCH.

ham, with its wayside church, and Juniper Hall, red-faced, green-shuttered; perched above the roadside, redolent of memories of the French refugees,— of whom M. D'Arblay, the husband of Fanny Burney,

BURFORD BRIDGE.

was one,—and still wearing a fine and most unmistakable eighteenth-century air, even though, as we pass, an equally undoubted nineteenth-century telegraph-boy comes walking, with the leisurely air peculiar to telegraph-boys, out of its carriage-drive into the road.

"Now we are nearing our journey's end. The glorious woodlands of Norbury Park—that old-time resort of literary ladies and gaping gentlemen, who stapped their vitals and protested monstrously that the productions of those blue-stockings were designed

THE "WHITE HORSE," DORKING.

for immortality, long before the modern woman was thought possible—the woods of Norbury come in view, and the great swelling side of Box Hill rises in front, with the Burford Bridge Hotel beneath, shaded by lofty trees which take their nourishment from the Mole, bridged here by a substantial brick-and-stone structure that gives that hostelry its name.

"No more pleasant week-end resort than the Burford Bridge Hotel—'providing always,' as the lawyers might say, that you do not make your week-end coincide with one of Sir John Lubbock's popular carnivals. Then———! But enough, enough. Hie we onwards, casting just one backward glance towards

The Road to Dorking.

that hotel which was just a decent road-side inn when Keats wrote 'Endymion' there, coming in from moonlit walks across Box Hill, inspired to heaven knows what unwritten poesy. Also, the Burford Bridge Hotel has a claim upon the patriotic Englishman, who, thank goodness, is not extinct, although Mr. Grant Allen thinks the generous feeling of patriotism is unfashionable. For here Nelson slept during his last night on English soil. The next day he embarked from Portsmouth, and—the rest is history!

"Dorking at last! We pull up, with steaming cattle, at the old 'White Horse,' where lunch is spread. We speculate upon the theory (one of many) that the real original Weller inhabited here, but come, of course, to no conclusion, where so many learned doctors in Dickens disagree. We adventure down to Castle Mill; yea, even to the picturesque Brockham Bridge below the town, beyond the foot of Box Hill. The town of Dorking stretches out its more modern part in this direction, halting within sight of Castle Mill, whence its *avant-garde* is seen stalking horribly across the meadows. For the rest, Dorking is pleasant enough, though containing little of interest; and the parish church of St. Martin has been rebuilt. Yet the long High Street still contains a few quaint frontages of the seventeenth century, and our halting-place has a curious sign of wrought ironwork. Those who do not pin their faith to the 'White Horse' as the original of the 'Marquis of Granby' in the 'Pickwick Papers,' elect to swear by the 'Red Lion,' once owned by a coach-proprietor who *might* have sat for Samivel's father.

"The town and district have, indeed, many literary associations. Some of these authors are now forgotten, or were never of more than local celebrity; but what generation will that be which forgets old John Evelyn, the diarist and author of 'Sylva,' and many other works, who must often have ridden into the town from Wotton House, near by? He was a friend of another congenial worthy, John Aubrey to

BROCKHAM BRIDGE.

wit. That amusingly quaint, but not strictly reliable, old chronicler, says of this town :—' Dorking is celebrated for fowls. The kine hereabout are of a sandy colour; the women, especially those about the hill, have no roses in their cheeks.' I do not notice that, however true may be his remarks about the fowls.

"Defoe, among others, lived here; and Benjamin Disraeli at Deepdene conceived the idea of 'Coningsby,' and wrote part of that work under its roof, as may be seen set forth in his dedication. The fame of Madame D'Arblay belongs more correctly to Mickleham. Then there were at Dorking many disciples of the Aikins and Barbaulds, those Clarissas and Laetitias of a pseudo-classic age whose dull wit was as forced as were the turgid sentiments of the eminently proper characters in their writings. Theirs was an age whose manners were as superficial as was the stucco upon the brick walls of their neo-classic mansions and quasi-Greek conventicles; and, for frankness' sake, I think I prefer our own times, when we have no manners and make no pretensions that way.

"However, time is up. The guard winds his horn up the street, and we take our seats again. The coachman gathers up his reins and shakes squarely down into his seat; the ostlers step back. 'Good-bye, good-bye,' and we are off at a quarter-past three on the return journey. We halt our team by the way at a cheerful inn. The air bites shrewdly, and—— 'Well, yes; I don't mind if I do!' 'Here's confusion to the Apostles of the Pump; a health to our driver; prosperity to the "Tally-ho," and——' 'Hurry up, please, gentlemen!' We take our seats once more with alacrity, and another hour sees us again at Hampton Court."

To show the manner in which coach accounts were kept in the coaching age, I append a copy of an old statement now in my possession. It is a "sharing account," and details a month's takings and expenses in the expiring days of road travel.

Meanwhile we resume our itinerary of the Portsmouth Road where we broke off, at Esher.

At Esher the fallen Cardinal Wolsey lived awhile when Providence frowned upon him—and for Providence in this connection read Henry VIII., who filled that position towards the great prelate, with

COACH ACCOUNTS

Dr.   LONDON AND *Dorking* COACH.   *Cr.*

Account for 4 Weeks, ending the 5th Day of August 1837, both inclusive.

RECEIPTS.				DISBURSEMENTS.					
Messrs. Horne	82	17	6						
Mr. Walker	75	12	–	**Messrs. Horne.**					
				Duty	16	17	–		
				Mileage					
				Tolls and Wages					
				Booking and Settling Accounts	3	3	–		
				Washing and Greasing	1	1	–	21	1	–
				Mr. Walker.					
				Wages and Tolls	13	4	–		
				Booking	–	–	–		
				Washing and Greasing ...	7	–	–		
				Mileage					
				Touter		16	–	21	–	–
				SHARES.					
				Miles.					
				8 Messrs. Horne	37	5	2		
				17 Mr. Walker	79	3	4	116	8	6
				25 Miles @ £4 13 1½ 18/25 a mile.					
	£158	9	6					£158	9	6

Dr. Mr. Walker,
To Receipts of Messrs. Horne   82 17 6
Do.   of Mr. Walker   75 12 –
    £100   3   4

By Shares   79 3 4
Disbursements   21 – –
    Cr. £100 3 4

great *éclat* and an altogether overwhelming success.
When the King commanded Wolsey to retire hither,
the Cardinal lived in the old building of Esher Place,
whose only remains are seen at this day in the Gate-
house standing in the damp and watery meadows
beside the Mole. He found the place little to his
liking, and displayed his sorrows in a letter to
Gardiner, Bishop of Winchester, wherein he complains
of the "moist and corrupt air." That he was quite
in a position to appreciate the dampness of his
residence, we may well believe when we read that
he was "without beds, sheets, table-cloths, or dishes";
and that he presently "fell sore sick that he was
likely to die" creates, under the circumstances, no
surprise.

The place of Wolsey's compulsory retirement was
almost completely destroyed when the modern mansion
of Esher Place was built, and the chief historic house
of Esher is now Claremont.

XII

CLAREMONT is a house of sad memories, destined,
so it might seem to the superstitious, to witness a
succession of tragedies and sorrows.

Neither the house nor the estate are of any considerable age; the estate originating in a fancy of
Sir John Vanbrugh,—that professional architect and
amateur dramatist of Queen Anne's time,—for a
suburban retreat. He purchased some land at Esher,
between the village and the common, and, foregoing

Ruins of Cardinal Wolsey's Palace Esher.

his usual ponderous style of piling up huge masses of stone and brickwork, put up quite a small and unpretentious brick house upon it. Sir John Vanbrugh died in 1726, and posterity seems still in doubt as to whether he excelled in writing comedies or in designing ponderous palaces of the type of Blenheim and Castle Howard. Certainly his writings are as light as his buildings heavy, and though a wit might justly compose an epitaph for him as an architect,

" Lie heavy on him, Earth, for he
Laid many a heavy load on thee,"

the application can extend no further.

Before he died, Vanbrugh's estate was sold to the Earl of Clare, who added a banqueting-hall to the architect's modest dwelling, purchased additional land, and, after the custom greatly honoured in the observance during the eighteenth century, stole much more from the neighbouring common, until he brought the palings of the park coterminous (as the political geographers might say) with the Portsmouth Road. In midst of the land he had thus filched from the commoners of Esher, the Earl of Clare built a kind of belvidere on a pleasant eminence overlooking the country-side, and called it Clare Mount. Thus arose the name of the house and park. Soon afterwards, however, the Earl was created Duke of Newcastle, and, to honour his new pomp and circumstance the more, employed Kent, the celebrated landscape gardener, to re-arrange the grounds and gardens, until their magnificence called forth this eulogium from Sir Samuel Garth, a dabbler both in medicine and metre:—

> "Oh! who can paint in verse those rising hills,
> Those gentle valleys, and their silver rills;
> Close groves and opening glades with verdure spread,
> Flow'rs sighing sweets, and shrubs that balsams bleed?"

Ah! who indeed? Not Sir Samuel Garth, though, if this be a representative taste of his quality.

The Claremont that we see now was built by the "heaven-born general," Clive, who purchased the estate upon the death of the Duke of Newcastle in 1768. He built, with the aid of Lancelot Brown (Capability Brown his contemporaries eke-named him), in a grand and massive style that excited the gaping wonder of the country folk. "The peasantry of Surrey," says Macaulay, in his "Essay on Clive," "looked with mysterious horror on the stately house which was rising at Claremont, and whispered that the great wicked lord had ordered the walls to be made so thick in order to keep out the devil, who would one day carry him away bodily." This unenviable reputation for wickedness was the work of Clive's enemies, of whom, perhaps, from one cause and another, no man has possessed so many. The men above whose heads his genius and daring had carried him, and the Little Englanders of that day, both hated the hero of Plassey with a lurid and vitriolic vehemence. They circulated strange tales of his cruelty and cupidity in India, until even well-informed people regarded Clive as an incarnate fiend, and "Capability" Brown even came to wonder that his conscience allowed him to sleep in the same house with the notorious Moorshedabad treasure-chest.

Clive ended his brief but glorious career, slain by

LORD CLIVE.

his own hand, in November 1774, but none the less murdered by the ingratitude of his country, a country so prolific in heroes that it can afford, for the sport of factions, to hound them occasionally to ruin and to death, coming afterwards in recriminating heart-agony to mourn their loss. Clive died, not yet fifty years of age, killed by constitutional melancholia, aggravated by disease and the yelpings of politicians, eager to drag down in the mire the man who gave us India. The arms of Clive still decorate the pediment of Claremont, the only house, so 'tis said, that "Capability" Brown ever built, though he altered many.

In the forty years that succeeded between the death of Clive and the purchase of the estate by the Commissioners of Woods and Forests, Claremont had a succession of owners; and upon the marriage of the Prince Regent's only daughter, the Princess Charlotte, in 1816, it was allotted to her for a residence. It was in May of that year that the Princess Charlotte of Wales was married to Prince Leopold of Saxe-Coburg, the petty German Duchy that has furnished princelings innumerable for the recruiting of kingdoms and principalities, and has given the Coburg Loaf its name.

But within a year of her marriage the Princess died in child-birth, and was buried in a mausoleum within the park. Then Claremont was for long deserted. There is a much-engraved portrait of the Princess, painted by Chalon, R.A., which shows a pleasant-faced girl, with fine neck and full eyes,—the characteristic eyes of the Guelphs,—and a strong facial resemblance to her father and grandfather, the Third and Fourth Georges. She is represented as habited in the indecent dress of the period, with ermined robe, and wearing a velvet hat with an immense plume of ostrich feathers. But a much more pleasing portrait is that by an unnamed artist, " a Lady," reproduced here, which gives a representation of the Princess without those elaborate feathers and showy trappings of Court ceremonial.

The circumstances that attended the death of this Princess, to whom the nation looked as their future Queen, were not a little mysterious, and gave rise to many sinister rumours and scandals. Sir Richard Croft, a fashionable *accoucheur* of that time, was in attendance upon her with other physicians. He was one who signed the bulletins announcing her steady progress towards recovery after the birth of a dead child ; but on the following day the news of the Princess's death came as a sudden shock upon England, whose people had but recently shared in the joy and happiness of her happy marriage, doubly welcome after the sinister quarrels, estrangements, and espionages that marked the wedded life of the Regent. Scarce had the tidings of the Princess Charlotte's death at Claremont become public property than all manner of strange whispers became current as to the causes of it. The public mind was, singularly enough, not satisfied with the medical explanations which would ordinarily have been accepted for very truth; but became exercised with vague suspicions of foul play that were only fanned into further life by the mutual recriminations

PRINCESS CHARLOTTE OF WALES.

K

of medicos and lay pamphleteers. Even those who saw no shadow of a crime upon this bad business were ready to cast blame and the bitterest reproaches upon Sir Richard Croft, in whose care the case chiefly lay, for his mistaken treatment. And this was not the first occasion upon which Croft's conduct had been looked upon with suspicion, for, years previously, a scandalous rumour had been bruited about with regard to two of his noble patients,—the Duchess of Devonshire and an unnamed lady of title,—by which it would seem that he was privy to a supposititious change of children at the Duchess of Devonshire's accouchement, when it was believed that the Duchess exchanged a girl for her friend's boy.

But on this occasion the affair was much more serious, whether blame attached to him solely for mistaken treatment, or whether scandal whispered at criminal complicity. The Princess Charlotte died on November 6, 1817; three months later—on February 13, 1818—Sir Richard Croft, in despair, shot himself. He was but fifty-six years of age.

Years later—in 1832—when Lady Ann Hamilton's extraordinary scribblings were published in two volumes under the title of "A Secret History of the Court of England, from 1760 to the Death of George IV.," these old rumours were crystallized into a definite charge of murder against some nobleman whose name is prudently veiled under a blank. The Princess, says Lady Hamilton, was in a fair way of recovery, and a cup of broth was given her; but after partaking of it she died in convulsions. The nurse who handed her the cup noticed a dark red sediment at the bottom, and on tasting it found her tongue blistered ! This peer, according to Lady Hamilton, acted with the connivance of the King, George III., and his glorified German *hausfrau*, and with the approval of the Princess's father, the Regent, who, it is asserted in those pages, was heard to say some time previously at Esher that " no child of the Princess Charlotte shall ever sit upon the throne of England." Lady Ann Hamilton, however, was a malevolent gossip, holding the most extreme Radical views, and as a personal friend and uncompromising partisan of Caroline, Princess of Wales,—that silly and phenomenally undignified woman—was eager to believe anything, no matter how atrocious, of her husband and his people.

No member of the Royal Family was present at the Princess Charlotte's death-bed. She died, with the sole exception of her husband, Prince Leopold, amid physicians and domestics.

The King and Queen were (says Lady Hamilton) a hundred and eight miles away, and the Regent was either at Carlton House or staying with the Marquis of Hertford (or rather the *Marchioness*, she adds, in significant italics).

It is said that Lady Ann Hamilton's writings, published as a " Secret History," were given to the world, without her knowledge or consent, by a gentleman who had obtained the manuscript. Certain it is that when these two volumes appeared, in 1832, they were suppressed ; and some four years later, when some other manuscripts belonging to the author were advertised for sale by auction, they were hastily bought up on behalf of a royal personage, and, it is believed, destroyed.

It is difficult to understand the hardihood which asserted at that time that the Princess Charlotte had been the victim of a murderous conspiracy between her nearest relatives; the more especially because her death would not seem to have been any one's immediate great gain. Had it been of great advantage to any prominent member of the Royal Family, the suspicion might have been better founded, for royalty has no monopoly of virtue, while the temptations of its position are a hundredfold greater than those of lower estate. The history of royal houses shows that murder has frequently altered the line of succession, but surely the House of Brunswick (that heavy and phlegmatic line) never soared to this tragic height, or plumbed such depths of crime in modern times.

For many years after the death of the Princess Charlotte, Claremont was closed, the rooms unoccupied, and left in much the condition they were then. Prince Leopold became, by the death of his wife, life-owner of the place, but its sad memories led him to leave it for ever. In after years the Prince became King of the Belgians, and, in 1832, a year after this advancement, married the eldest daughter of Louis Philippe, King of the French. Sixteen years later, during the stress of the French Revolution of 1848, that *bourgeois* King fled from Paris and crossed the Channel as "Mr. Smith," and his son-in-law placed Claremont at the disposal of the *émigré malgré lui.* Here he died in 1850. In 1865 the King of the Belgians died, and Claremont reverted to the Crown. Six years later the Marquis and Marchioness of Lorne stayed here on the occasion of their marriage, and when the Queen's youngest son, Prince Leopold, Duke of Albany, was married, Claremont became his home. But the Duke died in 1884, and the house is now in the occupation of his widow.

Claremont, indeed, is a place weighted with memories and sad thoughts of the "might have been." If only the intrepid Clive had lived to take the field against our rebellious colonists, as it was proposed he should do, it seems likely that the New England States had yet been ours, and Washington surely hanged or shot. Then North America had not become the safe refuge of political murderers commanding sympathetic ears at the White House, nor had we ever heard of the *scagliola* fripperies of a Presidential Reception. But a dull and obstinate King, a stupid ministry, and incompetent generals combined to lose us those colonies, and death snatched away untimely the foremost military genius of the time, to leave statesmen in despair at what they thought was surely the decay of a glorious Empire.

How changed, too, would have been the succession had the Princess Charlotte lived! The Sailor King —that most unaffected and heartiest of monarchs, whom the irreverent witlings of his day called "Silly Billy," for no particular reason that I know of— would have still remained Duke of Clarence, and the Princess Victoria would have been but a mere cousin of another Queen. But no matter what Fate has in store for other Houses, the Coburger reaps an advantage, whate'er befalls; and though one is relegated to a less distinguished career by the death of his consort, another of that prolific race becomes the husband of a Queen, and the father of our future Kings.

XIII

BUT it is a long way yet to Guildford, and eight miles to our next change, at the "Talbot" Hotel, Ripley; equally with the Esher "Bear" a coaching inn of long and honourable lineage. Let us then proceed without more ado down the road.

Fairmile Common is the next place of note, and it is especially notable from the coaching point of view, by reason of the flatness of the road that is supposed to be the only level mile between London and Guildford. Along this Fair Mile, then, the coachmen of by-past generations generally took the opportunity of "springing" their cattle, and as they were "sprung" then, so they are to-day, over this best of galloping-grounds, the said "springing" bringing us, in less than no time, to Cobham Street, where there is a very fine and large roadside inn indeed, called the "White Lion." If the coach stopped here, you would be able to verify this statement by an exploration of the interior, which is as cosy and cheerful within as it is bare and cold and inhospitable-looking without—at least, those are my sentiments. But, then, the coach doesn't stop, but goes dashing round the corner and over the river Mole and up Pain's Hill in the "twinkling of a bed-post," that somewhat clumsy *façon de parler*.

Now, if you walked leisurely this way, there would be time for talking of many interesting things. Firstly, as to Fairmile itself, which is worth lingering over upon a fine summer's day.

Fairmile Common is associated, in local tradition, with the following tragedy. Two young brothers of the Vincent family of Stoke D'Abernon, the elder of whom had but just come into possession of his estate, were out on a shooting expedition from that village. They had put up several birds, but had not been able to get a single shot, when the eldest swore with a great oath that he would fire at whatever they next met with. They had gone but little further when the miller of the neighbouring mill passed them and bade them good-day. When he had passed, the younger brother jokingly reminded the elder of his oath, whereupon the latter immediately fired at the miller, who fell dead upon the spot. The murderer escaped to his home, and, by family influence, backed by large sums of money, no effective steps were taken for his arrest. He was concealed upon his estate for some years, when he died from remorse. To commemorate his rash act and his untimely death, a monument was placed in Stoke D'Abernon Church, bearing the "bloody hand" which no doubt gave rise to the whole story.

The red hand of Ulster, badge of honourable distinction, is not understood by the country folk, and so, to account for it, the Stoke D'Abernon villagers have evolved this moving tale. That is my view of the legend. If you are curious concerning it, why, Stoke D'Abernon is near at hand, and there, in as charming a village church as you could wish to see, filled, beside, with archæological interest, is this memorial. Did space suffice (which it doesn't) much might be said of Stoke D'Abernon, of Slyfield Farm, and of Cobham village; which last must on no

COBHAM CHURCHYARD.

account be confounded with Cobham Street. The latter place is, in fact, just an offshoot (though an old one 'tis true) of the original village, and it arose out of the large amount of custom that was always going along the Portsmouth Road in olden times.

Cobham Street stood here in receipt of this custom and of much patronage from that very fine high-handed gentleman, the Honourable Charles Hamilton, who in the reign of George II. filched a large tract of common land just beyond the other side of the Mole, enclosed it, and by the expenditure of vast sums of money caused such gardens to blossom here, such caves and grottoes to be formed, and such cunning dispositions of statuary to be made (all in the classic taste of the time) that that carping critic, Horace Walpole, was compelled to a reluctant admiration. And this was the origin of the estate still known as Pain's Hill.

> " 'Tis very bad, in man or woman,
> To steal a goose from off the common :
> But who shall plead that man's excuse
> Who steals the common from the goose ? "

Thus the metrical moralist. But this was common sport (no joke intended here !) during last century and in the beginning of this, and if a man stole a few hundred acres in this way, he was thought none the worse of for it. For all that, however, the Honourable Charles Hamilton was nothing more, in fact, than a common thief, with this difference—that the poor devil who "prigged" a handkerchief was hanged for petty larceny, while the rich man who stole land on a large scale, and converted it to his own uses, was hailed as a man of taste and culture, and his robbery commended.

Pain's Hill looms up finely as one turns the corner of Cobham Street and crosses the Mole by the successor of the bridge built here by the "Good Queen Maud," in place of the ford where one of her maids-of-honour was drowned. There are more inns here, and their humped and bowed roofs make an excellent composition in a sketch, with the remarkable moplike trees of Pain's Hill Park seen in silhouette beyond. To Pain's Hill succeeds Tartar Hill and Wisley Common; sombre fir trees lining the road

PAIN'S HILL.

and reflected in the great pond that spreads like some mystic mere over many acres. The "Huts" Hotel, however, rebuilt and aggressively modern, is not at all mystic, and neither are the crowds of thirsty, dusty cyclists who frequent it on summer days.

XIV

THE Portsmouth Road, from London to Ripley, has, any time these last twenty years, been the most frequented by cyclists of any road in England. The "Ripley Road," as it is generally known among wheelmen, is throughout the year, but more especially in the spring and summer months, alive with cycles and noisy with the ringing of cycle-bells. On Saturday afternoons, and on fine Sundays, an almost inconceivable number take a journey down these twenty-three miles from London, and back again in the evening; calling at the "Angel," at Ditton, on the way, and taking tea at their Mecca, the "Anchor," at Ripley. The road is excellent for cycling, but so also are a number of others, equally accessible, around London, and it must be acknowledged that the "Ripley Road" is as much favoured by a singular freak of fashion in cycling, and as illogically, as a particular walk in Hyde Park is affected by Society on Sundays. But in cycling circles (apt phrase!) it is quite the correct thing to be seen at Ditton or at Ripley on a Sunday, and every one who is any one in that sport and pastime, be-devilled as it is now-a-days with shady professionalism and the transparently subsidized performances of the makers' amateurs, must be there. The "Ripley Road," now-a-days, is, in fact, the stalking-ground of self-advertising long-distance riders, of cliquey and boisterous club-men, and of the immodest women who wear breeches awheel. The tourist, and the man who only has a fancy for the cycle as a means of healthful exercise, and does not join the membership of a club, give the "Ripley Road" a wide berth.

The frequenters of this road became in 1894 such an unmitigated nuisance and source of danger to the public in passing through Kingston-on-Thames, that the local bench of magistrates were obliged to institute proceedings against a number of cyclists for furious driving, and for riding machines without lights or bells. According to the evidence given by an inspector of police, no fewer than twenty thousand cyclists passed through Kingston on Whit Sunday, 1894.

Coaching men hate the cyclist with a bitter hatred, and he will ever be to them a *bête noir* of the blackest hue. It may not be generally known that the contumelious expression of "cads on castors," which has become so widespread that it has almost obtained the popularity of a proverb, originated with Edmund Yates; but he was really the author of that scornful epithet, whose apt alliteration will probably never be forgotten, though the "castors" be evolved into hitherto undreamed-of patterns, and the race of cads who earned the appellation be dead and gone. The expression "cads on castors" will, with that other humorous epithet, "Brompton boilers," achieve immortality when cycling is obsolete, and the corrugated iron roofs of the Bethnal Green Museum are rusted away. The objectionable phrase of "bounders on box-seats," which some cycling journalists have flung back at their coaching critics has not run to anything like the popularity of the other, and more apt, effort of alliterative conciseness; for the prejudices of the lieges have, up to now, been chiefly in favour of the whips and horsey men to whom the cycle is the "poor man's horse," and therefore to be condemned. Will the sport and pastime of cycling ever become aristocratic? It is to be feared or hoped

FAME UP-TO-DATE.

(accordingly as you admire or detest the cycle) that it will never win to this regard: at least, not while the road-racing clubs and individual cyclists continue to render the Queen's highway dangerous for all other travellers; not so long as that peculiar species of Fame, which is more properly Notoriety, continues to be trumpeted abroad concerning the doings of

racing cyclists who strive, not for the English love of sport, but for the cheques awarded them by the long-headed manufacturers whose machines they ride—and advertise.

But cycling has brought much prosperity to Ripley village and its two antiquated inns, the "Talbot" and the "Anchor." A few years ago, indeed (before cycling had become so popular), the "Talbot" was closed and given over to solitude and mice, but now-a-days one may be as well served there as at any country hostel you please to mention. The company, however, of the "Talbot" is not exclusively made up of wheelmen of the gregarious (or club) species, and a decent tourist who is neither a scorcher nor a wearer of badges, nor anything else of the "attached" variety, may rest himself there with quiet and comfort, except on high days and Bank holidays: on which occasions the quiet and peaceable man generally stays at home, preferring solitude to the over-much company he would find on the road.

But if you wish to see the club-wheelman in his most characteristic moods, why then the "Anchor" is your inn, for in the low-ceiled rooms that lurk dimly behind the queer, white-washed gables of that old house, cycling clubmen foregather in any number, limited only by the capacity of the inn. The place is given over to cyclists, and beside the road, behind the house, or on the broad common upon which this roadside village fronts, their machines are stacked as thickly as in the store-rooms of some manufactory.

L

At the further end of the village stands the ancient but much-restored chapel of Ripley, interesting to cyclists by reason of the memorial window inserted here to the memory of an early cycling hero of the race-path—Herbert Liddell Cortis—who died, shortly after reaching Australia, at Carcoar, New South Wales, on December 28, 1885. Interest of another kind may be found in the architecture of the Earl of

HERBERT LIDDELL CORTIS.

Lovelace's beautiful seat, Ockham Park, that borders the road, just before entering the village; and in the ruins of Newark Abbey, that lie on the banks of the Wey, across Ripley Green. But time and tide wait for no man, and the "New Times" coach is equally impatient of delay. Two minutes suffice for changing teams at the "Talbot," and off that heir of the coaching age goes again.

XV.

For six miles the road runs level, from Ripley to Guildford, forming excellent galloping ground for the horses of the "New Times" coach. All the way the scenery is pretty, but with no very striking features, and villas dot the roadside for a considerable distance. On the left hand the coach passes Claudon Park, and on the right comes Mr. Frederic Harrison's historic house, Sutton Place, and Stoke Park, that takes its name from the village of Stoke-next-Guildford.

Past some outlying waste lands and over railway bridges, the coach rattles down the sharp descent into Guildford town; down the narrow High Street—the steepest, they say, in England, and certainly the stoniest—to draw up before the "Angel," punctually at two o'clock.

Guildford is no more than thirty miles from London, and yet it remains to this day as provincial in appearance as ever it could have been in the olden times of road-travel. Provinciality was the pet bugbear of Matthew Arnold, but he applied it as a scornful term only to literary and critical shortcomings. To him the vapourings of modern poetasters would have been provincialisms, and the narrow-minded criticisms of Mr. George Howells, who can see nothing in Shakespeare, but perceives a wealth of genius in his fellow-novelists of the United States, would have been provincialisms of the worst order.

But the provinciality of places, as distinguished

from minds, can be no reproach in these latter days, when all the great towns, with London at their head, have grown so large and congested that a sight of God's pure country and a breath of healthy air are only to be obtained by most townsfolk with infinite pains and great expenditure of time. It was an evil day when the great cities of England grew so large that one who ascended a church steeple in their midst could discover nothing on the horizon but chimney-pots and bricks-and-mortar; and the best of times were those when weary citizens took their pleasure after the day's work in the fields and groves that bordered upon the habitations of men. What are Progress and Civilization but will-o'-wisps conjured up by the malignity of the devil to hide the degeneration of the race and the starvation of the soul, when the outcome of the centuries is the shutting out from the face of nature of three-fourths of the population? What else than a sorry jest is the boast of London's five millions of people, when by far the greater proportion of those five millions never know what country life means, nor even what is the mitigated rusticity of a provincial town in whose centre you can open your casement of a morning and welcome the sun rising in a clear sky, listen to the morning chorus of the birds, and see, though you be in the very midst of the provincial microcosm, the fields and hedge-rows, the streams and rural lanes of the country-side?

Guildford, then, is provincial in the best and healthiest sense; for though your habitat be in the High Street, which here, as in all other properly-constituted

GUILDHALL, GUILDFORD.

towns, is the very nucleus of the borough, you need never be longer than ten minutes in leaving the town behind if you are so minded. Guildford is a town of very individual character. Godalming folks will tell you that Guildford is "cliquey," by which term I understand exclusiveness to be meant. It may be so, in fact I believe this to be one of Guildford's most marked social characteristics; but exclusiveness implies local patriotism, which is a refreshing spirit for a Londoner to encounter once in a way. At any rate, he will find no spirit of this description in what Cobbett satirically termed "the Wen." The patriotism of Peckham has yet to be discovered; the local enthusiasm of Camberwell is as rare as the song of the lark in London streets; and the man who would now praise what was once the country village of "merrie" Islington is not to be found.

It is difficult to pluck even one greatly outstanding incident from Guildford's history wherewith to enliven these pages, for although Guildford possessed a strong and well-placed castle from Norman times, it cannot be said that the annals of the town are at all distinguished by records of battle, murder, and sudden death, or by military prowess. So much the better for Guildford town, you will say, and the expression may be allowed, for this old borough has ever been eminently peaceful and prosperous in the absence of civil or military commotion. Its very name is earnest of trade and merchandise; and the guilds of Guildford were very powerful bodies of traders who dealt in cloths and wool, at one time the chiefest of local products, or in the minor articles that ministered to the wants of those great staple trades.

Meanwhile the guardians of the old Castle, whose keep still dominates Guildford from most points of view, had little enough to do but to keep the place in order for such occasions when the King came a-hunting in the neighbourhood, or progressed past here to some distant part of the realm. King John seems to have been by far the most frequent royal visitor to Guildford Castle, and almost the last, for the cold comforts of Norman keeps went very early out of fashion with kings and queens, and domestic hearths began to replace dungeon-like apartments in chilly towers as soon as social conditions began to settle down into something remotely resembling tranquillity.

Guildford Keep stands at this day in gardens belonging to the Corporation, and free to all. It is of the Norman type, familiarized to many by prints of such well-known Norman towers as those of Rochester and of Hedingham Castles, and is at this time a mere shell, open to the sky. Within the thickness of the walls are staircases by which it is possible to climb to the summit and gaze thence down upon the red roofs of the town that cluster so picturesquely beneath. Here, too, is a Norman oratory, whose narrow walls are covered with names and figures scratched deeply into the stone, "probably," says a local guide, "the work of prisoners confined here." But "J. Robinson, 1892," was surely no prisoner within these bounds, although he should have been who thus carved his undistinguished name here.

CASTLE ARCH.

Beside the keep there remains but one archway of all the extensive military works that at one time surrounded the Castle. This is in Quarry Street, and is known as Castle Arch. The chalk caverns close at hand, and the vaulted crypt beneath the "Angel," although they have long been looked upon as dungeons, had, according to the best-informed of local archæologists, no connection whatever with the Castle. Perhaps even before the Castle keep, the delightfully quaint old Guildhall is the most characteristic feature of Guildford's architecture. Compared with that old stronghold, the Guildhall is the merest *parvenu*, having been built in 1683; but, comparisons of age apart, there is no parallel to be drawn between the two. The old tower is four-square and stern, with only the picturesqueness that romance can find, while the belfried tower and the boldly-projecting clock that impends massively over the pavements of the High Street, and gives the time o' day to the good folks of the town, are the pride of the eye and the delight of the artistic sense of all them that know how to appreciate at their true æsthetic value those memorials of the old corporate spirit of business and good-fellowship that have long since vanished from municipal practice. The legend that may still be read upon the Corporation mace, of Elizabethan date, is earnest of this old-time amity. Thus it runs: "Fayre God. Doe Justice. Love thy Brether." Set against this, the proceedings of the Kingston-upon-Thames Town Council of some few weeks back make ugly reading, and at the same time illustrate the new spirit very vividly indeed. You who list to learn may read in the records for the present year of that old borough, that while one member of the Council stigmatized another member's statements as falsehoods, the first rejoined that his accuser was, in plain English, "a liar." Appealed to by the Mayor to withdraw the offensive expression, he refused, and the Mayor and Corporation filed out of the Council-chamber, leaving him to his own reflections.

That the burghers of Guildford were always the best of friends one with another is not my contention; that the dignity of their ancient surroundings should conduce to loving-kindness may remain unquestioned.

XVI

THE greatest of Guildford's worthies was George Abbot, the son of Maurice Abbot, a clothworker of this town, and his wife Alice. He was born in 1562, the eldest of that "happy ternion of brothers," as Fuller quaintly describes him and his two younger brothers, who became respectively Bishop of Salisbury and Lord Mayor of London. The parents of these distinguished men came very near to martyrdom in the reign of Queen Mary, for they were both ardent Protestants; but, escaping the fate that befell many others, they had the happiness of seeing their children rise in the world far beyond all local expectations. Alice Abbot, indeed, had a singular dream which foretold that "if she could eat a jack or pike, the first son she should bring into the world would be a great man." A few days afterwards (so runs the story) she drew up a pike from the river Wey while filling buckets for household use; and, in accord with the promptings of her dream, ate it. "Many people of quality offered themselves to be sponsors at the baptism of Mistress Alice's son—the future Archbishop," says Aubrey; and if the dream itself was nothing but the result of a late supper acting upon a vivid imagination, certainly local interest in "Mistress Alice's" account of it procured for her firstborn quite an exceptional degree of favour and consideration. He was educated first at the Free Grammar School of Guildford, and was sent at the age of sixteen to Balliol College. Thenceforward his rise was rapid. He studied theology, and became tutor to the sons of influential personages. Excellent preferments in the Church became his at an early age, and through many stages of favour he became Archbishop of Canterbury in his forty-ninth year. His rise was undoubtedly due to native worth, for Abbot was a scholar of the foremost rank, and well equipped, both by study and by force of character, to hold his own in the fierce religious controversies of his time. He was, moreover, honest, and had little of the truckler or the time-server in his nature, as his opposition both to James I. and Charles I. showed, on occasion. It is to his righteous opposition that Charterhouse School, now down the road at Godalming, owes its very existence; for, when the cupidity of James I. was aroused over the provisions of Thomas Sutton's will, and when he attempted to divert that pious founder's money to his own uses, Abbot withstood the attempt, and the King was fain to give way—with an ill grace, 'tis true, but effectually enough.

Abbot was nothing of a courtier, and, indeed, no very pleasant-natured man. He was sour of aspect and morose; gloomy and fanatic in religion, and no less swift to send religious opponents to the stake than the Catholic inquisitors of a generation before his time. He had a strong and militant affection for the reformed religion, and held a singularly lonely position between the levelling puritanical-democratic doctrines of the age and the High Church party. A Calvinistic narrowness distinguished this great man's public acts, and he was sufficiently Puritan in spirit to look with disfavour upon, and to absolutely forbid, Sunday sports. His truculent religious views appeared in a lurid light shortly after he became Archbishop, when he condemned two Arians to death for what he held to be "blasphemous heresy." These two unfortunate men, Bartholomew Legate and Edward Wightman, were burnt in 1614, three years after their sentence, as the "recompence of their pride and impiety."

Meanwhile, the mind of the Archbishop was liberal enough in other directions. He could send religious dissenters to a horrible death, and look back with satisfaction upon his handiwork, while, at the same time, he was maturing the plans and provisions for the noble almshouse that still stands in Guildford High Street and bears the honoured name of Abbot's Hospital.

In 1619 he laid the first stone of his "Hospital," and three years later had the satisfaction of seeing it incorporated by Royal Charter; a satisfaction clouded by an accident that embittered the remainder of his life. The story of this untoward event illustrates at once the morbid habit of his mind and the bitter passions of those times. It was in 1621, while with a hunting party in Bramshill Park, that this thing befell. A large party had assembled by the invitation of Lord Zouch, and chased the deer through the glades of that lovely park. The Archbishop drew his bow at a buck, and at the same time that the arrow sped, a gamekeeper, one Peter Hawkins, darted forward between the trees, and received the shaft in his heart.

A coroner's jury returned a verdict by which the accident was attributed to the man's negligence in exposing himself to danger after having been warned; but Abbot was greatly distressed, and so heavily did the occurrence weigh upon him that, to the time of his death, in 1632, he kept a monthly fast on a Tuesday, the day of the gamekeeper's death. He also settled an annuity of £20 upon the man's widow.

The King declared that "an angel might have miscarried in such sort," and that "no one but a fool or a knave would think worse of a man for such an accident"; but it suited Abbot's religious rivals and opponents to regard with public aversion one "whose hands were imbrued with blood"; and his clergy, who had felt the curb of the Archbishop's discipline too acutely to let this chance slip, felt or expressed a horror of their spiritual head ever afterwards. Others even went so far as to refuse ordination at the hands of a homicide, and bishops-elect scrupled to receive consecration from him, until the Royal Pardon had been obtained and the conscience of the Church satisfied.

For all his opposition to James I., the Archbishop lost a good friend when that pragmatical monarch died, and gained an enemy when Charles I. came to the throne. The High Church party were then in the ascendant, and Abbot, from various causes, declined from favour. In 1627 he was sequestered, and the Archbishopric of Canterbury put into commission of five bishops, of whom Laud, Abbot's particular enemy, was one.

These misfortunes at length broke Abbot's health, which finally failed in 1632. At the beginning of that year he seemed upon the point of death, but revived somewhat, and a letter, still preserved, written by an especial friend at this juncture, hinted at the indecency of those who expected his end, and says—"If any other prelate gape at his benefice, his Grace perhaps may eat the goose which shall graze upon his grave."

But death came upon Abbot that same year. He made an edifying end at Croydon, and was buried, by his own request, in Trinity Church, opposite the Hospital he had founded in his native town.

Eight years afterwards, the Archbishop's brother, Sir Maurice Abbot, erected the sumptuous monument there which Pepys admired on one of his visits to Guildford. It still remains, although the church itself (one of Guildford's three churches) has been rebuilt.

XVII

GUILDFORD has many old inns, as befits an old town which lay directly upon an old coach-road. Of these the chiefest lie in the High Street, and they are the "Angel," the "Crown," the "White Hart," and the "Red Lion." The "Red Lion" has a modernized frontage, but within it is the same hostelry at which Mr. Samuel Pepys stayed, time and again; the others are more suggestive of the flower of the coaching age and of Pickwickian revels; but in these latter days the wide race of "commercial gentlemen" and the somewhat stolid and beefy grazier class are their more usual guests. Behind their prosperous-looking fronts are the vast stable-yards, approached from the High Street by yawning archways that "once upon a time" admitted the coaches, and whence issued the carriages and post-chaises of a by-gone day; now echoing with the rumble of the omnibus that plies between the town and the railway-station, laden chiefly with the sample-boxes of enterprising bagmen. But in that "once upon a time," whose chronology finally determined and came to an end in the '40's, there was a superabundance of coach traffic here.

Hogarth has left a picture of a typical country inn-yard of his time which shows, better than any amount of unaided description, what manner of places they were whence started the lumbering stages of last century. No one has yet identified the picture, reproduced here, with any particular inn, although some have sought to place it in Essex, because of the election crowd seen in the background carrying an effigy and a banner inscribed with the weird, and at first sight incomprehensible, legend "No Old Baby." A candidate named Child stood for one of the Essex boroughs about this date, and, according to Hogarth commentators, this group was intended as an incidental satire upon him. On the other hand, the likelihood of this being really an inn-yard upon the Portsmouth Road is seen by the sailor who occupies a somewhat insecure position upon the roof of the coach beside a French valet, and whose bundle is inscribed "Centurion." The "Centurion," one of Anson's squadron, put in repeatedly at Portsmouth, and the sailor is apparently on a journey home, fresh from the sea and from Anson's command.

The scene is very amusing, and most of the interest centres in the foreground, where a coach is seen, about to start. An old woman sits smoking in the rumble-tumble behind, while a traveller looks on and pays no heed to the post-boy who holds his hat in readiness for a tip. A guest is about to depart, and the landlord is seen presenting his bill. He seems to be assuring his customer that his charges are strictly moderate; but, judging from the sour expression of the latter's face, mine host has been overcharging him for a good round sum. Meanwhile, the devil's own din is being sounded by the fat landlady, who is ringing her bell violently for the chambermaid, and by a noisy fellow who is winding a horn out of window with all his might. The chambermaid is otherwise engaged, for an amorous spark is seen to be kissing her in the open doorway.

AN INN-YARD, 1747. *After Hogarth.*

So greatly was Guildford High Street crowded in the old coaching times that, just about a hundred years ago, it was widened at one point by the slicing off of a portion from one of Guildford's three churches which projected inconveniently into the roadway. To gaze upon what is still a very narrow street, and to remember that this is its "widened" state, is calculated to impress a stranger with the singular parsimony of our ancestors, when land was comparatively cheap and considerations of space presumably not so pressing.

The pressure of traffic here in the Augustan age of coaching will be better understood when it is learned that not only did the Portsmouth coaches pass through Guildford, and the numerous local stages that ran no further than Guildford and Godalming, but that the Southampton coaches came thus far, and only turned off from this road at a point just beyond the town. The celebrated "Red Rover" Southampton coach came this way, and so did the equally famous "Telegraph"; and, leaving Guildford behind, they pursued their way to Southampton by way of Farnham and Winchester. To this route belonged many celebrated whips of those times whose names are almost unmeaning now-a-days; and some of the best of these once well-known wielders of the whipcord were stopped by Fate and the Railway in the full force of their careers. Happy the man whose spirit was not too stubborn to submit gracefully and at once to the new dispensation, and to seek employment on the rail. Good servants of the road found equally good places on the railways—if they chose to take them. But (and can you wonder at it?) they rarely chose to accept, having naturally the bitterest prejudices against the railways and everything that belonged to them; and many men wasted their energies and expended their savings in a fruitless endeavour to compete with steam, when they could have transferred their allegiance from the road to the rail with honour and profit to themselves and no less to their employers. John Peers, a well-known coachman, and driver of the London and Southampton "Telegraph," was reduced by the coming of the railway to driving an omnibus. From this position, being scornful and quarrelsome, unable to adapt himself to changed circumstances, and altogether "above his station," he drifted finally into the workhouse. A gentleman who had known him well upon the box-seat in more prosperous days, discovered him in this refuge of the poverty-stricken and superseded; started a subscription for him amongst his former patrons, and rescued him from the small mercies and little ease of the Guardians of the Poor. He was housed upon the road he had driven over so often in the days before steam had come to ruin the coaching interest, and there, in due course, he died.

And his was a fate happier than that of most others—coachmen, guards, post-boys, and ostlers—thrown out of employment by railways, and unable or unwilling to adapt themselves to new surroundings. Many of these soured and disappointed men lived on and on in a vain hope of "new-fangled notions" coming to a speedy and disastrous failure. When accidents occurred and lives were lost by railway

THE "RED ROVER" GUILDFORD AND SOUTHAMPTON COACH.

smashes, their faces were lit up with a wintry joy, and they wagged their heads with an air of profound wisdom, and said individually, "I told you so!" When the "Railway Mania" of 1844 and succeeding years collapsed and brought the inevitable financial crash, they chuckled, and felt by anticipation the ribbons in their hands again. But though financial disasters came on top of collisions, and though the system of railway travel seemed for a while like a bubble on point of bursting, the promise was never fulfilled, and the old coachmen who actually did drive the roads once more did so as ministers to the amateur spirit that has since 1863 caused so many coaches to be put upon the country roads of Old England.

XVIII

DIRECTLY the river Wey is crossed, either in leaving or entering Guildford, the road begins to rise steeply. Going towards Godalming, it brings the traveller in a mile's walk to the ruined chapel of St. Catherine, standing on a sandstone hill beside the highway, whose red sides are burrowed by rabbits and sand-martins. The chapel has been ruined time out of mind, and is to-day but a motive for a sketch. One of Turner's best plates in his "*Liber Studiorum*" has St. Catherine's Chapel for its subject, and to the criticism of Turner's work comes the Rev. Mr. Stopford Brooke, in this wise:—"It is no picturesque place. Turner painted English life as it was; and the struggle of the poor is uppermost in his mind in all these rustic subjects .... pathetic feeling is given them by Turner's anxious kindness."

No picturesque place! Where, then, do you find picturesqueness if not here? And as for Turner, the man who dares to say that he "painted English life as it was," dares much. It is the chiefest glory of Turner that he painted or drew or etched things, not as they were, but as they might, could, should, or would be under an artist's direction. He was, in short, an idealist, and cared nothing for "actuality," and perhaps even less for the "struggle of the poor." It is possible to read anything you please into Turner's work, for it is chiefly of the frankest impressionism; but to say that *he* felt and did all these things is criticism of the most inept Penny Reading order. Turner was an artist of the rarest and most generous equipment, and he *had* to do what he did, and never reasoned *why* he did it. Ruskin surprised him with what he read into his work; how much more, then, would he have been astonished at Mr. Stopford Brooke's "Notes on the *Liber Studiorum*," had he lived to read them! But angels and ministers of grace defend us from ministers of religion who essay art criticism!

And now, having descanted upon the wisdom of the cobbler sticking to his last, or of the clergyman adhering rigorously to his spiritual functions, let us proceed to Godalming on foot.

"Everybody that has been from Godalming to Guildford knows," says Cobbett, "that there is hardly another such a pretty four miles in all England. The

ST. CATHERINE'S CHAPEL. *After J. M. W. Turner.*

road is good; the soil is good; the houses are neat; the people are neat; the hills, the woods, the meadows, all are beautiful. Nothing wild and bold, to be sure, but exceedingly pretty; and it is almost impossible to ride along these four miles without feelings of pleasure, though you have rain for your companion, as it happened to be with me."

There! is that not a pretty testimony in favour of this stretch of road? And it is all the prettier, seeing from what source it comes; a source, to be sure, whence proceeded cursings and revilings, depreciations, and a thorough belittling of most things. Cobbett, you see, was a man with an infinite capacity for scorn and indignation, and that bias very frequently led him to take no account of things that a more evenly-balanced temper would have found delight in. But here is an altogether exceptional passage, and therefore let us treasure it.

When within sight of Godalming, the road descends suddenly and proceeds along level lands through which runs the winding Wey. All around, a bold amphitheatre of hills closes the view, and the queer little town is set down by the meadows beside the river in the most moist and damp situation imaginable. It is among the smallest and least progressive of townships; with narrow streets, the most tortuous and deceptive, paved with granite setts and cobble-stones in varied patches. Godalming is a town as old as the Kingdom of the South Saxons, and indeed derives its name from some seventh-century Godhelm, to whom this fair meadow-land (or "ing") then belonged. Godhelm's Ing remains in, probably, almost the same condition now as when, a thousand years and more ago, the Saxon chieftain squatted down beside the Wey in this break of the hills and reared his flocks and herds, and was, in the fashion of those remote times, the father of his people. The little river runs its immemorial course, gnawed by winter flood and summer spate, through the alluvial soil of the valley; the grass grows green as ever, and the kine thrive as they have always done upon its succulent fare; the hoary hills look down upon the lowlands in these days, when agitators would restore the Heptarchy, just as they did when the strife of the Eight Kingdoms watered the island with blood. Only Godhelm and his contemporaries, with his descendants and many succeeding generations, are gone and have left no trace, save perhaps in the ancient divisions and hedges of the fields, like those of the greater part of England, old beyond the memory of man, or the evidence of engrossed parchments. Where the Saxon chieftain's primitive village arose, on a spot ever so little elevated above the grazing grounds beside the river, there run Godalming streets to-day; their plan, if not so old as the days of this patriarch farmer, at least as ancient as the Norman Conquest, when the invaders dispossessed his descendants and kept them overawed by the strong castle of Guildford, perched in a strategic position, four miles up the road.

Not that those stolid agriculturists required much repression. Malcontents there might be elsewhere, but here, upon the borders of the great Andredwald—the dense forest that stretched almost continuously from the Thames to the South Coast—the peaceful herdsmen were content to acknowledge their new masters, so only they might be left undisturbed.

And respectable obscurity has ever been the distinguishing characteristic of Godalming. At intervals, indeed, we hear of it as the site of a hunting-lodge of the Merry Monarch; and once, in 1726, "Godliman" (as the vulgar tongue had it then)[1] was the scene of a most remarkable imposture; but, generally speaking, the town lived on, the world forgetting and by the world forgot, saving only those whose business carried them here by coach on their way to or from Portsmouth; and Godalming remained in their memories chiefly, no doubt, by reason of the excellent fare dispensed at the "King's Arms," where the coaches stopped. The "King's Arms" is there to this day, in one of the passage-like streets by the Market House; this last quite a curiosity in its way. The "King's Arms," doubtless so called from the frequent visits of Charles II. and his Court on their hunting expeditions, has a quite wonderful range of stables and outhouses, reached through a great doorway from the street, through which the mails and stages passed in days when road-travel was your only choice who journeyed to and fro in the land. It is a matter of sixty years since those capacious stalls and broad-paved yards witnessed the stir and bustle of the stablemen, coachmen, post-boys, and all the horsey creatures who found employment in the care of coach and horses, and they are so many lumber-rooms to-day.

---

[1] This corrupt pronunciation is perpetuated in "Godliman" Street, by St. Paul's Churchyard, in London.

But Godalming was a place notorious in the eighteenth century as the scene of one of the most impudent frauds ever practised upon the credulity of mankind. There have been those who have said that

MARKET-HOUSE, GODALMING.

such trickery as that to which Mary Tofts, the "rabbit-breeder" of Godalming, lent herself, would meet with no success in so enlightened an age as this; but in so saying those folk have done a little less than justice to the eighteenth century, and have been particularly lenient to the nineteenth, which has proved itself, in the matter of Mahatmas, at least as credulous as by-gone ages were.

The story of Mary Tofts, if not edifying, is at least interesting. She was the wife of Joshua Tofts, a poor journeyman cloth-worker of this little town, and was described as of "a healthy, strong constitution, small size, fair complexion, a very stupid and sullen temper, and unable to write or read." Stupid or not, she possessed sufficient cunning to maintain her fraud for some time, and even to delude some eminent surgeons of the day into a firm belief in her pretended births of rabbits. For this was the preposterous nature of the imposition, and she claimed to have given birth to no less than eighteen of them. She attempted to account for this remarkable progeny by recounting how, "when she was weeding a field, she saw a rabbit spring up near her, after which she ran, with another woman that was at work just by her: this set her a-longing for rabbits. . . . Soon after, another rabbit sprang up near the same place, which she likewise endeavoured to catch. The same night she dreamt that she was in a field with those two rabbits in her lap, and awoke with a sick fit, which lasted till morning; from that time, for above three months, she had a constant and strong desire to eat rabbits, but being very poor and indigent, could not procure any." A Mr. Howard, a medical man of Guildford, who claimed to have assisted Mary Tofts in giving birth to eighteen rabbits, seems, from the voluminous literature on this subject, to have been something of a party to the cheat; and even if we did not find him a guilty accomplice, there would remain the scarce more flattering designation of egregious dupe. But Mr. Howard, dupe or rogue, was extremely busy in publishing to the world the particulars of this extraordinary case. The woman was brought over from Godalming to Guildford, so that she might be under his more immediate care, and he wrote a letter to Dr. St. André, George I.'s surgeon and anatomist, asking him to come and satisfy himself of the truth of this marvel. St. André went to Guildford post-haste, and returned to London afterwards with portions of these miraculous rabbits, and with so firm a belief in the story that he wrote and published a pamphlet setting forth full details of these wonders —the first of a long series of tracts, serious and humorous, for and against the good faith of this story.

Public attention was now roused in the most extraordinary degree, and the subject of Mary Tofts and her rabbits was in every one's mouth. The caricaturists took the matter up, and Hogarth has left two engravings referring to it: a small plate entitled "Cunicularii, or the Wise Men of Godliman," and another, a very large and most elaborate print, full of symbolism and cryptic allusions, entitled "Credulity, Superstition, and Fanaticism."

Even the clergymen of the time rushed into the fray, and one went so far as to assert that Mary Tofts was the fulfilment of a prophecy in Esdras.

The King, too, was numbered among the believers, and things came to such a pass that ladies began to

MARY TOFTS.

be alarmed with apprehensions of bringing into the world some unnatural progeny. "No one presumed to eat a rabbit," and the rent of rabbit-warrens sank to nothing. But a German Court physician—a Dr. Ahlers—who had proceeded to Guildford in order to report upon the matter to his Majesty, was rendered sceptical as much by the behaviour of Mr. Howard as by that of his interesting patient. He returned to town, convinced of trickery, and finally Mary Tofts and her medical adviser were brought to London and lodged in the Bagnio, Leicester Fields, where, in fear of combined threats of punishment and an artfully-pictured operation darkly hinted at by Sir Richard Manningham, she confessed that the fraud had been suggested to her by a woman, a neighbour at Godalming, who, with the showman's instinct of Barnum, told her that here was a way to a good livelihood without the necessity of working for it. The part taken by Mr. Howard has never been satisfactorily explained, but as he was particularly insistent that Mary Tofts deserved a pension from the King on account of her rabbits, his part in the affair has, naturally, been looked upon with considerable suspicion. Doctor and patient were, however, committed to Tothill Fields, Bridewell.

Mary Tofts died many years later, in 1763, but a considerable time elapsed before she was forgotten, and portraits and pamphlets relating to her imposition found a ready sale. A rare tract, in which she is supposed to state her own case, still affords amusement to those who care to dig it up from the dusty accumulations of the British Museum. In it the interviewer of that age says, "It was thought fit to print her opinions *in puris naturalibus*, (*i. e.*) in her own Stile and Spelling"; and a taste of her "stile" may be had from the following elegant extract:—

"Thof I be ripurzentid as an ignirunt littirat Wuman, as can nethur rite nor rede, yet I thank God I can do both; and thof mahaps I cant spel as well as sum peple as set up for authurs, yet I can rite trooth, and plane *Inglish*, wich is mor nor ani of um all has dun. As for settin my Mark to a papur, it was wen I wont well, and wos for goin the shortist wa to work: if tha had axt me to rite my name, I wood hav dun it; but tha onli bid me set my mark, as kunclooding I cood not rite my nam, but tha was mistakn."

And here is emphasis indeed!—

"All as has bin sad, except what I have here written, is a damd kunfounded ly.
"MERRY TUFT."

Mary Tofts made one more public appearance before she joined the great majority, and that was an occasion as little to her credit as the other. Thus we read that, in 1740, she was committed to Guildford Gaol for receiving stolen goods!

XIX

IN a more than usually quiet street, upon the edge of the town, stands the old church of Godalming, dedicated to SS. Peter and Paul, whose tall leaden spire rises with happy effect above the roofs, and gives distant views of Godalming a quiet and impressive dignity all its own among country towns. Vicars of

Godalming have not infrequently distinguished themselves; some for piety, one for piety combined with pugnacity, two for literature and learning, and at least one for "pride, idleness, affectation of Popery," and for refusing to preach. This last-named divine, Dr. Nicholas Andrews, had the misfortune to have been born out of due time, for had he but held the living in the sceptical eighteenth century instead of exactly a hundred years earlier, when piety was particularly aggressive, his passion for fishing on Sunday would have done him no harm. As it happened, however, his era fell in the midst of Puritan times, and the Godalming people of that day were at once godly and vindictive: a combination not at all uncommon even now. At any rate, they petitioned Parliament for the removal of this too ardent fisherman, and he was sequestered accordingly.

The times were altered when the Rev. Samuel Speed, grandson of Speed the historian, held the living. He was, according to Aubrey, a "famous and valiant sea-chaplain and sailor," whose deeds are handed down to us in the stirring lines of a song "made by Sir John Birkenhead on the sea-fight with the Dutch"; in which we hear of this doughty cleric praying and fighting at one and the same time:—

> "His chaplain, he plied his wonted work,
> He prayed like a Christian and fought like a Turk;
> Crying, 'Now for the King and the Duke of York,'
> With a thump, a thump, thump," &c.

This worthy was at one time a buccaneer in the West Indies, and later, while he held the living of Godalming, was imprisoned several times for debt.

He died, indeed, in gaol, and was buried in London, in the old City church, since demolished, of St. Michael, Queenhithe, in 1682.

Manning, scholar and historian of Surrey, was vicar here, and also the Rev. Antony Warton. Their virtues and their attainments are duly set forth upon cenotaphs within the church, as also is the discovery of a certain cure for consumption by

> "Nathaniel Godbold Esqr.
> Inventor and Proprietor
> of that Excellent Medicine
> The Vegetable Balsam
> For the cure of Consumption and Asthmas."

He died in December 1799, aged sixty-nine, and his appreciative relatives caused to be engraved on his epitaph, *Hic cineres, ubique Fama*; which really is very amusing, because his fame is now-a-days as decayed as are his ashes.

And yet they say these latter days of ours are distinguished above all else by shameless puffery! At least we spare the churches and do not use their walls as advertisement hoardings. And, despite Godbold and his Balsam, consumption still takes heavy toll, and not all the innumerable remedies nor all the Kochs in creation seem able to prevail in any degree against the disease.

At a short distance from the church, on the edge of a thickly-wooded hill overlooking New Godalming station, stands the house and small estate of Westbrook, once belonging to the Oglethorpes, who settled here from Yorkshire in the seventeenth century. Of this family was that notable octogenarian, General

NEW GODALMING STATION.

Oglethorpe, the literary discoverer of Dr. Johnson, friend of Whitefield and founder of Georgia. During a long and active life that extended from 1698 to 1785, Oglethorpe had many experiences. He warred with the Indians who threatened the North American Colonies; he was secretary and aide-de-camp to Prince Eugene, when, according to the alliterative poet, that " good prince " bade

> " An Austrian army, awfully arrayed,
> Boldly by battery bombard Belgrade."

He was suspected of Jacobite leanings, and was court-martialled for want of diligence in following up the Pretender's forces in their retreat from Derby; but he is memorable from a Londoner's point of view chiefly because he claimed to have, when a young man, shot woodcock on the spot where in his old age rose the fashionable lounge of Regent Street.

Westbrook, too, has some slight connection with the Stuart legend; for General Oglethorpe's father— Sir Theophilus Oglethorpe—was a devoted partisan of that unlucky House, and it was whispered that one of his sons was the famous child smuggled into Whitehall Palace in a warming-pan, and known afterwards as the Old Pretender.

One of the most pleasing views of Godalming is that from the grounds of Westbrook, above the railway-station, and the station of New Godalming itself and its situation are distinctly picturesque, composing finely with the Frith Hill and the uplands away in the direction of Charterhouse.

And Godalming is celebrated in modern times on

two distinct counts: firstly for having been a pioneer in lighting street-lamps by electricity, and secondly for being the new home of Charterhouse School, removed from London in 1870, under the care of the Rev. W. Haig Brown, who still remains head-master of Thomas Sutton's old foundation. The school-buildings stand on the plateau of a down, at a distance of about a mile from Godalming, and occupy a site of about eighty acres.

Here the Carthusians carry on the traditions of their old home in London, and some of the stones of the old school, deeply carved with the names of by-gone scholars, have been removed from old Charterhouse to the new building, where they are to be seen built into an archway. Charterhouse School numbers five hundred scholars, and its lovely situation, amid the Surrey Hills, together with its finely-planned buildings and spreading grounds, render this amongst the foremost public schools of the time.

One of the most interesting features of the school is its museum, housed in a building of semi-ecclesiastical aspect, built recently in the grounds. Here are many relics of old times and old scholars, together with the more usual collections of a country museum: stuffed birds, chipped flints, and miscellaneous antiquities; or, to quote the sarcastic Peter Pindar:—

> "More broken pans, more gods, more mugs;
> Old snivel-bottles, jordans, and old jugs;
> More saucepans, lamps, and candlesticks, and kettles;
> In short, all sorts of culinary metals!"

Among the *alumni* of Charterhouse were Addison and Steele; John Wesley, the founder of Methodism;

Chief Justice Blackstone, Sir Henry Havelock, Grote, Thackeray, and John Leech. Several of these distinguished Carthusians are represented here, in a fine collection of autographs and manuscripts. First, in point of view of general interest, is a collection of drawings and poems in their original MS. by Thackeray. Some thirty of his weird sketches are here, with the manuscript of "The Newcomes," bound

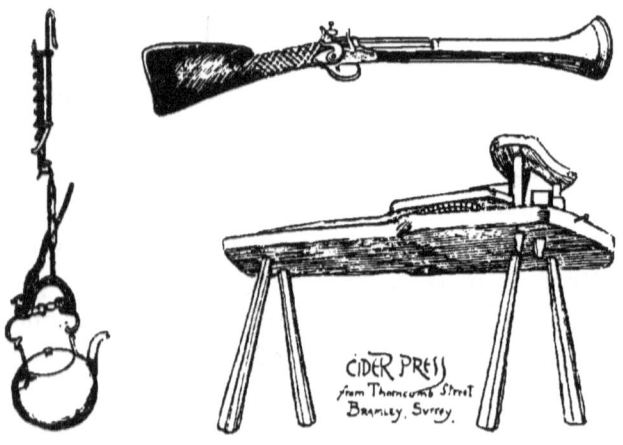

CHARTERHOUSE RELICS.

up in five volumes. Here also is Thackeray's Greek Lexicon, covered thickly with school-boy scrawls and scribbles.

Leech, the caricaturist,—one of the most absurdly over-rated men of this century,—was at Charterhouse from 1825 to 1831. Here are two letters from him, written, it would seem, when he was ten years of age, and apparently before he had been taught the use of capital letters. In one to "my dear mama," he seems to have been in a far from happy frame of mind. His "mama" had been to the school, but had not seen him, "me being in the grounds." "That," he adds, "made me still more unhappy." Writing to "my dear papa," young Leech is "happy to say I am promoted, because I know it pleases you very much. allow me to come out to see you on saturday because I have a great deal to tell you, and I want some one to assist me in the exercises because they are a great deal harder."

GOWSER JUG.

There is a very characteristic letter by John Wesley, and close by it a letter by Blackstone, part of which is worth reproducing. Writing on August 28, 1744, Blackstone, then a Fellow of All Souls, Oxford, says: "We were last Friday entertained at St. Mary's by a curious sermon from Wesley ye Methodist. Among other equally modest particulars, he informed us (1) that there was not one Christian among all ye heads of houses; (2) that pride, gluttony, avarice, luxury, sensuality, and drunkenness were ye whole characteristics of all Fellows of Colleges, who were useless to proverbial uselessness; lastly, that ye younger part of ye University were a generation of triflers, all of them perjured, and not one of them of any religion at all. His notes were demanded by ye Vice-Chancellor, but on mature deliberation it has been thought better to punish him by mortifying neglect." Which is all very humorous, and the phrase " mortifying neglect "

WESLEY.

distinctly good, as showing that the authorities had taken Wesley's measure to a nicety, and were maliciously aware that neglect *would* mortify a person of his essential vanity a great deal more than persecution.

A striking bust of Wesley stands beside a statuette of Thackeray; but among the chiefest articles of interest in the School Museum are the curious objects illustrating the rural life of Surrey in the olden times:

a primitive hand cider-press, from Bramley, a "pot-hook hanger" from Shamley Green, and a "baby-runner" from Aldfold. Other curiosities are a bust of Nelson, cut by a figure-head carver from the main-beam of the "Victory"; "Gowser" jugs and cups, formerly used by gown boys of Charterhouse, and decorated with the arms and crest of Thomas Sutton, together with his pious motto, *Deo dante dedi;*

BUST OF NELSON, CARVED FROM MAIN-BEAM OF THE "VICTORY."

and an Irish blunderbuss of the most murderous and forbidding aspect.

So much for Godalming, its sights and its memories. But we have halted here longer than the most dilatory coach that ever rumbled into the "King's Arms" Hotel, that house of good food and plenty in days when men had robust appetites, fit to vie with that of Milo the Cretonian. What glorious twists (for instance) must Peter the Great and his suite have possessed when they lodged here, twenty-one of them, all told, on their way from Portsmouth to London;—that is to say, if we are to take this breakfast and this dinner as sample meals :—

Breakfast.

Half a sheep.
A quarter of lamb.
10 pullets.
12 chickens.
3 quarts of brandy.
6 quarts of mulled wine.
7 dozen of eggs,
   with salad in proportion.

Dinner.

5 ribs of beef, weighing 3 stone.
1 sheep.
56¾ lbs. of lamb.
1 shoulder of veal, boiled.
1 loin   ,,   ,,
8 rabbits.
2 dozen-and-a-half of sack.
1   ,,   claret.

These details are from a bill now in the Bodleian Library, at Oxford, and are earnest of Gargantuan appetites that have had their day. If only we could compare this fare with the provand supplied to the Allied Sovereigns at the same house by Host Moon when those crowned heads and their suites were travelling to Portsmouth for the rejoicings over the final overthrow of the Corsican Ogre! Their Majesties must have had a zest for their banquets that had been a stranger to them all too long in the terrible years when Napoleon was hunting their armies all over Europe, from Madrid to Moscow.

XX

FROM Godalming the old coachmen had an easy run until they passed the hamlet of Milford, in those days a very small place indeed, but grown now to the importance of a thriving village, standing amid level lands where the road branches to Chichester. Once past Milford, however, they had need of all their skill, for here the road begins to rise in the long five miles ascent of Hindhead, and they found occasion for all their science in saving their cattle in this long and arduous pull through a stretch of country that for ruggedness has scarce its compeer in England.

Up to this point the villages and roadside settlements are numerous; but now we leave the "White Lion" at Moushill behind, the more ordinary signs of civilization are missing, and long stretches of heath and savage hill-sides become familiar to the eye. On the right of the road lies Thursley Common, a perfectly wild spot occupying high ground covered with sand hummocks and tangled heather, and wearing all the characteristics of mountain scenery. To the left stretches Witley Common, in the direction of artist-haunted Witley and beautiful Haslemere, and in the distance are the sandy hillocks known as the Devil's Jumps.

No road so wild and lonely as the Portsmouth Road, from the time when mail-coaches first travelled along it, in 1784, until recent years, when houses began to spring up in the wildest spots. From Putney Heath to Portsdown Hill the road runs, for more than three-quarters of its length, past ragged

THE DEVIL'S PUNCH BOWL.

heaths, tumbled commons, and waste lands, chiefly unenclosed; and the sombre fir tree, with its brothers, the larch and pine, is the predominant feature of the copses and woodlands that line the way. See what a long list the wayside commons make from London to Portsmouth. To Putney Heath succeeds Wimbledon Common, Ditton Marsh, Fairmile Common, and the commons of Wisley and Peasmarsh, all this side of Godalming; while those of Witley, Hindhead, and Milland, with the bare and open downs of Rake and Chalton, and the remains of Bere Forest, render the remainder of the way one long expanse of free and open land.

Hindhead is the culminating-point of all this agriculturally barren, but artistically delightful, country, and to see Hindhead aright requires the grey and tender mists of late autumn. This road, in fact, is seen at its best, from start to finish, in the last days of October or in the first weeks of November, when the red sun sets in the early evening like a huge fiery globe across the wastes and the darkling coppices, and gleams like molten metal between the tall straight trunks of the melancholy fir trees that stand like dumb and monstrous battalions deployed across the tangled crofts. So much has been said and written in praise of Hindhead, that I have known people to come away from it with a disappointed surprise. They looked for a deeper profundity in the Devil's Punch Bowl, and saw but a cup-like depression (marked on the maps as Haccombe Bottom), where they expected to find the beetling cliffs and craggy precipices of the Pyrenees, with, perhaps, the Foul Fiend himself waiting below amid the scrub and the heather for any one more adventurous than his fellows who should essay to climb down and investigate the scene. I will allow that the tourists who come here at mid-day of some blazing summer, and gaze with an air of disappointment at what some reckless writers have called "these awful depths." have a right to their dissatisfaction, for the Punch Bowl is least impressive at such a time, when never a shadow throws aërial perspective into the view, nor mists hide with a delicate artistic perception the prosaic fields which the merely utilitarian instincts and industry of the farmer have created from the surrounding waste. The imagination is curbed at this bald statement of facts under a cloudless sky, and I may confess that a first sight of this famous spot under similar conditions sent me away with no less a sense of disappointment. But try the same scene on an autumn evening, when a grey-blue haze in the atmosphere meets the white ground-mists, and your imagination has then a free rein. There is no telling at such a time what may be the depths of the Punch Bowl; and as for the houses that stand upon the topmost ridge of Hindhead, why, they wear all the appearance of romantic castles, in which not nineteenth-century villadom dwells, but where daredevil barons of Rhine-legend, or of the still more terrible Mrs. Radclyffe type, exercise untrammelled their native ferocity, even unto the colophon of the third volume.

The wild grandeur of Hindhead and the gloomy depths of the Devil's Punch Bowl are rendered additionally impressive by the memory of a particularly brutal murder committed here, in 1786, upon an unknown sailor, who was walking to Portsmouth to rejoin his ship.

HINDHEAD. *After J. M. W. Turner.*

On the 24th of September in that year three men—Edward Lonegon, Michael Casey, and James Marshall—were tramping to Portsmouth in search of employment, when they met the sailor near Esher. He treated them to drink, and offered to bear the expense of their journey, and they continued together down the road. At the "Red Lion," in Road Lane, beyond Godalming, where they stopped for refreshment, they were observed by two labouring men who chanced to be in the house, and who, later in the day, followed in their footsteps when returning home. On coming to the Devil's Punch Bowl they noticed something lying below, amid the heather, that looked like a dead sheep, but on climbing down to examine it, they found it to be the dead body of the sailor they had seen drinking in the "Red Lion." His villainous companions had knocked him down and killed him, "each agreeing to have two cuts at his throat," and after stripping the body they had rolled it into the hollow.

An alarm was raised, and the three murderers were overtaken at the hamlet of Sheet, near Petersfield, where they were actually selling the clothes of their victim in a public-house. Arrested here, they were tried at the Spring Assizes of 1787, held at Kingston-on-Thames, were sentenced to death, and hanged on April 7, their bodies being afterwards gibbeted on Hindhead, the scene of their crime. For years afterwards the place was known as Gibbet Hill, and, indeed, the country folk still speak of it by that name. The tall post of the gibbet appears in Turner's view of Hindhead in the "*Liber Studiorum,*" and the road is shown winding amid the downs, with a coach in the distance. Turner's view must be accepted with all reserve, *as a view*, for he never sank the artist in the mere topographical draughtsman; and the gibbet is quite an effort of his imagination, for even so early as Gilbert White's time, it was shattered in a terrific thunderstorm, as the old naturalist relates.

But although Turner has exaggerated the ruggedness of Hindhead in his picture, the place is not at all gracious or suave. Cobbett roundly declared that it was "certainly the most villainous spot that God ever made"; and how wild it was in the seventeenth century, before even the old high-road was in existence, we may gather from an entry in Pepys' Diary of August 6, 1668 : "So to coach again, and got to Liphook, late over Hindhead, having an old man, a guide, in the coach with us; but got thither with great fear of being out of our way, it being ten at night." Hindhead was in the direct line of signalling semaphores between Greenwich and Portsmouth before the days of the electric telegraph, and every day at one o'clock the time was passed down from the Observatory. People used to set their watches by the waving semaphore arms.

Until 1826 the old Portsmouth Road went along the very summit of Hindhead, and its course, although deeply rutted and much overgrown with grass, can still be readily traced near by the great cross of Cornish granite, erected here, 345 feet above the deepest depths of the Devil's Punch Bowl, by Sir William Erle, Chief Justice of the Common Pleas, in 1851, in memory of the murdered sailor. The Latin inscriptions, *In luce spes, Post tenebras lux*, and others, do not seem particularly appropriate to either the place or the occasion.

The old highway followed the very brink of the Punch Bowl, and was in winter-time extremely dangerous for coaches. To avoid the chance of accident a new roadway was constructed some sixty feet lower, with a substantial earthen embankment on the outer side, to prevent any unlooked-for descent into this precipitous gulf.

The headstone which was set up to mark the spot where the sailor was murdered has been removed, and placed beside this newer road, where its position renders its legend peculiarly vivid and terrible, although it is couched only in the plainest and least affected of phrases. One side is shown in the illustration, the other repeats the date of its erection, and invokes a curse upon "the man who injureth or removeth this stone"; but whether or no the man who thus invites the wrath of heaven would have included the Ordnance Surveyors, I cannot say. Certainly *they* have "injured this stone" by carving upon it the Governmental "broad arrow." The body of the murdered sailor was buried at the little village of Thursley, some two miles distant, and there, in the churchyard, shadowed by dark fir trees, stands a gruesome tombstone, an unconscionable product of local art, with a carving in relief of the three murderers in the act of dispatching their victim. Beneath this melodrama, the circumstances are recounted at great length, and some halting verses conclude the mournful narration.

Thursley itself is situated on an old road that branches from the newer highway upon entering Witley Common, and rejoins the ordinary route near the "Royal Huts" Hotel. The village is rarely visited by strangers. The old church stands in a commanding position, overlooking a wide tract of country, including the Hog's Back, by Guildford, and the

TOMBSTONE, THURSLEY.

scattered ponds of Frensham. An old sun-dial on the tower has the inscription *Hora pars vitæ*, and, like most of our clocks and watches, perpetuates in the numeral "IIII" the long-exploded fiction of the infallibility of kings. I wonder if any one remembers the origin of the substitution of "IIII" for "IV" on nearly all the dials, whether sun-dials or clock-faces, of civilization? Here is the story. The first clock that kept anything like accurate time was constructed by a certain Henry Vick, in 1370. It was made to

THURSLEY CHURCH.

the order of Charles V. of France, who was known as "the Wise." Wise he certainly was, in some respects; but Roman numerals were not within the sum of his knowledge. When Vick brought the King his clock, he looked at its movements awhile. "Yes," said he, at length, "it works very well; but you have got the figures on the dial wrong." "Surely never, your Majesty," said Vick. "Yes," replied the King, "that IV should be IIII." "But your Majesty is wrong," rejoined that not very tactful clockmaker. "Wrong!" answered outraged majesty, "I am never wrong! Take it away and correct the error." Vick did as he was commanded, and so to this day we have IIII where we should really have IV.

SUN-DIAL, THURSLEY.

There is a certain interest bound up with the name of Thursley, for it affords an excellent example of the lengths to which antiquaries will go, to scent derivatives. Kemble, the learned author of a deep and scholarly book, "The Saxons in England," derives the name of Thursley from the Scandinavian god

Thor, whose equivalent in Saxon mythology was Thunor. The name of Thunder Hill, a height near the village, has the same origin; but the clinching argument of the neighbouring "Hammer Ponds," which Mr. Kemble assumes to have been named after Thor's hammer, spoils the reasoning of the theory altogether, for the "Hammer Ponds" are nothing but the remains of the old forges that were thickly spread over the surface of Kent, Surrey, and Sussex during a period from three centuries to one hundred years ago.

Just where the road from Thursley rejoins the highway stands the "Huts" Inn, now enlarged and refurbished, and nothing less, if you please, in these days than the "Royal Huts" Hotel. "Ma conscience!" I wonder what friend Cobbett would have thought, *and* said. But, believe me, nothing less than this would serve the turn of Hindhead district now-a-days, for it is fast becoming as suburban as (say) Clapham. Do you want a building-plot, carved out of a waste, where nothing has yet bloomed but the tiny purple bells of the heather or the golden glory of the gorse? Here, then, is your chance, for building-plots fringe the road where, indeed, the trim-built villa has not already risen. Professor Tyndall, who built a house for himself just here, in 1882, selected the situation both for its health-giving air and for its seclusion, but his example served only to advertise the attractions of the place, and the astonishing favour with which Hindhead is now regarded as a residence is directly attributable to him. No one was less pleased than himself at this sudden popularity of a district that had but a few years previously been a more or less "howling" wilderness, for "he was always curiously sensitive to the beauty of scenery," disliked suburbs, and was also singularly sensitive to being overlooked from any neighbouring house. This preference for reclusion led to the building of the hideous screens which hid from his gaze an ugly house close at hand, and created so much angry controversy a few years ago: screens that to-day remain an unfailing reminiscence of the Professor. *Sic monumentum requiris, circumspice*, to quote the old tag.

XXI

AND now, save for the slight rise of Cold Ash Hill, it is all down-hill to Liphook, and excellent going, too, on a fine gravelly road, closely compacted and well kept. The country, though, is still wild and unfertile, and for long stretches, after passing the "eligible plots" of Hindhead, the road is seen narrowing away in long perspectives with never a house in sight. In midst of all this waste stands a lonely roadside inn—the "Seven Thorns" a wayside sign proclaims it to be—which draws its custom the Lord only knows whence. It is frankly an inn for refreshing and for passing on your way: no one, I imagine, ever wants to stay there; and by its cold and cheerless exterior appearance one might readily come to the conclusion that no one even lived there. The sign is singular, and seems either descriptive or legendary. If legend it has, no whisper of it has

ever reached me; while as for descriptiveness, the "seven thorns" are simply non-existent; and so the sign is neither more nor less a foreshadowing of the place than the average Clapham "Rosebank" or the Brixton "Fernlea."

Even on a summer's day one does not find the immediate neighbourhood of the "Seven Thorns" Inn particularly exhilarating or cheerful, for, although the country is open and unspoiled by buildings, yet the scenery lacks the suavity of generous land, prolific of fine timber and graceful foliage. The soil is ungrateful and unproductive; nourishing only the gorse and the hardy grasses that grow upon commons and cover the nakedness of the harsh sand and gravel of the surrounding country-side. Such trees as grow about here are wind-tossed and scraggy, bespeaking the little nutriment the land affords, and the greater number of them are firs and pines, which, indeed, are the chiefest of Hampshire's sylvan growths.

But in winter-time this unsheltered tract is swept with piercing winds that know no bulwark, nor any stay against their furious onslaughts; and here, in the great snow-storm of Yule-tide 1836, the Portsmouth coaches were nearly snowed up. "The snow," says a writer of local gossip, "was lying deep upon Hindhead, and had drifted into fantastic wreaths and huge mounds raised by the fierce breath of a wild December gale. Coach after coach crawled slowly and painfully up the steep hill, some coming from London, others bound thither. But as the 'Seven Thorns' was neared, they one and all came to a dead stop. The tired, wearied, exhausted cattle refused to struggle through the snow-mountains any longer. Guards, coachmen, passengers, and labourers attacked those masses of spotless white with spade and shovel, but all to no purpose. It seemed as if a way was not to be cleared. What stamping of feet and blowing of nails was there! Women were shivering and waiting patiently; men were shouting, grumbling, and swearing; and indeed the prospect of spending a winter's night upon the outside of a coach on such a spot was, to say the least of it, not cheerful. At last a brave man came to the rescue. The 'Star of Brunswick,' a yellow-bodied coach that ran nightly between Portsmouth and London, came up. The coachman's name was James Carter, well known to many still living. He made very little to-do about the matter, but, whipping up his horses, he charged the snow-drifts boldly and resolutely, and with much swaying from side to side opened a path for himself and the rest."

And so the Portsmouth Road was kept open in that wild winter, while most of the main roads in England were hopelessly snowed up. But memories of coaching days on this old road are rather meagre, for, although sea-faring business sent a great many travellers journeying between London and the dockyard town, the Portsmouth Road was never celebrated for crack coaches or for record times, and when coaching was in full swing, men saw as little romance in being dragged down the highways behind four horses as we can discover in railway travelling. With coach-proprietors, the horsing and equipping of a coach were matters of business, and beyond looking shrewdly after that business, the most of them cared little enough for coaching history. With the passengers, too, travelling was an evil to be endured. It irked them intolerably: it was a necessity, a duty,—what you will for unpleasantness,—and so, when the journey was done, the better part of them immediately dismissed it from their minds, instead of dwelling fondly upon the memories of perils overcome and rigours endured—as we are apt to imagine.

It was only when the Augustan age of coaching had dawned that travellers began to feel any delight or exhilaration in road-travel; and that age was cut short so untimely by the Railway Era that the young fellows and the middle-aged men whose blood coursed briskly through their veins, and who knew a thing or two about horse-flesh, felt a not unnatural regret in the change, and conceived an altogether natural affection for the old *régime*. Their regret can be the more readily understood when one inquires into the beginnings of railway travel; when conveyance by steam *might* have been more expeditious than the coach service (although what with delays and unpunctuality at the inauguration of railways even *that* was an open question), but certainly was at the same time much more uncomfortable. For, in place of the sheltered inside of a coach, or the frankly open and unprotected outside, the primitive railway passenger was conveyed to his destination in an open truck exposed to the furious rush of air caused by the passage of the train; and, all the way, he employed his time, not in admiring the landscape, or, as he was wont to do from a coach-top, in kissing his hand to the girls, but fleeted a penitential pilgrimage in scooping out from his eyes the blacks and coal-grit liberally imparted from the wobbly engine, own brother to the "Rocket," and immediate descendant of "Puffing Billy."

No wonder they regretted the more healthful and cleanly journeys by coach, and small blame to them if they voted the railway a nuisance; believed the country to be "going to the dogs," and agreed with the Duke of Wellington, when he exclaimed, upon seeing the first railway train in progress, "There goes the English aristocracy!"

For these men, and for the amateur coachees who during the Regency had occupied the box-seats of the foremost stages, this last period of coaching represented everything that was healthful and manly, and when the last wheel had turned, and the ultimate blast from the guard's bugle had sounded; when the roadside inn and its well-filled stables became deserted; and when the few remaining coachmen, post-boys, and ostlers had either accepted situations with the railway companies or had gone into the workhouse, a glamour clothed the by-gone dispensation that has lost nothing with the lapse of time. The pity is that these thorough-going admirers of days as dead as those of the Pharaohs were so largely "mute, inglorious Miltons," and have left so small a record of their stirring times awheel.

One of the last coachmen on this road was interviewed by a local paper some years ago, and the inclusion here of his reminiscences is inevitable. The "Last of the Old Whips" they called him:—

"He was sitting by a blazing fire, in a cheerful, pleasant room, evidently enjoying a glass of 'something hot' in the style that 'Samivel's father' would have thoroughly appreciated. But truth compels us to add that he had evidently seen better days, and that the comforts with which he was now temporarily surrounded had been strangers to him many a long day. Yet there were many still living who remembered 'young Sam Carter' as a dashing whip, who knew a good team when he sat behind them, and had handled the ribbons in a most workmanlike fashion. But the old fire and energy are still unquenched, either by the lapse of years or the pressure of hard times, and the veteran gladly gives the rein to memory and spins a yarn of the old coaching days.

"'The last conveyance of which I had charge,' said he, 'was the old "Accommodation." She was not a road wagon, but a van driven by five horses, three leaders abreast, and reaching London in sixteen hours. We used to start from the "Globe Inn," Oyster Street, Portsmouth, and finished the journey to London at the "New Inn," Old Change, or at the "Castle and Falcon," Aldersgate Street. Yes, I took to the road pretty early. I was only about sixteen or seventeen years of age when I took charge of the London mail for my father. Father used to ride to Moushill and back (that's seventy-two miles) every night for fifty years. He drove the night "Nelson" for thirty-two years. That was a coach with a yellow body, and about 1822 its name was altered to that of the "Star of Brunswick." It ran from the "Fountain" and the "Blue Posts," Portsmouth, to the "Spread Eagle," in Gracechurch Street. Its pace was about eight miles per hour, including changes. We only changed once between Portsmouth and Godalming, and that was at Petersfield, but the stages were terribly long, and we afterwards used to get another team at Liphook. The night coaches to London used to do the distance in about twelve hours, and the day coaches did it in nine hours; but the mails were ten hours on the road. The mail-coaches carried four inside and three out, with a "dickey" seat for the guard, who never forgot to take his sword-case and blunderbuss, though in my time we never had any trouble with highwaymen, and I never heard much about them stopping coaches in this neighbourhood. Of course every now and then a sailor would tumble off and break a leg, a head, or an arm, but that was only what you might expect. There were plenty of poachers and smugglers about, but no highwaymen. We did not have key bugles, as the books often say; the horn served our turn. William Balchin, who was guard with me as well as with father, was a good hand with his horn. I was guard for twelve months to the night " Rocket," which ran to the " Belle Sauvage," then kept by Mr. Nelson. It was established for the benefit of the people of Portsea, and only ran for six or seven years. The day " Rocket" was much older, and got a good share of the Isle of Wight traffic. Both these " Rockets" were white-bodied coaches. Francis Falconer, who died at Petersfield about 1874, drove the day

"Rocket" all the time it ran. Robert Nicholls was the only coachman that I ever knew to save money. He was a post-boy with me, and when he died he left a nice little fortune to each of his four daughters.

"'The "Independent" ran to the "Spread Eagle," and to the "Cross Keys," Wood Street. It was horsed by Mr. Andrew Nance as far as Petersfield, after which the two coachmen, Durham and Parkinson, found horses over the remaining stages. Yes, I knew old Sam Weller very well indeed. He drove the "Defiance" from the "George" and the "Fountain" to the Blue Coach Office, Brighton. The "Defiance" was painted a sort of mottled colour. Sam was a lame man, with a good-humoured, merry face, fond of a bit of fun, and always willing for a rubber. His partner was Neale, for whom I used sometimes to drive. He afterwards became landlord of the "Royal Oak," in Queen Street, Portsmouth. Do you see that scar, sir? I got that in 1841, through the breaking of my near hind axle as we came down through Guildford town. I was then driving the "Accommodation" between Ripley and Portsmouth. One night we were an hour late in starting. I had the guard on the box with me, and as we were going pretty hard down the High Street at Guildford I heard the wheel "scroop." The axle broke, and the next thing I remember was finding myself in bed at the "Ram" Hotel, where I had lain without speaking for a week. Whilst I was ill my wife presented me with twins, so that we had plenty of troubles at once. When I was driving the "Wanderer," a pair-horse coach, my team bolted with me near the "Seven

Thorns," and on another occasion a dog-cart got in the way of the "Star of Brunswick," and we capsized, and a lot of mackerel was spilt all over the road. That was about half-a-mile this side of Horndean. When I was first acting as post-boy my chaise got overturned, but on the whole I have been pretty fortunate. Once during a deep snow there was a complete block of coaches on the road at "Seven Thorns." My father undertook to lead the way, and he succeeded in opening the road for the rest. My father's name was James Carter. He was post-boy at the "Royal Anchor" Hotel, Liphook, at the time that the unknown sailor was murdered at the Devil's Punch Bowl. In fact, all my people belonged to Liphook. The names of the murderers were Michael Casey, James Marshall, and Edward Lonegon. They were captured the same day, in a public-house at Rake Hill, nearly opposite the present "Flying Bull," where they were offering a blood-stained jacket for sale. The poor fellow who was murdered was buried in Thursley churchyard.

"'I used to drive the "Tantivy,"—a day and night coach,—which afterwards ran only by day. We drove from Portsmouth to Farnborough station, then put the coach on the train, and drove into town from the terminus at Nine Elms.

"'Of course I remember the old "Coach and Horses," at Hilsea. It was afterwards burnt down. There was formerly a guard-house and picket at Hilsea Bridge, where the soldiers' passes were examined. Hilsea Green we used to reckon the coldest spot between Portsmouth and London. Once some bodysnatchers started from the "Green Posts," at Hilsea, with the officers in full cry after them, but the rascals had a famous mare, "Peg Hollis" (oh! she was a good 'un to go !), and got clear off.

"'Yes, I knew Lord Adolphus Fitzclarence well; he was a good friend to me. Many's the time he has sat beside me on the box, and at the end of the stage slipped a crown-piece into my hand.'"

XXII

AT the "Seven Thorns" Inn the three counties of Sussex, Surrey, and Hants are supposed to meet; but, like so many of the picturesque legends of county and parish boundaries that make one house stand in three or four parishes, this particular legend is altogether unfounded, for the three counties meet in a dell about two miles southward of the road, in Hammer Bottom, where once stood a lonely beer-house called the "Sussex Bell."

We will not turn aside to visit the site of the "Sussex Bell," or the remains of the Hammer Ponds that tell of the old iron-foundries and furnaces that were wont to make the surrounding hills resound and despoiled the dense woods of their noblest trees for the smelting of iron ore. We have no present business so far from the road in a place that has harboured no notorious evil-doer, nor has ever been the home of any distinguished man.

But we may well turn aside after passing Cold Ash Hill to explore a singular relic of monkish days that still exists, built into a comparatively modern farm-house and forgotten by the world.

Some three miles south of the road, reached by a turning below the "Seven Thorns" Inn, lies the little-visited village of Lynchmere, a rural parish, embowered in foliage and picturesquely situated amid hills; and in the immediate neighbourhood stand the remains of Shulbrede Priory, now chiefly incorporated with farm-buildings. The place is well worthy a visit, for the farm-house contains a room, called the Prior's Room, still decorated with monkish frescoes of a singular kind. These probably date almost as far back as the foundation of this Priory of Augustinian Canons, in the time of Henry III., and are unfortunately very much defaced. But sufficient can be discerned for the grasping of the idea, which seems to be a representation of the Nativity. The design introduces the inscription:— *Ecce virgo concipiet et pariet filium; et vocabitur nomen Jesus;* while a number of birds and animals, rudely drawn and crudely coloured, appear, with Latin legends issuing from their mouths. Uppermost stands the cock, as in the act of crowing, while from his beak proceeds the announcement, "*Christus natus est.*" Next follows a duck, from whose bill issues another label, inscribed "*Quando, quando?*" a query answered appropriately by a raven, "*In hac nocte.*" "*Ubi, ubi?*" asks a cow of a lamb, which rejoins, bleating "*In Bethlems.*"

But few other relics of this secluded priory are visible. Some arcading; a vaulted passage; fragments of Early English mouldings: these are all.

Somewhere underneath the pig-sties, cow-houses, and rick-yards of the farm rest the forgotten priors and the nameless monks of that old foundation. Haply this worn slab of stone has covered the remains of some jolly Friar Tuck or ascetic Augustine; this battered crocket, maybe, belonged to the tomb of some pious benefactor for whose benefit masses were enjoined to be said or sung for ever and a day; and I dare swear this obscure stone trough, filled with hog-wash, at which fat swine are greedily drinking, was once a coffin. Imperial Cæsar's remains had never so foul an insult offered them.

I lean across the fence and moralize; a most unpardonable waste of time at this *fin de siècle*, and I regret those old fellows whom Harry the Eighth in his reforming zeal sent a-packing, to beg their bread from door to door. I regret them, that is to say, from purely sentimental reasons, being, all the while, ready to allow the policy and the state-craft that drove them hence, and willing to acknowledge that the greasy cassocks and filthy hair-shirts of the ultimate occupants of these cloistral shades covered a multitude of sins.

I poke the porkers thoughtfully with a stick in the place where their ribs should be, but they are of such an abbatical plumpness that my ferrule fails to discover any "osseous structure." (I thank thee, Owen, for that phrase!) They respond with piercing cries that recall the shrieks and the yells of a witches' sabbath on the Brocken, as presented before a quailing Lyceum audience,—and their horrid chorus brings the farmer on the scene. "Who drives fat oxen should himself be fat," to quote the famous classical *non sequitur;* and how much more should it apply to him who fattens pigs to unwieldy masses of unconverted lard and pork! To do justice to the quotation, he *is* fleshy and of a full habit.

"Fine creeturs, them," says he. "Aye," say I. "Thirty score apiece, if they're a pound," he continues. They might be a hundred score for all I know; but no man likes to acknowledge agricultural ignorance, and so I agree with him, heartily, and with much appearance of wisdom. "Pooty creeturs, *I* say," continues the farmer, smacking a broad-bellied beast, with white bristles and pink flesh covered with black splotches. That dreadful creature looks up a moment from the trough, with ringed snout dripping liberally with hog-wash, and gazes pathetically at me for acquiescence. "Yes: fine animals," I say, in a non-committal voice.

"Pictures, they are," says their owner decisively. That settles the matter, and I am off, to seek the road to Liphook.

If the excellence of the great highways of England is remarkable, the tangled lanes and absolute rusticity of the roads but a stone's throw from the main routes call no less for remark. Here, just a little way from Liphook, and in the immediate vicinity of a railway, I might have been in the deepest wilds of Devon, so meandering were the lanes, so untamed the country. An old pack-horse trail, still distinct, though unused these many generations past, wandered along, amid gorse and bracken, and footpaths led in perplexingly-different directions.

Amid this profusion of wild life, with the dark foliage of the fir trees, the lighter leaves of the beech, and the gaily-flowered hedgerows on either hand, there appeared before me the most incongruous wayfarer: a Jingle-like figure, tall and spare, with a tightly-buttoned frock-coat, and a silk hat of another era than this, set well back upon his head—one who

"CONSIDERING CAP."

might have wandered here from Piccadilly in the '50's and lost his way back. I should not have been surprised had he asked news of the Great Exhibition; of Prince Albert, or the Emperor of the French. However, he merely said it was a fine day. "Yes, it was," I said; "but could he direct me to Liphook?" "Liphook?" said he, as though he had never heard the name; "I'm afraid I can't. I'm a stranger in these parts." And then he walked away. I believe he was a ghost!

XXIII

AND now the road brings us to the borders of Hants. It is no mere pose to assert that every English county has its own especial characteristics, an unmistakable and easily recognizable individuality: the fact has been so often noted and commented upon that it is fast becoming a truism. But of a county of the size of Hampshire, which ranks eighth in point of size among the forty English divisions, it would be rash to generalize too widely. One is apt to sum up this county as merely a slightly more gracious and generous variant of the forbidding downs and uplands of Wiltshire, but, although quite three-quarters of the area of Hants is poor, waterless, and inhospitable, yet there are fertile corners, nooks, and valleys, covered with ancient alluvial soil, that yield nothing to any other part of England.

Still, Fuller is a little more than just to Hampshire when he calls it "a happy countrey in the foure elements, if culinary *fire* in courtesie may pass for one, with plenty of the best wood for the fuel thereof; most pure and piercing the *aire* of this shyre; and none in England hath more plenty of clear and fresh rivulets of troutful *water*, not to speak of the friendly sea, conveniently distanced from London. As for the *earth*," he continues, "it is both fair and fruitful, and may pass for an expedient betwixt pleasure and profit, where by mutual consent they are moderately accommodated."

If old Fuller could revisit the scenes to which this

description belongs, he would indeed find profit but moderately accommodated, if at all; for as the greater proportion of the soil of Hampshire has always been notoriously poor, so now the farming of it has decayed from the moderately profitable stage to a condition in which the tenant farmer sits down in despair, and the landlord has to meet the changed conditions of the times with heavier reductions of rents than his contemporaries of more fertile counties are called upon to make. And even so, and despite the fifteen and twenty-five per cent. deductions that are constantly being made, innumerable farms have gone, or are going, out of cultivation in Hampshire, whose bare chalk downs and unkindly levels of sand are growing lonelier and more desolate year by year.

But a grateful and profitable feature of Hampshire are the water-meadows that border the fishful streams of the Itchen, the Test, and the Avon. They merit all the commendation that Fuller gives them, and more; but, so far as the Portsmouth Road is concerned, Hampshire exhibits its most barren, ill-watered, and flinty aspects; from the point where it enters the county, near Liphook, past the chalky excrescence of Butser Hill, through the bare and barren downs of Chalton, to Portsmouth itself.

Cobbett has not very much to say in praise of Hampshire soil, but he found a considerable deal of prosperity within its bounds in his day, when agricultural folk still delved, and rural housewives still kept house in modest fashion. Still! Yes, but already modern luxury and progress had appeared to leaven the homely life of the villager, when that

Q

indignant political and social censor was riding about the country and addressing the farmers on the State of Politics, the Price of Wheat, and the advantages of American Stoves.

Cobbett, writing in 1825, was particularly severe upon the farmers of his time, who were changing from the race he had known who sat with their carters and labourers at table; who, with their families, dined at the same board off fat bacon and boiled cabbage as a matter of course. "When the old farm-houses are down," he says, "(and down they must come in time), what a miserable thing the country will be! Those that are now erected are mere painted shells, with a mistress within who is so stuck-up in a place she calls the *parlour*" (note, by the way, the withering irony of Cobbett's italics), "with, if she have children, the 'young ladies and gentlemen' about her; some showy chairs and a sofa (a *sofa* by all means); half-a-dozen prints in gilt frames hanging up; some swinging bookshelves with novels and tracts upon them; a dinner brought in by a girl that is perhaps better 'educated' than she; two or three nick-nacks to eat instead of a piece of bacon and a pudding; the house too neat for a dirty-shoed carter to be allowed to come into; and everything proclaiming to every sensible beholder that there is here a constant anxiety to make a *show* not warranted by the reality. The children (which is the worst part of it) are all too clever to *work*; they are all to be *gentlefolks*. Go to plough! Good God! What! 'young gentlemen' go to plough! They become *clerks*, or some skimmy-dish thing or other. They flee from the dirty *work* as cunning horses do from the bridle. What misery is all this! What a mass of materials for proclaiming that general and *dreadful convulsion* that must, first or last, come and blow this funding and jobbing and enslaving and starving system to atoms!"

One only wonders, after reading all this, what Cobbett would have said at this time, when things have advanced another stage towards the millennium; when nick-nackery is abundant in almost every farm-house; when every other farmer's wife has her drawing-room ("parlour," by the way, being vulgar and American), and every farmer's daughter reads,—not tracts, my friend Cobbett,—but novelettes of the pseudo-Society brand.

Hampshire cottages remain practically the same, only the dear, delightful old thatches are gone that afforded pasturage for all sorts of parasitic plants and mosses; harboured earwigs and other insects too numerous to mention, and divided the artist's admiration equally with the rich red tiling of the more pretentious houses.

Hampshire cottage architecture is peculiarly characteristic of the county. The wayside villages and the scattered hamlets that nestle between the folds of its chalky hills are made up of cottages built with chalk rubble, or with black flints and red brick mixed. The flints being readily obtained, they form by far the greater portion of Hampshire walls; the red brick being used for dressings and for binding the long, flinty expanses together, or occupying the place taken by stone quoins, in counties where building-stone is freely found. Thus, the homely architecture of the greater part of Hants is mean and uninteresting, for black flint is not beautiful and has never been used with good effect in modern times, although in ancient days the mediæval builders and architects of East Anglia—notably in Ipswich and Bury St. Edmunds—contrived some remarkably effective work in this unpromising material. Some old work in the larger Hampshire towns, notably at Hyde Abbey, Winchester, shows an effective use of black flint in squares alternating with squared stone, —a method known as diaper work,—but the elaborate flint panelling of Norfolk and Suffolk is unknown in Hampshire.

And this brings me to Liphook, a roadside village perhaps originally sprung from the near neighbourhood of the old deer-forest of Woolmer, when half-forgotten Saxon and Norman kings and queens, earls and thanes, hunted here and made the echoes resound with the winding of their horns—"made the welkin ring," in fact, as the fine romantic writers of some generations ago said, in that free and fearless way which is, alas! so discredited now-a-days. And this is so much more a pity, because along this old road, upon whose every side the hallooing and the rumour of the hunting-field were wont to be heard so often and so loudly, one could have worked in that phrase about "the welkin" with such fine effect, had it not been altogether so battered and worn-out a literary *cliché*. This it is to be born a hundred years later than Sir Walter Scott!

The Royal Forest of Woolmer lies partly in this

parish. It is a tract of land about seven miles in length by two and a half in breadth, running nearly north and south. In the days of William and Mary the punishments of whipping and confinement in a house of correction were awarded to all them that should " burn on any waste land, between Candlemas and Midsummer, any grig, ling, heath, and furze, goss or fern"; yet in this forest, about March or April, according to the dryness of the season, such vast heath-fires were lighted up that they frequently became quite unmanageable, and burnt the hedges, woods, and coppices for miles around. These burnings were defended on the plea that when the old and coarse coating of heath was consumed, young and tender growths would spring up and afford excellent browsing for cattle; but where the furze is very large and old, the fire, penetrating to the very roots, burns the ground itself; so that when an old common or ancient underwoods are burnt, nothing is to be seen for hundreds of acres but smother and desolation, the whole extent of the clearance looking like the cinders of an active volcano.

One of these great fires broke out on May 22, 1881, and consumed over 670 acres. It was originated by the keepers of the Aldershot Game Preserving Association, for the purpose of obtaining a belt of burnt land around the Forest, to prevent the straying of the pheasants; but the fire, fanned by a wind, grew entirely out of hand and quite uncontrollable. Great damage was occasioned by this outbreak, and the Earl of Selborne's plantations were destroyed, together with those of the vicar, whose very house and stabling had a narrow escape. The Forest was the picture of desolation for a long time afterwards. The oaks were either dead or dying, and the whole district had an inexpressibly blasted and weird appearance.

"I remember," says Gilbert White, of a fire that occurred in his time, "that a gentleman who lives beyond Andover, coming to my house, when he got on the downs between that and Winchester, at twenty-five miles distance, was surprised with much smoke, and a hot smell of fire, and concluded that Alresford was in flames, but when he came to that town, he then had apprehensions for the next village, and so on to the end of his journey."

When the forest was enclosed, in 1858, about one thousand acres were allotted to the Crown.

XXIV

LIPHOOK is the centre of a tract of country thickly settled with "men of light and leading." From Hindhead and Haslemere on one side, to Rake and Petersfield on the other, are the country homes of men well known to fame. Away towards Haslemere, on the breezy heights of Blackdown, stands the picturesque modern house of Aldworth, the home, in his later years, of Tennyson; and on the very ridge of Hindhead is the obtrusive and still more modern house built by the late Professor Tyndall, with his hideous screens of turf and woodwork, set up by the Professor with the object of shielding his privacy from the curious gaze of the vulgar herd. Near by is a house lately built by Mr. Grant Allen, while Professor Williamson, the well-known professor of chemistry, resides close at hand, and conducts experiments with chemical fertilizers over some forty acres of wilderness and common land, which his care and long-enduring patience have at last made to "blossom like the rose." At Blackmoor, towards Selborne, Sir Roundell Palmer, Q.C., afterwards Lord Chancellor and Earl of Selborne ("the mildest-mannered man that ever helped to pass a Reform Bill or disestablish a Church"), has created a fine estate out of a waste of furze-bushes and heather; while he had for many years a neighbour at Bramshott in that eminent lawyer, Sir William Erle, who died at the Grange in 1880. Professor Bell, a natural historian after Gilbert White's own heart, and the editor of a scholarly edition of the "Natural History of Selborne," lived for many years at that village, in White's old home, the Wakes; and at Hollycombe, down the road, Sir John Hawkshaw, the well-known engineer and designer of the Victoria Embankment, had a beautiful demesne. Artists in plenty, including Vicat Cole, R.A., Mr. Birket Foster, and Mr. J. S. Hodgson, have delighted to make their home where these three counties of Sussex, Surrey, and Hampshire meet; and among literary men, the names of G. P. R. James and of Anthony Trollope occur. Some years ago, one who was familiar with the country-side said, while standing on the tower of Milland new church:—"Within a circle of twelve miles from here there are more brains than within any other country district in England," and if we read *quality* for quantity, I think he was right.

But if the neighbourhood of Liphook is the favoured home of so many distinguished men of our own time, the annals of that famous old hostelry, the " Royal Anchor," in Liphook village, can boast quite a concourse of royal visitors, from the first dawn of its history until the childhood of Queen Victoria; while as for historic people of less degree (although very great folk indeed in their own way), why, they are to be counted in battalions. In fact, had I time to write it, and you sufficient patience to read, I might readily produce a big book of bigwigs who, posting, or travelling by stage or mail to Portsmouth, have slept over-night under this hospitable roof. As for the royalties, one scarce knows where to begin: indeed, almost every English sovereign within the era of history has had occasion to travel to Portsmouth, and most of them appear to have been lodged at the "Anchor," as it was called before Mr. Peake very rightly, considering the distinguished history of his house, affixed the " Royal " to his old sign.

Records are left of a sovereign as early as the unfortunate Edward II. having visited Liphook, although we are not told by the meagre chronicles of his remote age whether the King, who came here for sport in his Royal Forest of Woolmer, stayed at an inn, nor, indeed, if there was any early forerunner of the " Anchor " here in those times. Edward VI. passed down the road to Cowdray, and Elizabeth, who was always "progressing" about the country, and, like the Irishman, never seemed so much at home as when she was abroad, halted here on her way to that princely seat, and put in a day or so hunting in the Forest.

Beyond the fact that the "Merry Monarch" journeyed to Portsmouth and stayed once at the "Castle" Inn, at Petersfield, we have no details of his hostelries. He was in a hurry when he came thus far, and troubled the Woolmer glades but little at any time. Queen Anne, who, after all, seems rather less of a sportswoman than any other of our Queens, came to Liphook and Woolmer for the express purpose of seeing the red deer whom her remote ancestor, the Conqueror, "loved like a father"; and after her time royal personages came thick and fast, like swallows in summer, and we find them conferring a deathless fame upon the old inn by the feasts they ordered, the pretty things they said, and the number of equipages they hired for the conveyance of themselves and their trains towards the sea-coast. But never was there in the history of the "Anchor" a more august company than that assembled here in 1815, after Waterloo, when the Prince Regent, journeying to Portsmouth to take part in the rejoicings and the reception of the Allied Sovereigns, entertained at luncheon these crowned heads, together with the Duchess of Oldenburg and Marshal Blucher. Afterwards came William IV., who, when Duke of Clarence and Lord High Admiral, had frequently stayed in the old house and taken his meals in the kitchen, sitting sometimes, with commendable and endearing *bonhomie*, on the edge of the kitchen table, gossiping with the landlord, and eating bread-and-cheese with all the gusto and lack of ceremony of a hungry plough-boy. The last royal personages to stay at the old inn were the Duchess of Kent and the Princess Victoria, who walked in the garden or showed themselves at the windows before the crowds who never failed to obstruct the roads, eager for a glance at their future Queen.

I must confess, however, staunch Tory of the most crusted and mediæval type though I be, that all this array of sovereigns *in esse* or *in posse* seems very dull, and bores me to yawning-point. With the exception of those two royal brothers, George IV. and the Fourth William, they seem not so much beings of flesh and blood as clothes-props and the deadly dull and impersonal frameworks on which were hung so many tinselled dignities and sounding titles. I turn with a sigh of relief to a much larger and a great deal more interesting class of travellers who have found beneath the hospitable roof of the "Royal Anchor" both a hearty welcome and the best of good cheer; travellers who, however much we may like or dislike them, were men of character who did not owe everything to the dignities to which they were born; who, for good or ill, carved their own careers and have left a throbbing and enduring personality behind them, while a king or a queen is usually remembered merely by a Christian name and a Roman numeral.

The guest-rooms of the "Royal Anchor" are called by regal names, and their titles of "King," "Queen," "Crown," or "George" are blazoned upon the doors with great pomp and circumstance; but as I have retired between the sweet-smelling, lavender-scented sheets in one or other of the spacious up-stair rooms and have dowsed the glim of my bedroom candle, I have considered with satisfaction not so much that "Farmer George" and his snuffy old *hausfrau* may have slept here, as that the dearest of old sinners and inconsequent gossips—I name Samuel Pepys—came to Liphook and "lay here" o' nights, in receipt of many conjugal reproaches, I doubt not, for certain gay vagaries, darkly hinted at with many "God forgive me's," in the pages of those confessions which men know by name as "Pepys' Diary."

Mr. Samuel Pepys, Secretary to the Admiralty first, and amiable gossip afterwards—although I fancy we generally reverse those titles to recognition—was among those travellers who have left some sign of their travels along these miles of heaths and open commons—this wildest high-road in all England. Apart from his suburban trip to Putney, we find the diarist chronicling journeys to and from Portsmouth.

On May 4, 1661, he left Petersfield. "Up in the morning," says he, "and took coach, and so to Gilford, where we lay at the 'Red Lyon,' the best inne, and lay in the room where the King lately lay in, where we had time to see the Hospital, built by Archbishop Abbott, and the free schoole, and were civilly treated by the Mayster.

"So to supper and to bed, being very merry about our discourse with the Drawers" (as who should say the Barmen) "concerning the minister of the towne, with a red face and a girdle.

"*5th, Lord's Day.* Mr. Creed and I went to the red-faced Parson's church, and heard a good sermon of him, better than I looked for. Anon we walked into the garden, and there played the fool a great while, trying who of Mr. Creed or I could go best over the edge of an old fountaine well, and I won a quart of sack of him. Then to supper in the banquet-house, and there my wife and I did talk high, she against and I for Mrs. Pierce (that she was a beauty), till we were both angry."

Seven years later, on August 6, 1688, to wit, Mr. Samuel Pepys was called on business to Portsmouth, and Mrs. Pepys determined to go with him, at an hour's notice. You may notice that Pepys says her readiness pleased him, but that would seem to be a shameless want of frankness altogether unusual in that Diary, wherein are set forth the secret thoughts and doings, not altogether creditable to him who set them down so fully and freely.

He did not travel as an ordinary commoner, being properly mindful of his dignity as Secretary of a Government Department, a dignity, be it observed, which it had been well if he had maintained more constantly before him. Thus he was not a passenger in the Portsmouth "Machine," which preceded the mail-coaches, but travelled in his own "coach" or "chariot," as he variously describes his private carriage. He would probably have fared better, swifter, and more certainly if he had used the public conveyance, but in that case we should have been the poorer by his description of a journey in which his coachman lost his way for some hours in the district

SAMUEL PEPYS.

between Cobham and Guildford, and the party came late for dinner to the "Red Lion":—

"*August 6th, 1688.* Waked betimes, and my wife at an hour's warning is resolved to go with me; which pleases me, her readiness. . . . To St. James's to Mr. Wren, to bid him 'God be with you!' and so over the water to Fox Hall; and then my wife and Deb. took me up, and we away to Gilford, losing our way for three or four miles about Cobham. At Gilford we dined; and I showed them the hospitall there of Bishop Abbot's, and his tomb in the church; which, and all the rest of the tombs there, are kept mighty clean and neat, with curtains before them. So to coach again, and got to Lippook, late over Hindhead, having an old man a guide in the coach with us; but got thither with great fear of being out of our way, it being ten at night. Here good, honest people; and after supper to bed.

"*7th.* To coach, and with a guide to Petersfield. And so," he says, "took coach again back" after dinner, and "came at night to Gilford; where the 'Red Lyon' so full of people, and a wedding, that the master of the house did get us a lodging over the way, at a private house, his landlord's, mighty neat and fine: and there supped; and so" (the usual formula) " to bed."

XXV

ANOTHER celebrated (or rather, notorious) person was used to lie here frequently on his journeys between town and the Isle of Wight. "Liberty"

Wilkes had an estate at Sandown (*he* calls it "Sandham"), and when he was not busy agitating and be-devilling ministers in London, he was taking the sea-breezes in the Wight and writing innumerable letters to his daughter, Polly.

Statesmen must have breathed much more freely when the demagogue had left London and they were rid for a while, however short, of "his inhuman squint and diabolic grin." If we are to believe his contemporaries and the portrait-painters, he was the ugliest man of his time, with the countenance of a satyr, to match and typify the low cunning and the obscenity of his crooked mind. "His personal appearance," wrote Lord Brougham, "was so revolting as to be hardly human;" and, indeed, apologists for Wilkes' character and appearance are singularly few among historians in these days, when it is the fashion to review by-past notorieties with the whitewash brush.

John Wilkes was born in 1727, and married, when in his twenty-second year, a lady of considerable fortune, who afterwards separated from him, chiefly owing to the disgust and abhorrence with which she looked upon his dissolute habits and profligate acquaintances, amongst whom he counted three of the most notorious rakes of the time, a time excelled in profligacy only by the reign of Charles II. Shortly after this separation, Wilkes joined a burlesque monastery, founded, amongst others, by those three vicious creatures and notorious rakes, Lord Sandwich, Thomas Potter, son of the Archbishop of Canterbury, and Sir Francis Dashwood. They occupied the ruins of an old Cistercian monastery that still stands on

JOHN WILKES.

the banks of the Thames at Medmenham, and passed their time in a blasphemous travesty of religion and the monastic life. The "Medmenham Monks," they called themselves, but were known generally as the "Hell-Fire Club."

If the Earl of Sandwich was the champion *roué*, rake, and profligate of a vicious age, certainly Wilkes almost bore away the distinction from him; as we may judge from the result of the election amongst the Medmenham revellers as to who should be chosen to take a place among the round dozen who played a leading part in their midnight orgies.

The Earl of Sandwich, as the greater reprobate of the two, was chosen, and Wilkes revenged himself upon the company by a practical joke, which admirably illustrates the nature of their proceedings. "While the profane revellers were feasting and uttering impious jests, Wilkes let loose, from a chest wherein he was confined, a baboon dressed according to the common representations of the Evil One. The moment chosen was during an invocation addressed by Lord Sandwich to his master, the devil. The consternation was indescribable. The terror communicated itself to the baboon, which bounded about the room and finally lighted on Lord Sandwich's shoulders, who in a paroxysm of terror recanted all he had been saying, and, in an agony of cowardice, prayed to Heaven for mercy."

Some years later, in 1757, Wilkes entered Parliament as member for Aylesbury, and became a supporter of the elder Pitt. When Pitt was in opposition and the scandalously venal, corrupt, and utterly incompetent ministry of Lord Bute misgoverned the country, Wilkes started the "North Briton," a periodical satire, both in its contents and its title, upon Scotchmen, who were then bitterly hated by the English, and upon the Scots in Parliament and in politics, among whom Bute was the most prominent. The persistent abuse which Wilkes showered upon the ministry had successfully damaged the Government by the time that his forty-fourth number had been published, and upon the appearance of the famous "Number 45," in 1763, containing criticisms of the King's Speech, it was resolved to prosecute him for seditious libel, to search his house, and to arrest himself, his printers, and publishers.

Wilkes desired nothing better than persecution. He was nothing of a patriot, but only a vulgar schemer who worked for notoriety and gain, and his craft, together with the inconceivable stupidity of the Government in making a martyr of him, assured him of both. The warrants for his arrest and for the seizure of his papers were declared illegal, and the numerous actions-at-law which he brought against members of the Cabinet and prominent officials in respect of those illegal proceedings, cost the Government which defended them no less than £100,000. Wilkes now reprinted "Number 45," and a majority in the House of Commons ordered the paper to be burned by the common hangman, and on January 19, 1764, voted his expulsion from the House, as the author of a scandalous and seditious libel. He was convicted in the Court of King's Bench for having re-published the obnoxious "Number 45," but did not present himself to receive sentence. He fled, in fact, to France, and resided there for four years, an outlaw. Twice he returned to England and unsuccessfully petitioned an incredibly obstinate and stupid King for a pardon, which, it is scarcely necessary to add, George III. refused to grant. On the second occasion a general election was in progress, and this agitator then sought re-election to Parliament, and stood for the City of London. Defeated in the City, he issued his election address the following day as a candidate for the county of Middlesex, and was returned triumphantly at the head of the poll. "Wilkes and Liberty!" was now the popular cry, and the member for Middlesex became more than ever the darling of the mob, the idol of the populace. But the extraordinary stupidity of King, Court, and Government, that had raised so utterly worthless and degraded a fellow as Wilkes to this high pinnacle, kept him there by another expulsion from the Commons, and by fines and imprisonment inflamed the anger of the crowd to such a pitch that Benjamin Franklin said, with every appearance of conviction, "that had Wilkes been as moral a man as the King, he would have driven George III. out of his kingdom." So strong were prejudices in favour of superficial morality in even that licentious age!

So sensible was Wilkes of the advantages conferred upon him by imprisonment, that when the savage mob rescued him from the coach that was conveying him to gaol, he escaped from them and gave himself up, rather than lose the advertisement of an incarceration. He had his reward subsequently, when, offering himself for re-election for Middlesex, he was returned with an enormous majority over Colonel Luttrell. The House of Commons, however, by a vain and impotent resolution, declared the latter to have been duly elected, and now, chiefly by the aid of folly and fortuitous circumstances, Wilkes found his fortunes identified with the cause of the Constitution and the liberty of the subject. He was elected Sheriff of London, and became in 1774 Lord Mayor, being returned as a member for Middlesex in the same year, unopposed, and for the fifth time. At this period the citizens of London conferred upon him the post of Chamberlain of the City, a position of great profit and consideration, which must have made amends for many inconveniences in the past.

And now, having attained all he could desire, Wilkes sank the patriot in the courtier. "Hush! you old fool!" said he at this period to an old woman who raised the stale cry of "Wilkes and Liberty" in the street; "that was all over long ago;" and, upon his being presented at Court during his Mayoralty, he made himself so agreeable to the King that the old Monarch declared he had never met so well-bred a Lord Mayor! Wilkes, not to be out-shone when compliments were going free, assured his Majesty that he had never been a Wilkite; and so, as in the fairy tales, "they lived happily ever afterwards."

Wilkes is seen to best advantage in his letters to his daughter. In them he dropped the turgid vehemence which characterized his public utterances, and became a quiet, mildly humorous gossip, concerned deeply about all manner of insignificant domestic details, the incidents of his journeys, and his sojournings in town or country. But from time to time the leer of the elderly satyr is seen in this correspondence, and passages are not infrequent in which the most frank and unlooked-for things, as between father and daughter, may be read. But you shall judge for yourself.

He writes from Newport, Isle of Wight, on June 9, 1772 :—

"MY DEAREST POLLY,

"I arrived at Cobham on Sunday before twelve, and dined, like a sober citizen, by one ; then sauntered through the elysium of Mr. Hamilton's gardens till eight in the evening, like the first solitary man through Paradise ; and afterwards went to bed before ten. Yesterday I got to Guildford by eleven, and paid my compliments to our good friend, Mrs. Waugh and her family: reached Portsmouth at five."

At a later date he writes from "Sandham" (Sandown) Cottage, a country retreat which he occupied frequently in these latter days, and several references to the Portsmouth Road occur from time to time, as he journeyed between Sandham Cottage and Prince's Court, London. He lay generally at the "Anchor," Liphook, where the landlady, Mrs. Keen, "dull and sour" though she might have been, according to one of Wilkes' letters, seems to have made the triumphant demagogue and his daughter sufficiently comfortable. Writing on September 14, 1788, he says :—

"My dearest Polly,

"I arrived at Sandham yesterday afternoon at three, after a lucky passage of an hour and five minutes. There was very little wind, and that quite adverse. I therefore hired for four-and-sixpence a wherry with two oars not larger than a Thames boat, and committed myself to our English deity, Neptune, who favourably heard my prayers. The opposition of a little wind to the tide at high water made the beginning of this long voyage rather rough; but the rest was exceedingly pleasant.

"The preceding day I lay at Liphook, and directed Mrs. Keen to send you this week a fine goose, and a brace of partridges. . . .

"The road from Guildford quite to Portsmouth is really enchanting. But I wanted you to enjoy with me these glorious scenes of Nature. I hope, however, that the quiet of your present situation" (Miss Wilkes was visiting the Duchess de la Vallière) "has chased away your feveret, and restored you to sweet sleep, Nature's best nurse. Pray send me such welcome news."

And then this agitator and sometime blasphemous member of the Medmenham Hell-Fire Club goes on to write verses appreciative of the scenery on the Portsmouth Road. In this wise :—

> "Ever charming, ever new,
> The landscape never tires the view :
> The verdant meads, the river's flow,
> The woody vallies warm and low ;
> The windy summit, wild and high,
> Roughly rushing on the sky :

> The pleasant seat, the ruin'd tower,
> The naked rock, the shady bower;
> The town and village,"——

But enough, enough. This "poetry" is but journalism cut into lengths and rhymed.

We find Wilkes as a *poseur* on literature in one of these entertaining letters to "dearest Polly." He indites from his cottage of Sandham a June letter wherein he says how impatient he is for " the descending showers to call forth all Nature's sweets, and waken all her flowers, for the earth is as thirsty as Boswell, and as cracked in many places as he certainly is in one. His book, however, is that of an entertaining madman. Poor Johnson! Does a friend come and add to the gross character of such a man the unknown trait of disgusting gluttony? I shall bring his two quartos back with me, and will point out numberless mistakes; but there are many excellent things in them. I suspect, not unfrequently, a mistake in the *Dramatis Personæ*. He has put down to *Boswell* what was undoubtedly said by *Johnson*; what the latter did, and what the former could not say. The motto to his book should have been the two lines of Pope,

> ' Who tells whate'er you think, whate'er you say,
> And if he lies not, must at least betray.' "

But he has a playful and somewhat engaging style of writing, on occasion. Perpend :—

> "' *Anchor,*' *at Liphook,*
> " *Friday Afternoon,* July 8, 1791.

"My dearest Polly,

" I have found the tench here so remarkably delicate, that nothing could add to their flavour on a certain Alderman's palate but the eating them in your company. They were, indeed, exquisite, and I see a brace playing about, which seem to promise equally. I have therefore spoiled their sport in the watery element, and as they set out this evening, before ten, it is thought they will arrive in Grosvenor Square to-morrow morning, in time for you to decide, at four, if their personal merit is equal to that of their late companions. Two little feathered folks, young and tender, of the same farm, accompany them in their journey, and I hope are not unworthy of being *croqués*.

"My best compliments to the nymph of the bosquets in Grosvenor Square.

"Adieu!"

The inclemency of the merry month of May is not of modern date, for Wilkes, who had been travelling from Grosvenor Square to Sandown on the sixth of that treacherous month, in the year of grace 1792, found a fire at the hospitable "Anchor" as welcome as fires generally are in dreary autumn.

"After I left Grosvenor Square," he says, "quite to Liphook, it rained incessantly, and I enjoyed a good fire there as much as I should have done on a raw day of the month of November. I found the spring very backward, except in the immediate environs of London; and nothing but a little purple heath and yellow broom to cheer the eye in the long dreary extent from Guildford to Liphook."

Some few days later, he writes a gossipy letter to his daughter, full of little domestic details, most strange and curious to find flowing from the pen of Liberty Wilkes. We find, for instance, "that the gardener's wife increases in size almost as much as his pumpkins," and that " there are thirteen pea-fowls at the cottage, between whom some solemn gallantries are continually passing; and the gallinis are as brisk and amorous as any French *petits-maîtres*. The consequences I foresee.

> 'Un et un font deux,
> C'est le nombre heureux,
> En galanterie, mais quelquefois,
> Un et un font trois.'"

On another occasion we learn that " the farmers are swearing, the parsons praying, for rain; neither hopeful of any result until the weather changes." About this time—on July 7, 1793—Mr. Wilkes has been returning along the Portsmouth Road from London to the Isle of Wight. He found the dust and heat almost overpowering, and the highway crowded with recruits, both for army and navy, who were no small inconvenience to his progress. Portsmouth was full of warlike preparations, Lord Howe expecting to sail the same day with a fleet of twenty sail, perfectly well-conditioned, and the men in high spirits at the prospect of coming to blows with the French.

Similarly, the next year, he found the July heat almost beyond endurance. " I almost melted away," he tells Polly, " from the extreme of a suffocating heat before I arrived at Cobham, and a large bowl of lemonade was scarcely sufficient to wash away the dust, which I had been champing for above three hours." A Mr. Hervey, "brother-in-law to Mr. Lambe, a silversmith, and Common Councilman of my ward," was at that time landlord of the "White Hart," at Cobham. "I was well used by him," says Wilkes, "and the house has a very decent appearance, but the poor fellow had tears in his eyes when he told me of thirty-five horse quartered on him." When he reached Liphook, what with two hounds, chained together in the outhouses of the "Anchor," yelping all night, and the intolerable heat, the patriot had no sleep the livelong night, and so resorted to his post-chaise and departed for Portsmouth at an early hour of the morning.

Those were busy days in the history of the "Anchor," and the constant stream of poorer wayfarers added to the bustle. Poor folk took a shakedown, with what grace they might summon up, in some clean straw on the floor of outhouses and barns, and in this manner slept the sailor-men who were continually tramping up the road or down. Not that sailors were necessarily poor, but the bedrooms that held royalty were judged to be above the tastes and circumstances of poor Jack, to whom, certainly, clean straw in a barn would seem at any rate infinitely better than the gloomy forecastle which he had just left.

But if the sailors a hundred years ago, or thereby, were denied the luxuries of sheets and coverlets, they were free to drink as much as they pleased at the public bar, so long as they had the wherewithal to settle the score. Rowlandson, who travelled this very road, has left a sketch of "Sailors Carousing," by

SAILORS CAROUSING. *From a Sketch by Rowlandson.*

which you can see that Jack was, at any rate, not one of Luther's fools, for the picture shows that he loved "women, wine, and song" to a riotous extent. And Jack come home from a long cruise, with prize-money in his pockets, was as ostentatious as any *nouveau riche*. He would damn expense with any lord, and has been known to call for sandwiches at the "Anchor" to place five-pound notes between, and to eat the whole with an insane bravado.

Those brave days were done when the railway came and left the roads silent and deserted. Old inns sank into obscurity and neglect, and for many years afterwards the sight of a solitary stranger wanting a bed for the night would have aroused excitement in a place where, in the old days, one more or less was a matter of little import. The "Anchor" for a time shared the fate of its fellows, and its condition in 1865 is eloquently pictured by the Hon. Grantley Berkeley. He says—

"I was travelling about the country, and it so happened that railway time, as well as inevitable time, chose to make me

> 'The sport of circumstances, when
> Circumstances seemed most the sport of men,'

and I found myself belated and tired in the vicinity of the little rural village of Liphook, on the borders of Hampshire and Surrey, and forced by time and circumstances to put up at a well-known inn.

"Now, time was when no traveller would have found fault with this, for the inn I thus allude to was then the great posting and coaching house of 'the road,' and the roar of wheels and the cries of 'first and second turn out,' either 'up or down,' rang through the merry air, and kept the locality in loud and continuous bustle, night and day. Now, however, the glory of the roadside inn was gone; its site seemed changed to grief, and the great elm tree [1] that had formerly during the heat of summer shed a cooling shade over panting steeds and thirsty, dusty-booted men, luxuriously grasping a fresh-drawn tankard of ale, stood sorrowing over the grave of the posting and coaching trade, a tearful mourner on every rainy day.

"There were the long ranges of stables, once filled by steeds of every step and temper, curious specimens of every blemish under the sun. Some that ran away the whole way, others that would be run away with by the rest of the team; some that kept the whip in action to send them to the collar, and others that kept the whip still, lest its touch should shut them up to stopping, and give them no collar at all.

"These stables were a melancholy sight to me. They reminded me of my own. Where, in my full stalls, twenty goodly steeds used to feed, little else than a mouse stirs now; and that mouse may be a ghost for all I know, haunting the grave of the last oat eaten a quarter of a century ago. In this long line of disused stabling I paused. There was a thin cat there, deceived to expectation by the long-deserted hole of a rat. A broken broom, covered with very ancient cobwebs, lay under one manger, and the remnants of a stable-bucket under another. Farmers came in and farmers went out occasionally and tied up their horses

---

[1] This "elm" is a chestnut.

anywhere ; so that all the tumbling-down stalls were dirty, and the whole thing given up to dreary desolation.

"A musing and a melancholy man, I left the stables, went into the house, and called for dinner and a bed. No smart waiter, with a white napkin twisted round his thumb, came forth to my summons; the few people in the house looked like broken-down farming-men and women, and seemed to be occupied in the selfish discussion of their own tap.

"'Yes,' they said, as if astonished by the unwonted desire for such refreshment, 'I *could* have a bed; and what would I like for dinner?'

"Now, that question was very well for them to ask, when they knew its meaning to be very wide; but the real dilemma was, what could they get to set before me? a point on which I at once desired information. 'A fowl.' 'What, ready for dressing?' 'Oh yes, quite.' Spirit of Ude—that King of Cooks (when he chose it)—if you still delight in heat, then grill these people; or when you 'cook their goose,' teach them to know the difference between a fowl hung for a time and picked for the spit, and a poor dear old chuckie, seated at roost in all her feathers, and 'ready' certainly; for her owner has only to clutch her legs and pull her screaming from her perch, to roast or boil, and send her, tough, to table.

"Well, up came my hen at last, flanked by some curious compound, dignified by the name of sherry, which I exchanged for some very nearly as bad spirits and water; when, having gone through the manual—

not the mastication—of a meal, I walked forth, and mused on the deserted garden and paddock in the rear of all; and in the dusky hue of night fancied that I saw the shadows of galled and broken-kneed posters limping over the grass to graze, as no doubt they had done in former times. In short, dear reader, from this last retrospection, hallucination, or what you will, I regained mine inn, and, calling for a candle, went to bed."

There is a sad picture of decadence for you! But in two years' time all this was changed, for in 1867 the present landlord, Mr. Peake, took the fortunes of the old house in hand, and restored, as far as possible, the old-time dignity of the place. He has brought back many of the glories of the past, and still reigns. I have met many sorts of hosts, but none of them approach so nearly the ideal as he, to whom the history and the care of this fine old inn are as much a religion as the maintenance of their religious houses was to the old monks of pre-Reformation days. And no post more delightful than this, which gives one fresh air, leisure for recreation, and nearly all the advantages of the country gentleman, to whom, indeed, mine host of the "Anchor" most closely approximates in look and speech. Long may the pleasant white face of the "Anchor" be turned towards the village street, and, friend Peake, may your shadow, with the grateful shade of the glorious chestnut tree that fronts your hostelry, never grow less!

XXVI

LEAVING Liphook, where, in the coaching revival of the '70's, Captain Hargreaves' "Rocket" coach between London and Portsmouth stopped forty minutes for lunch, we take to the road again, and come presently to Milland Common. This is splendid galloping ground, and coaches always made good time here, both in the old times and the new. Halfway across the Common (being, not coach-passengers, but merely pedestrians whose time is their own) we will step aside to investigate the two ecclesiastical-looking buildings that are seen between and beyond the trees on the left hand. Here, then, are the two chapels of Milland, with the adjoining "habitable parsonage," to quote the somewhat vague description of the "Clergy List." The new chapel, opened in 1880, although a fair specimen of modern work and the design of the late architect of the Royal Palace of Justice in London, is uninteresting; but the old, barn-like building that served the scattered inhabitants of Milland so many years and yet remains beside its modern successor, is worthy a glance, if only for its extremely small and simple (not to say primitive) design. It is so small that it could not conveniently contain a congregation of more than fifty people; its plan, shaped like the letter L, is surely unique, and altogether, the interior, with its plain high pews and meagre pulpit, and its plastered, whitewashed walls, is of the most unusual and secular appearance. Yet this diminutive building served the needs of the place from the days of Edward VI. until recently, and to it trudged on Sundays those of the Liphook folk who did not care to tramp to their own distant church of Bramshott; and even some pious souls from Rake (who, perhaps, valued public worship overmuch)

MILLAND CHAPEL.

performed a six-miles journey hither and home again.

But here let us leave the Portsmouth Road awhile for an expedition of some five miles into the still wild and rarely-travelled tract of country in whose midst lies the village of Selborne, memorable as the home, during his long life, of that most amiable and placid student of Nature and her works, the Rev. Gilbert White, D.D. When you have passed through the village of Liss, you come at once into a broad expanse of country whose characteristics resemble the typical scenes of Devonshire rather than those of Hants. Swelling hills and fertile vales, still intersected by the deeply-rutted lanes of which Gilbert White speaks,

THE WAKES, SELBORNE

lead on to the sequestered village of Selborne, as remote now from the rumours and alarums of the outer world as when the naturalist penned his "Natural History of Selborne," over a hundred years ago.

The village occupies, with its few cottages, its church and vicarage, and Gilbert White's home, "The Wakes," a long and narrow valley. The Hanger, covered now as in White's time with his favourite tree, the beech, rises at the back of the village street, and trees indeed abound everywhere, coming even to aid the simple architecture of the place.

The butcher's shop at Selborne rests its front on three polled limes which form living pillars to the roof, and give, apart from their rustic appearance, a welcome shade and grateful coolness to that country shop in the heats of summer. But the most remarkable tree in Selborne, as indeed anywhere in Hampshire, is the noble churchyard yew, mentioned by the naturalist, and still standing to the south-west of the church. This remarkable tree has a circumference of twenty-five feet two inches at a height of four and a half feet from the ground; it rises to a total height of sixty-two feet, and its great branches spread a distance of twenty-two yards from north to south. It is still in the perfection of good health, and its foliage wears the dark and lustrous appearance characteristic of the yew when in a thriving state. It must have been a remarkable tree even in Gilbert White's time, and its age can only be counted by centuries.

The Wakes, where this simple soul lived so long, stands in the village street, by the open grass-plot, familiar to readers of the "Natural History" as the Plestor. Additions have been made to the house since White's time, but so judiciously that its appearance is little altered. His summer-house is gone to wreck, but the sunny garden, with its narrow redbrick path, remains, and so does the American juniper tree, together with the sculptured sun-dial, both set up by this quiet curate-in-charge.

His life in this quiet and isolated parish, wherein his observation of and delight in the living things of garden and lane, hanger and pond, were mingled with the duties of a country clergyman and the contemplative recreations of the book-lover, was suave and untroubled. Of the events—so to call them—of this calm and kindly life there is but a slender outline to record. He was born here, at the Wakes, the residence of his father and his grandfather before him, on July 18, 1720. Educated first at Basingstoke, under the care of the Rev. Thomas Warton, father of Warton the Poet Laureate, he was entered at Oriel College, Oxford, in 1739; took his B.A. in 1743; obtained a Fellowship in the succeeding year, and the degree of M.A. in 1746. He was ordained as a priest in 1747, and subsequently served, it is said, as curate to his uncle, the Vicar of Swarraton. He soon removed to Selborne, where he lived the remainder of his days, dying here on June 26, 1793. It has been said that he accepted the College living of Moreton Pinkney in Northamptonshire, but he certainly never went into residence there, and refused other offers of preferment. A Fellow of his College, he never forfeited his fellowship by marriage, and he was never Vicar of Selborne, but only curate-in-charge.

His only regret seems to have been that he had no neighbours whose pursuits resembled his own in any way. Thus, one of his letters records the regret that it had been his misfortune "never to have had any neighbours whose studies have led them towards the pursuit of natural knowledge": to which he attributes his " slender progress in a kind of information to which I have been tenderly attached from my childhood."

But it was owing to this seclusion and want of companionship that we are become the richer, by his letters to Thomas Pennant and the Hon. Daines Barrington, which have delighted successive generations. Little has come down to us concerning the personal attributes of Gilbert White. No portrait of him is known. We are told that he was a little man—some say but five feet three inches in height—who wore a wig and rode on a pony to Farringdon Church, where he officiated for a quarter of a century, or ambled benignantly about the lanes and by-ways of the neighbourhood. In one of his letters to a friend in Norfolk, he speaks of himself as riding or walking about the parish " attended daily (for although not a sportsman I still love a dog) by a beautiful spaniel with long ears, and a spotted nose and legs," and watching the village folk " as they sit in grave debate while the children frolic and dance before them." All that remains of his memory in village traditions and recollections indicates the modest, kindly nature of a courteous gentleman, such as peeps out from the pages of the " Natural History of Selborne."

Selborne Church is a roomy and handsome building in the Transitional Norman and Early English styles. It consists of a nave of four bays, a south aisle, chancel, and massive western embattled tower. It has, however, a somewhat unfortunate effect of newness, owing to the restoration of 1883, when the south aisle was almost completely rebuilt, under the direction of a grand-nephew of the naturalist—Mr. William White, architect.

A memorial slab to the memory of Gilbert White is placed within the altar-rails, on the south wall of the chancel, and records that he was the son of John White, of Selborne, and Anne, daughter of Thomas Holt, Rector of Streatham. Another tablet, on the north wall, records the death, in 1759, of John White, barrister-at-law; and an earlier Gilbert White, Vicar of Selborne and grandfather of the more famous naturalist, lies in the chancel, beneath a ledger-stone bearing the date 1727.

Gilbert White is buried in the churchyard, among the tall grasses and waving wild-flowers, in a manner peculiarly fitting for that simple soul; and his grave —one of a row of five belonging to the White family —has a plain headstone, grey and lichened now, with the simple inscription, " G. W., 26th June, 1793."

It seems strange that so simple and uneventful a chronicle of the lives and habits of familiar birds and " wee sma' beasties," together with the plain records of sunshine and storm, rains and frosts, the blossoming of flowers and the fall of the leaf, which the " Natural History of Selborne " presents, should have attained so great and lasting a popularity. This book is become as sure a classic as the " Pilgrim's Progress " or the " Compleat Angler," and no one would have been more surprised at this result of his patient labours, undertaken simply for the joy they gave him, than old Gilbert himself. You see, in every page, nay, in every line, that he wrote for himself and his friends alone, and not with an observant eye upon the booksellers and their clients. Nay, more! Had he written thus, we should have missed the better part of his book; the observation of years, which thought nothing of profit for labour and time expended; the just language, written without any cudgelling of the brain for effect, and the homely incidents that make him live more surely than aught else. You can claim Timothy the tortoise as a personal friend, and are thrilled with the curious annals of the idiot boy whose strange appetite for honey-bees excited the naturalist's sympathies, both for the bees and the boy. Colonies might revolt and become the "United States"; French Revolutions and other dreadful portents shake thrones and set the world in arms, but Gilbert was a great deal more interested in the butcher birds, and in predatory rats, than in soldiers or bloodboltered human tyrants. The mid-day snoring of sleepy owls in the dusky rafters of some capacious barn, the hum of the bees, the scream of the peewits, and the clattering cabals of noisy starlings were more to him than instrumental music or the disputes of parliaments. And so he lived an uninterrupted round for forty years and died peacefully at last, happy and contented always, while dwellers in towns, then as now, beat their hearts out in unavailing ambitions and fruitless hatreds.

Ornithology owes much to Gilbert White's patient observations, and his "Natural History" bids fair to become a possession for all time. Numberless editions of it have been issued, annotated by men of science, who have found little of import to add to his work; and other editions are constantly in the making.

But best monument of all is that association of friends to birds and beasts, the Selborne Society, that, taking its name from Gilbert White's old home, owns him as master in many branches and local centres throughout England. When the centenary of the simple naturalist's death was celebrated in 1893, the large attendance at Selborne of members of the Society showed that here lies one whose memory the lovers of nature and wild life will not willingly let die.

BADGE OF THE SELBORNE SOCIETY.

XXVII

Returning from this sentimental excursion to Selborne to the road at Rake, the pedestrian will notice a singular old cottage with many angles, fronting the highway. This is one of the old toll-houses left after the abolition of turnpike trusts, and of the vexatious taxes upon road-travel that only finally disappeared within comparatively recent years. Sixty, nay fifty, years ago, there were six toll-houses and turnpike bars between London and Portsmouth. They commenced with one at Newington, followed closely by another at Vauxhall, and one more at the "Robin Hood," in Kingston Vale. The next was situated at Cobham Street, and neither Cary nor Paterson, the two great rival road-guides of coaching days, mention another until just before Liphook. The next was at

Rake, but, singularly enough, neither of those usually unimpeachable authorities mention this particular gate, which would appear to have been the last along this route.

Just beyond the old toll-house, visible down the road in the illustration of the "Flying Bull," comes the rustic public-house bearing that most unusual, if not unique, sign. Here stands a grand wayside oak beside a steep lane leading down into Harting Coombe, and the bare branches of this giant tree make a most effective natural composition with the tiled front of the inn and its curious swinging sign. The present writer inquired the origin of the "Flying Bull" of a countryman, lounging along the road, and obtained for answer the story that is current in these parts; which, having no competing legend, may be given here for what it is worth.

"The 'Flying Bull,'" said the countryman. "Oh, aye, it *is* a curious sign, sure-ly. How did it 'riginate? Well, they *do* say as how, years ago, before *my* time, they useter turn cattle out to graze in them meadows down there;" and he pointed down the lane. "There wur a lot o' flies in those meadows in summer at that time, and so there is now, for the matter o' that. Howsomedever, when they turned them there cattle into these here meadows, the flies made 'em smart and set 'em racing about half mad. They *wur* flying bulls; but 'tis *my* belief it useter be the 'Fly *and* Bull' public-house. . . . Thankee, sir; yer health, I'm sure!"

The road now rises gradually to a considerable height, being carried along the ridge of Rake Down,

THE "FLYING BULL" INN.

an elevated site now covered with large and pretentious country residences, but less than fifty years ago a wide tract of uncultivated land that grew nothing but gorse and ling, grass and heather, and bore no houses. The view hence is peculiarly beautiful over the wooded Sussex Weald, towards Midhurst, whose name, even now, describes its situation amid woods. The hollow below is Harting Coombe, and the neighbouring villages of Harting and Rogate recall the time when wild deer roamed the oak woods and the jealously-guarded Chases of Waltham and Woolmer.

THE "FLYING BULL" SIGN.

Just beyond the long line of modern houses stands another roadside inn, the "Jolly Drovers," planted 'mid capacious barns and roomy outhouses, at the angle of another country lane, leading to Rogate. The "Jolly Drovers" looks an old house, but it was built so recently as the '20's, by a frugal drover named Knowles, who saw a profitable investment for his savings in building a "public" at what was then a lonely spot called Shrubb's Corner.

And now, all the remaining five miles into Petersfield, the road goes along a fine, healthy, breezy country, bordered for a long distance by park-like iron fences and carefully-planted sapling firs, pines, and larches. At a point three and a half miles distant from Petersfield comes the hamlet of Sheet, where the road goes down abruptly between low, sandy cliffs, and brings us into the valley of the Rother, here a tiny stream that trickles insignificantly under a

THE "JOLLY DROVERS."

bridge, and rises, some three miles away, behind Petersfield, amid the hills and hangers of Steep, on the grounds of Rothercombe Farm, and then flows on through Sussex. The Sussex and Hampshire borders have, indeed, followed the road nearly all the way from Milland, but now we plunge directly into Hants. The character of the country changes, too, almost as soon as we are over the line; the chalk begins to replace the sand and gravel hitherto met, and the trees are fewer. Only by Buriton and at Up Park, to the south, is there much woodland; but at the latter place the deep shady copses and the ferny dells where the red deer still browse are delightful. Up Park should hold a place in the memory of loyal sportsmen, for it was here, long before Goodwood was used as a running-ground, that many celebrated races were held; and here the Prince of Wales, afterwards George IV., won his first race, in 1784, when his "Merry Traveller" beat Sir John Lade's "Medly Cut." And so into Petersfield.

XXVIII

THE old market town of Petersfield is one of those quiet places which, to the casual stranger, seem to sleep for six days of the week, and for one day of every seven wake up to quite a sprightly and businesslike mood. But Petersfield is even quieter than that. Its market is but fortnightly, and for thirteen days out of every fourteen the town dozes tranquilly. The imagination pictures the inhabitants of this old municipal and parliamentary borough rubbing their eyes and yawning every alternate Wednesday, when the corn and cattle market is held; and when the last drover has gone, at the close of day, sinking again into slumber with a sigh of relief. Parliamentary, alas! the borough is no longer, since the latest Reform and Redistribution of Seats Act has snatched away the one member that remained of the two who represented these free and enlightened burgesses before the Era of Reform broke out so destructively in 1832, and has now left the representation of Petersfield merged into that of a county division. The town lives in these days solely upon agriculture, and the needs of neighbouring fox-hunters. Once upon a time it possessed a number of woollen manufactories, but industries of this kind have long since died out, or have been transferred to more likely seats of commerce; and cattle, sheep, pigs, corn, and similar products now most do exercise the minds and muscles of local folk. It is a substantial, well-built town, looking, for all its age, like some late seventeenth-century growth, and the stranger standing in the market-place finds it difficult, if not impossible, to realize an antiquity that goes back certainly as far as the twelfth century, and dimly to an age when primitive savages, naked and dyed a brilliant blue, lived here in some clearing of the dense forest that spread over the face of the country, and hunted with ill success, and the inadequate aid of flint weapons, the wild boars and other fearsome fauna of that remote time.

We know, chiefly from geological evidence, that when the Romans came and sailed up what is now Portsmouth Harbour, and cast anchor off the shore at Porchester, they found the southern face of Portsdown Hill as bare of trees as we see it to-day. Mounting to the crest of that imposing range, the legionaries looked down upon a forest that stretched, with few breaks, black and sullen, as far as eye could reach. This interior contained a settlement of the Belgæ at what is now Winchester, and, for the rest, unknown men and beasts; and was only to be penetrated by slow and laborious felling of trees, and clearing of tangled brushwood; while, every now and again, these determined pioneers would be startled by an irruption of ferocious Belgæ (those primitive Frenchmen), who with flint-tipped arrows sent many an invader to his long account. Those stubborn Romans, however, cleared a way, and, indeed, several ways. For, from this Portus Magnus, modern Porchester,—where their original fortress still stands, added to by mediæval builders,—Roman roads were made to Venta Belgarum (Winchester), Regnum (Chichester), and Clausentum, now known as Bitterne. On either side of these roadways to and from their armed camps still stretched the woodlands, and they remained, in greater part, when the Roman power declined and the legions were withdrawn, to give room, in due time, to the invading Saxons. All these hundreds of years the dark recesses of the forest remained practically unknown; but at some safe and convenient distance from the towns of Venta or Regnum—handy for support, and yet sufficiently rural—Roman generals, prefects, and rich merchants erected elaborate villas, whose ruins are even now occasionally discovered by the ploughman as he laboriously turns over the grudging soil of Hants. Hypocausts and elaborate mosaic pavements testify to the comfort and luxury with which they surrounded themselves in those truly spacious days, while abundant traces of their roads remain. It cannot have been until late Saxon times that the site of Petersfield became at all settled, and we first hear of it as a town when William, Earl of Gloucester, conferred a charter upon it, in the dawn of the twelfth century.

That ancient document is still in existence, as also is its confirmation by the Countess Hawyse, the Earl's widow in after years; and both these important parchments, together with any number of later documents, were produced in the locally-celebrated Petersfield petition in 1820 against the pretensions of the lord of the manor, who claimed rights over the municipal elections which the worthy burgesses and freeholders of the town successfully resisted.

The result of that contention is evident to-day only in a supremely dull book in which all the conflicting evidence is printed in page after page of portentous, though hazy, rhetoric. It is all very uninteresting, and the quantity of evidence so obscures the issues of the fight that he who, like the present historian, comes to a consideration of these things from the point of view of interesting the "general reader," may be very well excused for coming away from a survey of the fray with as little knowledge of it as old Kaspar, in the poem. You cannot know "all about the war and what they fought each other for" without delving very deep indeed into the mustiest by-ways of municipal history.

The Jolliffe, the lord of the manor whose claims were thus resisted by the good folk of Petersfield, was, singularly enough, a descendant of that lover of liberty and paragon of latinity, William Jolliffe, Esq., M.P. for the borough, and a knight in 1734, who presented the leaden equestrian statue of William III., that now stands in the market square, in admiration of that " Vindicator of Liberty."

This statue, bowed and bent and painted white, was originally set up in that part of the town known as "the New Way." In those days it was richly gilt, and doubtless excited the awe and admiration of the travellers who passed through Petersfield; but to-day, the attitude of the King is undignified, and the airy garb of old Rome in which he is represented, not only adds nothing to our reverence, but outrages our sense of the fitness of things under these cloudy skies.

The circumstances under which this statue was erected are recounted (in a manner dear to the heart of Dr. Johnson) in a Latin inscription of equal length and magniloquence, carved upon its stone pedestal. It veils with an impenetrable obscurity the identity of this classic horseman from nine of every ten people who behold him, and it runs thus :—

   Illustrissimo Celsissimo Principi
     GULIELMO TERTIO
  Qui ob plurima quam maxuma Officia
   De his Gentibus optime meritus est
   Qui Rempublicam pene labefactam
     Fortiter sustentavit
   Qui purum et sincerum Dei cultum
     Tempestive conservavit
Qui legibus vim suam Senatiq: auctoritatem
    Restituit et stabilavit
    Gulielmus Jolliffe Eques
Ne aliquid qualecumque deesset Testimonium
Quanto cum amore Studioq: tam ipsam Libertatem
  Quam egregium hunc Libertatis Vindicem
     Proseartus est
  Hanc Statuam Testamento suo dicavit

   Et in hoc Municipio poni curavit
Exts { Samuele Tufnel
   Edvardo Northey
   Johanne Jolliffe

It was in 1815 that this leaden presentment of Dutch William was removed to its present site, over against the "Castle" Inn, where a scion of the House he supplanted—Charles II.—had, years before, slept a night on his way to France through Portsmouth.

Gibbon's father was the fellow-member with Sir William Jolliffe in the Parliamentary representation of Petersfield from 1734 to 1741, when he finally resigned all ambition to take part in the councils of the nation. The historian, although for many years he had a seat in the House of Commons, never represented Petersfield, but only the remote Cornish borough of Liskeard. In this connection, the return for the three candidates who offered themselves for election in 1774 may be of interest. Between them they polled only a hundred and twenty-five votes, in the following order :—

> For Jolliffe ... 55
> „ Hume ... 53
> „ Sutton ... 17

And this is the number of the free and independent electors who at that time cared to exercise the glorious privilege of the franchise!

As showing the relative importance of towns and villages in olden times, it may be noted that Petersfield was an appanage of the manor of Buriton, and that the ecclesiastical parish was a part of the rectory of the same village until 1886. Yet the ancient parish church of St. Peter the Apostle at Petersfield is a fine building, parts of which go back to Norman times. Indeed, the chancel arch and some elaborate arcading in the church are very fine examples of that

PETERSFIELD MARKET-PLACE.

period, and tend to show the importance with which the early Norman builders invested this spot. But even to-day the living of the quiet village of Buriton is very much more valuable than that of the borough town of Petersfield.

So much for the history of Petersfield. Busy days it had in coaching times, and its inns were of the best, as befitted a place where the coaches stopped to change teams. They are still here: the chiefest of them, the "Castle," is now a school, and a very fine building it is, whether as school or hostelry. It stands boldly fronting the market-place, and is to be seen in the accompanying illustration, behind the statue of William III. It is the place where Charles II. stayed, on his way to Portsmouth, and is referred to by Pepys :—

"*May 1st.* Up early and bated at Petersfield in the room which the King lay in lately at his being there. Here very merry and played with our wives at bowles. Then we set forth again, and so to Portsmouth, seeming to me to be a very pleasant, strong place."

The other inns where the jaded traveller of fifty years ago was certain of being well and adequately received, were the "Dolphin," the "White Hart," and the "Red Lion," all of them flourishing still. Of these the "Dolphin" is the largest, standing at the corner of Dragon Street, where the high-road passes by. The courtyards and coach-houses of the "Dolphin" are a sight to see and to wonder at. You gaze at them, and presently the old times seem to come crowding back. The eight-and-twenty coaches (more or less, as you choose your period) that fared either way upon the Portsmouth Road seem more real to you who look upon these capacious stables; and the passengers, the coachmen and guards, the ostlers, and the horsey hangers-on of such places come upon the imagination with a great deal more of reality than is gained from the reading of books, howsoever eloquent.

Cobbett on one of his rides stayed at Petersfield, and put up at this old house. "We got," says he, "good stabling at the 'Dolphin' for our horses. The waiters and people at inns *look so hard at us* to see us so liberal as to horse-feed, fire, candle, beds, and room, while we are so very very sparing in the article of drink! They seem to pity our taste!"

The memory of old times dies hard, and they still tell you here of the wonderful goat that was used to take his pleasure in following the up-coaches from here to Godalming, returning day by day to sleep in the straw of the "Dolphin" stables. For years this singular animal escorted the coaches, until one day, after running some distance with the mail, he turned round three times, trotted off home, and during the rest of his life eschewed the delights of the road altogether. That was in 1825, and the tale has lost nothing in the telling these seventy years.

For the rest, the "Dolphin" is a singularly dull and unromantic-looking house, painted a leaden hue. Within, it is all long dark corridors and unexpected corners. Commercials frequent it; although inquiries have not yet discovered what commercial gentlemen sell at Petersfield. Sportsmen come here too, and tourists of the pedestrian variety. In the old days, of the period between the coaching era and the present time, the "Dolphin" was very much neglected; the flooring precipitous and mostly worn out, so that the unsophisticated guest who jumped incautiously from his bed in the morning would, very likely, thrust his foot through some unexpected hole, to the imminent danger of the ceiling of the room beneath; or else would find himself rushing, with the steep gradient of the floor, into obscure corners of his apartment. The mirrors, also, in those days, left much to be desired of the guest who shaved himself, for they were either cracked or wavy, or both; and the traveller who, greatly daring, reaped a stubbly chin with trouble and cold water before one of those uncertain looking-glasses, in which his features flickered dizzily, required both stout nerves and a steady hand.

The dullness of that time has gone, and the roads are tolerably travelled to-day. The "Dolphin" rejoices in level flooring and decent repair, but the town, although so neat and cleanly, and, withal, prosperous, is a town of few wayfarers. You stand in the chief street and look with some surprise at twin evidences of considerable commerce—a large and modern Bank building, and a larger and still more modern Post-office. At the farther end of this street is the market-place, a spacious square, in which the fortnightly market, already referred to, is held; and the high jinks of the July fair are performed. On market Wednesdays you can scarce move for drovers and farmers, for graziers, and for a peculiarly knowing-looking class of men who might be horse-dealers or jockeys, or 'bus-drivers, or even cabmen: all wear the unmistakable look that they acquire who have much acquaintance with the noble animal, the Friend

"SHAVED WITH TROUBLE AND COLD WATER."

of Man. A very specialist crowd, this; and what they are ignorant of in the way of swedes and turnips, oil-cake, corn, or top-dressing, is scarce worth the acquiring. The market-place is partly filled on these occasions with pens in which sheep are closely huddled together, while cattle occupy the remainder of the space. The lowing of the cattle in a resonant diapason, the barking of the drovers' dogs, the querulous bleating of the sheep, and the hum of the people, amount altogether to an agricultural *charivari* as typical of a rural market-day as may be found in England.

XXIX

A SHORT mile off the road, two miles below Petersfield, is the charmingly-situated village of Buriton. It is reached by a winding lane turning off the highroad, beside a finger-post and two ugly modern cottages. Hop-fields and maltings border the lane, which suddenly, at one of its turns, discloses the village, tucked away in the sheltered lower slopes of the rolling South Downs, clothed in places with short grass, and in others bald and showing the white chalk; while just above the village are woodlands of tall elm and branching oak, vociferous with rooks. These " hangers," as hillside woods are locally termed, are a special feature of this part of Hampshire, and are not to be found in anything like this profusion in any other part of the county. They form the loveliest setting imaginable to an old-world village of this character, and it is difficult to say at what season of the year such a place as Buriton, backed with its woods, is most beautiful. Spring finds the forest trees bare and black, with waving branches scraping, like wizard fingers, gnarled and crooked, the leaden skies of moist February and windy March; and with April comes the stirring of the sap that sets off every little twig with the fairy-like pale green buds of future leaves, until a distant view of the hanger seems clothed in a tender emerald mist. Spring passes and leaves the hillside trees clothed with a thick coat of summer foliage that forms the best of backgrounds to the red roofs of the village; and when leafy summer mellows into russet autumn the hanger is one mass of brilliant colour; gorgeous reds and yellows and tints of dull gold. When November fades away in mists and midnight frosts into Christmastide and the bleak days of January, when days draw out and "the cold begins to strengthen," as the country folk say, then the hanger is etched black and solemn against the snow-powdered downs, and you can discern every high-perched homestead of the rooks, swinging in the topmost branches of the tallest trees, and looking twice their actual size by this adventitious juxtaposition of black and white.

And, indeed, Buriton is as cheerful in winter's frosts as in summer's heat. The village itself is commendably old-fashioned and typically English of the eighteenth century. True, a post and telegraph office stands in the village street, but that is the only anachronism: for the rest, it is a picture by Caldecott come to life. Caldecott saw in his mind's eye a characteristically English village of the time of the Georges, and he crystallized his vision in many tinted drawings. Here, then, is such a village in very truth, with its ancient church fronting an open space in the village street, where a broad horse-pond, fed by a trickling rill, reflects the ivied church tower in summer, and in winter-time bears the shouting, red-faced urchins who come sliding upon its surface as merrily as English boys have done from time immemorial. Fronting the other side of the pond is the old farm-house of Mapledurham, stuccoed, 'tis true, and plebeian enough to a casual observer, but bearing traces of antiquity in its gables, whence Tudor windows peep from out the handiwork of the modern plasterer, and thereby indict him for an artless fellow, with never a soul above contracts and cheap utility.

Behind the church, in midst of rick-yards and their pleasing litter of fragrant straw, stands Buriton Manor House, a solid, staid, and comfortable four-square building of mellowed red brick, frankly unornamental, and therefore pleasing. Built in the days of Queen Anne, you can yet scarce imagine (being a Londoner, and used to the grime of the eighteenth-century houses of the capital), as you stand in front of it, these cleanly walls to be so old. Yet there are brilliant lichens upon the bricks that are not the growth of yesterday, and the cumbrous sashes of the tall plain windows are not of the fashion of to-day. Some windows, too, are blank and bricked up; reminiscences, these, of the days of the window-tax, days when the light of heaven was appraised by the Inland Revenue authorities, and to be bought at a price in coin of the realm. So here, in very truth, is the Manor House of Caldecott's fancy, and of Washington Irving's picture-like prose.

And here lived, for a time, Edward Gibbon, the historian, whose birthplace we passed at Putney; and it is for this personal interest, for this hero-worshipping object, that I have turned aside from the highroad to visit Buriton. Gibbon, you will say, is a quaint figure for the hero-worshipper to admire

outside his stately pages of Roman History, and I have no mind to deny your contention. He was, indeed, a humorous figure of a man, the more so, doubtless, because he was so supremely unconscious of the whimsical figure he cut before his contemporaries. The difference between the majestic swing and rounded periods of his literary style, and his personal appearance and his private habits of thought, is scarce less than ludicrous. Gibbon was, in fine, exceedingly human, and his person was almost grotesque. Do you, I wonder, conceive in that luminous optic, the "mind's eye," when thinking of the man who wrote the stately prose of the "Decline and Fall," the figure of a little snub-nosed gentleman, with a square head, a prodigious development of chins, and a wagging paunch? Surely never. Yet this was the appearance of the man, and portraits and caricatures of him all agree in showing this great literary figure of last century's close as a very whimsical-looking human figure indeed.

It cannot with certainty be said whence Gibbon derived his singular appearance. Not (one would say) from either his father or his mother, who were both, to judge from their portraits, very comely persons. But if neither his face nor his figure would have served to make Gibbon's fortune, certainly his agreeable manners stood him in good stead; and although Boswell describes him, in ferociously unfriendly terms, as "an ugly, affected, disgusting fellow," of the race of "infidel wasps and venomous insects," he seems to have been in good favour with polite society. But then Bozzy's mind had room for only one hero.

He was not (curiously enough) at all eager in the early part of his career to be recognized for his literary abilities, for, when a young man, he was solicitous to be known as a good figure in polite society. Thus when, in 1762, we find the French Ambassador, the

Duc de Nivernais, giving him introductions to the foremost French writers of the time, we hear him complaining that the Duke treated him "more as a man of letters than as a man of fashion." He was, indeed, *very* human! This quality (or defect?) is seen again in a letter, still extant, in which he says, years later, upon his determination not to stand again for Parliament:—"A seat in Parliament I can only value as it is connected with some official situation of emolument." Does that not endear him to you at once, who live in these Pharisaical times, when men seek election to the House on the score of philanthropy, of patriotism, of service to mankind; on any ground, in fact, but the fundamental consideration of self-interest?

Gibbon lived and wrote in the days when the literary patron still existed, and although the historian was a man of some pretensions in his own county, and on his ancestral acres at Buriton, yet he found the powerful friendship of Holroyd, afterwards first Earl of Sheffield, most useful, not only in literature, but in his career as a Member of Parliament. The almost lifelong friendship between the two was manifested even in death, for Gibbon sleeps, not in the Abbey, nor among his fathers at Buriton, but in the Sheffield vault at Fletching, in Sussex.

The mind of this singular man was, indeed, not apt to run in the direction of ancestor-worship, and old acres represented only so much money to him when, a year after the publication of his History, he sold the estate. Years before, in his father's time, he held the captaincy of a battalion of Hampshire Militia (a sort of bachelor Sir Dilberry Diddle), and thus he says of himself in the "Memoirs," in a manner unconsciously humorous:—" I for two and a half years endured a wandering life of military servitude." Thus seriously did he look upon the perfunctory drilling of yeomen; the pleasant field-days between Portsmouth and Petersfield, and the Sunday church-parades, in which the militia, gorgeous in sky-blue coats with red facings; in white breeches with black gaiters; with astonishing hats and careful perukes finished off daintily with pigtails and black silk ribbons, bore a gallant part, exciting the admiration of the ladies, and the scornful animosity of those sober bachelors who belonged neither to the Militia, the Fencibles, nor to that doughty body of men, the Petersfield Cavalry; all good men and true, ready to shed their last drop of blood for their country, in the unlikely event of an invasion; but, meanwhile, none the less averse from a little parade of pomp and circumstance and the showing off of fine feathers. They were gaudy and most remarkable figures, these old militia-men, and the modern "Saturday afternoon soldier" is to them as a London sparrow is to a peacock for comparison. Neither is there any adequate compare between the work done by these old fellows and the modern amateur soldier. Gibbon and his contemporaries may have boasted of their "military servitude," and the historian may have profoundly believed the statement, that hints more than it really expresses —"The captain of Hampshire grenadiers was not useless to the historian of the Roman Empire;" but their services were more to the eye than to practical efficiency, and they would have resented, even to the laying down of their firelocks, the hard work which a battalion of Cockney rifle volunteers endures with cheerfulness.

But Gibbon grew tired of his military exploits; and presently, when the militia were disbanded, his father sent him travelling on the Continent. It was at Rome, amid the ruins of the Capitol, that, in 1764, he conceived the first idea of his great work, but it was not until 1788 that the final volume was issued, after years of incredible toil and research.

Whatever the popularity of Gibbon may be now, a hundred years after his death, certainly his "Decline and Fall" had an extraordinary run when it first appeared. The entire impression was exhausted in a few days; a second and third edition were scarce adequate to the demand, and it was said at the time that "the book was on every table and on almost every toilet." From that day to this there have been well-nigh twenty editions, some of them consisting of as many as fourteen volumes, and, as a sign of Gibbon's sometime popularity, it may be mentioned that the entries under his name in the British Museum catalogue number about a hundred and twenty.

Not many pilgrims make their way to Buriton for Gibbon's sake, yet were you to turn aside from the high-road, you would find the place interesting beyond expectation. Lying *perdu* among the hills, although so near the traffic of the outer world, it is, and has ever been, but rarely visited by the stranger, and has thus come to retain a distinct and individual character.

Push open the old wrought-iron gates of the churchyard and look around. The church itself is just a typical building, with some few special features. It has, of course, been restored, but the fury of the restorer has been wreaked with greater effect elsewhere, and he has come to Buriton in a manner comparatively mild and harmless. He has left even the fine Decorated window of the south chapel, and has not cast out all the memorials of the dead and used their shattered fragments for mending the village street—as he has been known to do elsewhere. You can, in fact, discover the names of some of Gibbon's ancestors upon the walls, and not all the original encaustic tiles have been thrown away. Prodigious!

But others have (truth to tell) been less fortunate. Poor cadavers! laid to rest within the church, with storied ledger-stones above, decently recounting both virtues they had and had not, they have been ruthlessly removed, and as the stranger paces round the exterior of the church, he walks upon their memorials, laid end to end, to form a solid footpath for the good folks o' Sundays. The frosts of winter crack them; the nailed boots of the rustics wear down the well-cut inscriptions that date from the seventeenth century to within a few generations of ourselves; and they will presently be worn quite away.

Here—stop and look—is the epitaph of one, a considerable fellow in his day, a barrister of the Middle Temple. Here is his coat-of-arms, and here his panegyric, writ, doubtless, by loving hands, and cut, most certainly, by an artist in his mortuary craft. Ha! barrister, where are your fees, your brief-bag, your writs of escheat and *fi fa?* Would you could arise and with all your former eloquence denounce the paltry fellows who have filched your gravestone for the paving of a churchyard path, whereon the casual clodhopper thumps his ponderous way and the meditative tourist pauses to moralize, and with the ferrule of his walking-stick scrapes away the dirt that hides your identity.

Where this solemn paving was used to be, are spread now, over the nave of the church, coloured tiles that wear a neat and cleanly, but distressingly secular, look. You might be pacing the tiled hall of a suburban villa, rather than the House of God. "But one must live," the restoring architect will tell you. The greater the cost of his commission the larger will be the amount from his five-percentage; so, out go the old stones and in come the patent tiles, while that gentleman pockets his money and sets off to fresh fields and pastures new.

XXX

ANOTHER country lane affords the opportunity of regaining the Portsmouth Road from Buriton, without undergoing what always is the penance of retracing one's steps. It brings the traveller out into the highway just below where the railway crosses, underneath a bridge; while away in front lies the long slope that climbs steadily and straight towards the crest of Butser Hill, that tall knob of the South Downs rising to a height of nine hundred and twenty-seven feet above the Meonware country, and commanding views stretching to Salisbury in one direction, and in others extending to Andover, to the Isle of Wight, and to the rich lands of the Sussex Weald.

Butser Hill is the highest ground in Hampshire. Here the traveller enters upon the chalk country extending to the southern slopes of Portsdown Hill, and here the character of the scenery changes suddenly with the geological strata. Beech woods, oak and fir, give place to barren downs, clothed only with a short and scanty covering of grass, or with meagre patches of gorse. In favoured nooks, sheltered from the winds and brought by the painful unremitting labour of years to a condition not altogether prohibitive of cultivation, farmsteads stand, with their surrounding barns and cow-sheds, the whole comprised within walls constructed of flints picked plentifully from the land.

Here, on the incline leading across Butser Hill, may be noticed the beginning of these things. At one point, to the left hand, turns off what was once the old road, leading across the Hill, now a secluded track-way, bringing the explorer upon excavations in the chalk, and suddenly upon lime-kilns and lime-burners, working away in a solitude where every sound re-echoes from the enclosing chalk in gruff and hollow murmurs. The old road was in course of time abandoned for the new, which marches straight ahead and is carried in a deep and precipitous cutting through the hill-top. The winds whistle shrilly through this chalky gorge, and the frosts and thaws loosen great pieces of chalk which come down into the road with tremendous leaps, and break into a thousand fragments at the bottom. It is a lonely place. A single cottage stands some distance away; the lime-burners are hidden in their resounding dell, and the only company the wayfarer has on ordinary days through the cutting are the two notice-boards that, with a fine disregard of punctuation, caution folks "against Chalk falling from the Sides by Order." These, together with a board warning cyclists that "This Hill is Dangerous," are not cheering to the spirits on a winter's day.

It was on Butser Hill that a post-boy from the "Anchor," at Liphook, was stopped by an unmounted highwayman, who took the horse he was riding and cantered off upon its back, in the direction of London. The post-boy returned, sorrowful, to Petersfield, where he procured another horse and rode back to Liphook.

On his way, riding up to the turnpike-gate at Rake, he received information of the robber's passing through, and, upon reaching the "Anchor," told the landlord of what had happened. Immediately "mine host" organized pursuit, and so quickly did the party take to the road that they overtook man and horse at Hindhead. When the highwayman observed his pursuers gaining upon him, he lost his nerve, and did the very worst thing possible under the circumstances. He dismounted and attempted to conceal himself amid the gorse of that wild spot.

But he was soon discovered, captured, and hauled off in custody; afterwards receiving sentence of transportation at Winchester Assizes.

Passing through the precipitous cutting of Butser Hill, the road now comes upon the bare and windy expanse of Oxenbourne Downs, where, at a distance of fifty-eight miles from London, stands beside the road the "Coach and Horses" Inn, marked on the Ordnance maps "Bottom" Inn, and known in coaching days as "Gravel Hill" Inn, from the hill in the Downs rising at some distance to the rear, covered in patches with scrub and gorse. This is the roadside inn referred to by Dickens in "Nicholas Nickleby."

We left Nicholas and Smike looking down into the Devil's Punch Bowl, and now take up their journey over Rake Hill and the heights of Butser to this lonely roadside inn, which Dickens, using the latitude allowed to novelists, describes as twelve miles from Portsmouth. It is, in fact, thirteen miles, but its identity is unassailable, because there is no other house beside the road for miles on either hand.

"Onward they kept with steady purpose, and entered at length upon a wide and spacious tract of downs, with every variety of little hill and plain to change their verdant surface. Here, there shot up almost perpendicularly into the sky a height so steep, as to be hardly accessible to any but the sheep and goats that fed upon its sides, and there stood a huge mound of green, sloping and tapering off so delicately, and merging so gently into the level ground, that you could scarce define its limits.

Hills swelling above each other, and undulations shapely and uncouth, smooth and rugged, graceful and grotesque, thrown negligently side by side, bounded the view in each direction; while frequently, with unexpected noise, there uprose from the ground a flight of crows, who, cawing and wheeling round the nearest hills as if uncertain of their course, suddenly poised themselves upon the wing and skimmed down the long vista of some opening valley with the speed of very light itself.

"By degrees the prospect receded more and more on either hand, and as they had been shut out from rich and extensive scenery, so they emerged once again upon the open country. The knowledge that they were drawing near their place of destination gave them fresh courage to proceed; but the way had been difficult, and they had loitered on the road, and Smike was tired.

"Thus twilight had already closed in, when they turned off the path to the door of a roadside inn, yet twelve miles short of Portsmouth.

"'Twelve miles,' said Nicholas, leaning with both hands on his stick, and looking doubtfully at Smike.

"'Twelve long miles,' repeated the landlord.

"'Is it a good road?' inquired Nicholas.

"'Very bad,' said the landlord. As, of course, being a landlord, he would say.

"'I want to get on,' observed Nicholas, hesitating. 'I scarcely know what to do.'

"'Don't let me influence you,' rejoined the landlord. '*I* wouldn't go on if it was me.'"

And so here they stayed the night, much to their

THE "COACH AND HORSES" INN.

advantage, in a manner familiar to the readers of Dickens. Of their progress to Portsmouth the next day, with Mr. Vincent Crummles and his troupe, we will say nothing, for no other outstanding features of the road are described between this and Hilsea Lines.

Oxenbourne Downs are succeeded, on the map, by Chalton (originally "Chalkton") Downs; but they are all one to the eye that ranges over their almost trackless hills and hollows.

XXXI

IT was in the neighbourhood of Chalton Downs that a terrific, if, in some of its details, a somewhat farcical, encounter took place between two highwaymen and a mail-coach in the winter of 1791. The coach had set out from the "Blue Posts" at Portsmouth in the afternoon, and the coachman drove up through Purbrook and on, past Horndean, with the greatest difficulty, in face of a blinding snowstorm. But when he had come, as daylight faded away, to these bleak and open downs, he found it utterly impossible to lash his tired horses a step farther. The situation probably reads a great deal more interesting than those who experienced it had any idea of. To be snowed up on an open down, miles away from anywhere, reads prettily enough in Christmas numbers, but, as an experience, it does not bear repetition. There were, on this occasion, four "insides" and two "outsides"; and the lot of these last two, together with that of the coachman and guard, must have been simply Dantesque in its chilly horrors. The coachman was a humane creature, and determined, at any rate, not to expose his shivering horses to the storm; so he unharnessed them and was proposing to lead them into Petersfield, when two fellows, well mounted, and apparently furnished with a perfect armoury of pistols, rode up through the falling snow and the gathering gloom, and demanded the passengers' money, or the usual alternative.

But the guard was a fellow of courage and resolution, and so was one of the "insides," a midshipman journeying to London for his Christmas. Quick as thought, the guard whipped out his blunderbuss from its case, and, at the same time, the midshipman bounded out of the coach, and laid one fellow head downwards in the snow by leaping on his horse and delivering a scientific blow on the side of his face. The other highwayman was, meanwhile, in single combat with the guard, who having, so to speak, entrenched himself behind the half-buried coach, opened fire in answer to a pistol-shot from the enemy.

The blunderbuss of last century was an appalling weapon, with a bore like that of a small cannon, and a bell muzzle which poured forth slugs and small shot in a stream that spread, fan-like, until at the distance of a yard or so it could be confidently relied upon, not only to hit the object aimed at, but anything else within a space of six feet on either side. The guard fired, and when the smoke and roar of the discharge, like that of a piece of ordnance, had finally died away, the second highwayman's horse was discovered plunging in the snow, peppered with shot from shoulders to hind-quarters. The man himself was wounded in the leg, but was seen to be advancing through the snow upon the guard, with another pistol aimed at his head. He pulled the trigger, but the snow had damped his powder, and it snapped harmlessly. The guard was now in a somewhat similar position with the wasp who has delivered his sting, and is afterwards rendered comparatively harmless: for the loading of a blunderbuss was an operation that required time and care and a large quantity of powder and shot, and not a moment's grace was he granted. Meanwhile, he was required to act.

The blunderbusses of that time were furnished with a hinged bayonet, rather under a foot in length, and doubled back upon the barrel. To release the bayonet and bring it into an offensive position, one had but to touch a catch, and it sprang out with terrific force and remained fixed.

The guard, touching the spring, remained upon the defensive, with bayonet fixed, while the highwayman, dismounted, came trampling down the snow and leaving behind him a trail of blood, trickling from the slug-wounds in his leg. Arrived at the back of the coach, from which peered the guard's red nose and the gaping bore of his blunderbuss, he fired, and the guard would in all likelihood have been killed, had not the midshipman, by creating a diversion in the rear with the butt of the coachman's heavy whip, not only destroyed his aim, but stretched him senseless in the snow. The enemy were now utterly defeated.

The first highwayman, on recovering from the blow he had received, found his hands securely tied behind him, in a thoroughly efficient and workmanlike manner characteristic of a sailor, and the second was treated in

WINDY WEATHER.

the same way, with the help of the guard and the entirely unnecessary aid of the remaining passengers, who now crawled from under the seats, where they had taken refuge on the first alarm.

Waiting until the second assailant had recovered consciousness, the coachman and guard, with the coach-horses; the midshipman and the rest of the passengers, in charge of the two prisoners and their steeds, trudged through the gloom and the fallen snow to Petersfield, leaving the coach abandoned on the highway.

This party of ten reached the town late at night, almost exhausted, and handed over their prisoners to the civil power, which no doubt dealt with them in the time-honoured fashion of sending such gentry out of the world "stabbed to death with a Bridport dagger," as the humorists of the time termed execution by hanging, "hempen cravats" being usually of Bridport make.

XXXII

But they were not only highway robberies that gained the Portsmouth Road so unenviable a notoriety a hundred and fifty years ago. Smuggling was rife along the highway from Hindhead to Portsmouth in those days, and the whole sea-board, together with the forest villages that were then so untravelled, swarmed with the "free-traders," as they euphemistically called themselves. And this district was not alone, or even pre-eminent, in smuggling annals, either for the number or for the ferocity of those engaged in the illicit trade of importing wines, spirits, tea, or lace, without the formalities of entering their goods at his Majesty's Custom-houses, or of paying duty upon them. The whole extent of the south coast, from the North Foreland and Dungeness, in Kent, to the Dodman and the Land's End, in Cornwall, was one long line of resistance to the Excise. The people, groaning under a heavy taxation, whose proceeds went towards the cost of Continental wars and the perpetration of shameless and atrocious jobs at home, saw no crime in evading the heavy duties that took so much out of the pockets of a generation notoriously addicted to continuous drinking; and the wealthy middle-classes, the squires, even members of the Peerage, and not a few of the country clergymen (semi-pagan as they were in those days), purchased and consumed immense quantities of excisable goods that had never rendered unto Cæsar—if, indeed, that imperial term may be used of either the Second or the Third George.

The possession of a cellar well stocked with liquor that had never paid duty was, in fact, a source of genuine pride to the jolly squires who winked at each other as they caroused round the mahogany, and, holding their glasses up to the light, pronounced the tipple to be "the right sort," and as good stuff as ever came across the Channel on a moonless night; and madam or my lady wore her silks, her satins, or her lace with the greater satisfaction when she knew them to have been brought over from France secretly, wrapped around some bold fellow's body who would surely never have hesitated to put a bullet through the head of the first Excise officer that barred his path.

The risk of smuggling was great, the profits large,

and the men who, having counted the cost of their contraband trade, still persisted in it, were not infrequently well able to afford presents to those easy folks who might know a great deal of their midnight runs, and who, knowing much and suspecting more, were folks to be rewarded for past silence, or to be bribed into a passive acquiescence for the future. Thus the Parson Trullibers of that time who discovered the belfries of their churches crowded with strange kegs and unwonted packages and smelling to Heaven with the scent of other spirits than those usually associated with churches and churchyards, were not at all surprised at finding a keg in their pulpits, together with a package of silk or such similar feminine gauds, if their parsonages held any womenkind. The sexton was simply told to take the keg and the package up to the house, and if, some blusterous night, those easy-going clerics looked forth of their casements and saw strange processions of men passing along the road, hunched with tubs on their backs, and bound, strange to say, for the House of God, why, they said nothing, but thought with great complacency upon the certain prospect of some right Hollands or some generous brandy from over sea.

Smuggling, in fact, was not regarded as a crime by any considerable section of the public, and public opinion in the counties that gave upon the sea was altogether in favour of the "free-traders" up to a certain point. And if the squires, the clergy, and the tradesfolk largely sympathized with them and connived at the wholesale cheating of the Revenue that went on for a long period almost unchecked, certainly the licensed victuallers—the country innkeepers and the struggling pot-house landlords of the hamlets—were eager to buy goods that had never seen the inside of a custom-house. Even the officers and men of the Customs and the Excise were often found to be in league with notorious smugglers, and the early inadequacy of the Revenue sloops and cutters to prevent the clandestine landing of excisable goods is to be traced, in part, to bribes judiciously expended.

The loss to the Revenue during a long series of years must have been simply enormous, for the bulk of the hardy 'longshore men were engaged all the year round in running cargoes across from France; in landing them at unfrequented coigns and inlets of the sea; and in secreting them in the most unlooked-for recesses of the country, until such time as they could be safely disposed of. The fisheries, too, were neglected for this much more remunerative trade, and few men cared to earn an honest and meagre livelihood by day when anything from five shillings to a guinea might be the reward of a night's work, climbing up cliffs with kegs slung on back and chest.

The foremost smugglers were no men of straw, for, like all other trades, the free-traders' business had its capitalists and its middlemen, who financed the buying of cargoes and received their share of the plunder, taking their ease at home while their less wealthy fellow-sinners worked in fear of capture and condemnation. Others, anticipating the joint-stock companies of later years, formed themselves into bands or confederacies who shared both risks and gains, and kept up an armed organization that, particularly in the counties of Kent, Sussex, and Hampshire,[1] kept the law-abiding country-side in terror, and not infrequently offered battle to the officers of the Preventive Service. These organized gangs of desperadoes alienated from themselves much of the sympathy that was felt for the individual smuggler; for, as their power grew, they committed crimes, not only upon that impersonal thing, the Revenue, but robbed and despitefully entreated the lieges, and even overawed considerable towns.

One of the most daring exploits of these armed bands of smugglers was the famous attack upon the custom-house at Poole. This resistance in arms to the King's authority arose out of the capture by a Revenue cutter of a heavy cargo of tea shipped, in September 1747, by a number of smugglers from Guernsey. Captain Johnson, the commander of the Government vessel, brought the tea to the port of Poole, in Dorsetshire, and lodged it in the custom-house there. The loss of their entire venture was a very serious matter to the men who had paid for their tea over in the Channel Islands, and looked to selling it over here for a profit, and they resolved not to let their cargo go without an effort. Accordingly, a consultation was held among them, and they agreed to go and take away the tea from the warehouse where it was lodged. A body of no less than sixty armed and mounted smugglers assembled in Charlton Forest, and proceeded thence to Poole, posting half their number on the roads, in true

---

[1] The "County of Southampton," to speak by the card.

military fashion, to scout, and to report the movements of Revenue officers or soldiers who might hear of their expedition. Thirty of these bold spirits reached Poole on the night of October 6, and, meeting with no resistance, broke open the custom-house and removed all their tea, except one bag, weighing about five pounds.

The next morning they returned through Hampshire, by way of Fordingbridge, where the expedition was a matter of such common notoriety that hundreds of persons were assembled in the streets of that little town, to witness the passing of their cavalcade. Among the leaders of this body of smugglers was a man named John Diamond, and it so happened that this fellow was recognized by a shoemaker of the place, one Daniel Chater, who had turned out from his cobbling to witness the unusual spectacle of sixty "free-traders" riding away with their booty in broad daylight. Diamond and he had worked together at haymaking some years previously. Now, to be identified thus was an altogether unlooked-for and unlucky chance, and Diamond threw his old acquaintance a bag of tea, by way of hushing him, as he passed by.

Chater, however, was not gifted with reticence, or perhaps the good folk of Fordingbridge looked askance upon one of their fellow-townsmen being selected for so considerable a gift as a bag of tea was in those days, and they probably plied him with awkward questions. At any rate, Diamond was shortly afterwards arrested at Chichester, on suspicion of being concerned in the raid at Poole, and Chater having acknowledged his acquaintance with the man, the matter became the subject of local gossip and presently came to the ears of the Collector of Customs for Southampton. At the same time, a proclamation was issued, offering a reward for information as to the persons implicated in the affair, and Chater, in an evil moment for himself, offered to give evidence.

The shoemaker, then, in company of an Excise officer, William Galley by name, set out for Chichester with a letter for Major Battin, a justice of the peace for Sussex, who lived in that city, and before whom it was proposed to examine Chater, in relation to what he knew of the affair, and whether he could prove the identity of Diamond.

The two set out on horseback on Sunday, February 14, 1748, and, calling on their way at Havant, were directed by a friend of Chater's to go by way of Stanstead, near Rowlands Castle. They, however, lost their way, and calling at the "New" Inn, at Leigh, to get their direction, were met by three men, George Austin, Thomas Austin, and their brother-in-law, Mr. Jenkes, who accompanied Galley and Chater to Rowlands Castle, where they all drew rein at the "White Hart," a public-house kept by a Mrs. Elizabeth Payne, a widow, who had two sons, blacksmiths, in the village; both grown men, and reputed smugglers.

And now commences the horrible story of the two most dreadful and protracted murders that have ever set lonely folk shivering by their firesides, or have ever made philosophers despair for the advancement of the human race. It becomes the duty of the historian of the Portsmouth Road to chronicle these things, but here duty and inclination part company. The tale must be told; but for those who take a deeper interest in the story, let them procure, if they can, any one of the several rare editions of a dreadfully detailed pamphlet, entitled "A Full and Genuine History of the Inhuman and Unparalleled Murders of Mr. William Galley, a Custom-House Officer, and Mr. Daniel Chater, a Shoemaker, by Fourteen Notorious Smugglers, with the Trials and Execution of Seven of the Bloody Criminals, at Chichester." If a perusal of the gory details set forth in these pages does not more than satisfy curiosity, why, then the reader's stomach for the reading of ferocious cruelties must indeed be strong.

But to resume the account.

Shortly after the arrival of the party at the "White Hart," Mrs. Payne took Mr. George Austin aside and whispered him her fears that these two strangers were come with intent to do some injury to the smugglers. When he replied that she need not believe that, for they were only carrying a letter to Major Battin, the landlady's suspicions became more fully aroused, for what other particular business could Galley, who was dressed as a "riding officer" of the Excise, have with the Justice of the Peace? But, to make sure, she sent one of her sons, who was in the house, for William Jackson and William Carter, who lived within a short distance. While he was gone, Chater and Galley wanted to be going, and called for their horses, but the woman told them that the man who had the key of the stable was gone out, and would be back presently. Meanwhile the unsuspecting men remained, drinking and gossiping.

When the two arrived who had been sent for, Mrs. Payne drew them aside and told them her suspicions, at the same time advising Mr. George Austin to go away, as she respected him, and was unwilling that any harm should come to him by staying. Mr. George Austin had the saving virtue of prudence. He went away, as he was bid, and left his brother and his brother-in-law behind, which seems to have been unnecessarily selfish on his part. Then the other son came in and brought with him four more smugglers, and the whole company drank together. After a while, Jackson took Chater aside into the yard and asked him after Diamond, and the simple-minded shoemaker let fall the secret of his journey. While they were talking, Galley, uneasy about his companion, came out and asked him to rejoin them within, whereupon Jackson struck Galley a violent blow in the face that knocked him down. "I am a King's officer," said Galley, "and cannot put up with such treatment!"

"You a King's officer!" replies Jackson. "I'll make a King's officer of you; and for a quartern of gin I'll serve you so again!"

The others interfered, and the whole party set to drinking again until Galley and Chater were overcome by drunkenness and were sent to sleep in an adjoining room. Thomas Austin and Mr. Jenkes, too, were beastly drunk; but they had no interest in the smugglers, nor the smugglers in them, and so they drop out of the narrative.

When Galley and Chater were asleep the compromising letters in their pockets were found and read, and from that moment the doom of these unfortunate men was sealed, and the only question seems to have been the manner of putting an end to their lives. True, less ferocious proposals were made, by which it was suggested to send them over to France; but when it became evident that they would return, the thoughts of the company reverted to murder. At this juncture the wives of Jackson and Carter, who were both present during these consultations, cried out, "Hang the dogs, for they came here to hang us!"

Another proposition that was made—to imprison the two in some safe place until they knew what would be Diamond's fate, and for each of the smugglers to subscribe threepence a week for their keep—was immediately scouted; and instantly the brutal fury of these ruffians was aroused by Jackson, who, going into the room where the unfortunate men were lying, spurred them on their foreheads with the heavy spurs of his riding-boots, and having thus awakened them, whipped them into the kitchen of the inn until they were streaming with blood. Then, taking them outside, the gang lifted them on to a horse, one behind the other, and tying their hands and legs together, lashed them with heavy whips along the road, crying, "Whip them, cut them, slash them, damn them!"

From Rowlands Castle, past Wood Ashes, Goodthorpe Deane, and to Lady Holt Park, this scourging was continued through the night until the wretched men were three parts dead. At two o'clock in the morning this gruesome procession reached the Portsmouth Road at Rake, where the foremost members of the party halted before the "Red Lion," kept in those days by one Scardefield, who was no stranger to their kind, nor unused to the purchase and storing of smuggled spirits. Here they knocked and rattled at the door until Scardefield was obliged to get out of bed and open to them. Galley, still alive, was thrust into an outhouse while the band, having roused the landlord and procured drink, caroused in the parlour of the inn. Chater they carried in with them; and when Scardefield stood horrified at seeing so ghastly a figure of a man, all bruised and injured and spattered with blood, they told him a specious tale of an engagement they had had with the King's officers: that here was one comrade, wounded, and another, dead or dying, in his brew-house.

While it was yet dark they carried Galley to a place in Harting Coombe, at some distance from the "Red Lion," and, digging a grave in a fox-earth by the light of a lantern, they buried him, without inquiring too closely whether or not their victim was dead. That he was not dead at that time became evident when his body was found, with the hands raised to the face, as though to prevent the dirt from suffocating him.

The whole of this day this evil company sat drinking in the "Red Lion," having disposed of their other prisoner for a time by chaining him by the leg in a turf-shed near by. This was Monday, and at night they all returned home, lest their absence might be remarked by their neighbours; agreeing to meet again at Rake on the Wednesday evening, to consider how they might best put an end to Chater. When Wednesday night had come, this council of fourteen smugglers decided to dispatch him forthwith, and, going down in a body to the turf-shed where he had lain all this while, suffering agonies from the cruel usage to which he had already been subjected, they unchained him, and with the most revolting barbarities, set him across a horse and whipped him afresh all the way back to Lady Holt Park, where there was a deep, dry well. Into this they threw the wretched man, and by his cries and groans perceiving that he was not yet dead, they collected a great number of large stones, which, together with two great gate-posts, they flung down upon him, and then rode away.

Even in those times two men (and men who had set out upon public business) could not disappear so utterly as Chater and Galley had done without comment, and presently the whole country was ringing with the story of this mysterious disappearance. That it was the work of smugglers none doubted: the only question was, in what manner had they spirited these two men away? Some thought they had been carried over to France, and others thought, shrewdly enough, that they had been murdered. But no tidings nor any trace of either Galley or Chater came to satisfy public curiosity or official apprehensions until some seven months later, when an anonymous letter sent to "a person of distinction," and probably inspired by the hope of ultimately earning the large reward then being offered by the Government for information, hinted that "the body of one of the unfortunate men mentioned in his Majesty's proclamation was buried in the sands in a certain place near Rake." And, sure enough, when the authorities came to search they found the body of the Excise officer "standing almost upright, with his hands covering his eyes." Another letter followed, implicating one William Steel as concerned in the murder; and when Steel was arrested the mystery was discovered, for, to save himself, the prisoner turned King's evidence, and revealed the whole dreadful story.

One after another seven of the murderers were arrested in different parts of the counties of Hants and Surrey, and were committed to the gaols at Horsham and Newgate, afterwards being sent to Chichester, where their trial was held on January 18, 1749. They were all found guilty, and were sentenced to be hanged on the following day. Six of them were duly executed; William Jackson, the seventh, who had been in ill-health, died in gaol a few hours after condemnation. The body of William Carter was afterwards hanged in chains upon the Portsmouth Road, near the scene of the crimes; three of the others were thrown into a pit on the Broyle, at Chichester, the scene of the execution, and the rest were hanged in chains along the sea-coast from Chichester to Selsea Bill, at points of vantage whence they were visible for miles around. Another accomplice, Henry Shurman, was indicted and tried at East Grinstead, and being sentenced to death, was conveyed from Horsham Gaol by a strong guard of soldiers, and hanged at Rake shortly afterwards.

And so an end to incidents as revolting as anything to be found in the lengthy annals of crime. Country folk breathed more freely when these daring criminals were "turned off"; and numerous other executions for resisting the military and the Excise followed, thus breaking up the gangs that terrorized law-abiding people.

But the Customs officers were still so intimidated that few possessed hardihood sufficient to carry them on their duty into places beyond reach of ready help. The more remote roads and lanes were patrolled at night by the most daring fellows, who, despite the warnings visible on every side in the dangling bodies of their dead comrades, dealt largely in many kinds of crime beneath the very gallows-tree; smuggling, starting incendiary fires, and assaulting and intimidating those wayfarers whose only fault was being found on the road after night had fallen.

Few people cared to be out alone after the sun had set, for the more daring among the "free-traders" were wont to appear then, and stopped and interrogated every one they chanced upon, lest they might be Government agents. If a peaceable villager, jogging home after sundown, failed to give a good and ready account of himself and his business upon the highway at that moment, he stood an excellent chance of a crack across the skull with something heavy, in the nature of a pistol-butt, which rendered further explanation impossible; and so, things being still in this pass, we can afford sympathy for the wayfarer who, having missed his road, found himself, when night was come and the moon risen, at some remote cross-road, far removed from sight or sound of human beings, except the ominous pit-a-pat of distant hoofs upon the hard road that heralded the approach of

BENIGHTED.

the merry men who played hide-and-seek with death and the gallows; to whom daylight was as unwelcome as to the predatory owl, and whose high noontide stress of business fell at dead of night.

XXXIII

CHALTON DOWNS is the ideal tract of country for so heart-stirring an encounter. Never a considerable tree for miles in any direction: only bushes and sparse clumps of saplings, and, for the rest, undulations of chalk as bare as the back of your hand, save for the short and scanty grass that affords not even a good mouthful for sheep. Here, where the Downs are most barren, a rough country lane dips into the hollow that runs parallel with the right-hand side of the highway, where a gaunt finger-post points the way to "Catherington and Hinton." On the corresponding ridge stands the small and scattered village, but large parish, of Catherington, whose church, dedicated to St. Catherine, is the parish church of modern Horndean and of other hamlets, a mile or more down the road.

The church of Catherington, so far as outward appearance goes, may be taken as amongst the most representative of Hampshire village churches, standing on the hill-brow, its graveyard separated from ploughed fields only by a hedge, its tombs overshadowed by two great solemn yew trees, its situation, no less than its shape and style, suggesting thoughts of Gray's "Elegy," and the peaceful rural lives of them that sleep beneath the skies in this retired God's acre. It is, therefore, with nothing less than a start of surprise that the wayfarer, weighted with obvious moralizings, discovers first the tomb of Admiral Sir Charles Napier, and then the resting-place of Charles Kean, his mother, and his wife. What do they

CATHERINGTON CHURCH.

here, who lived so greatly in the eye of the world? Here is the epitaph "to the memory of Mary, relict of the late Edmund Kean, who departed this life March 30, 1849, in or about the 70th year of her age"; and from her grave one can view the ridge along which runs the road to Portsmouth, tramped by Edmund Kean in 1795, when he, as a boy of eight or nine years, ran away from his home in Ewer street, Southwark, and shipped as cabin-boy on a vessel bound for Madeira. He lies at Richmond: his widow was buried here, close to the small estate upon which she had lived in retirement for years.

In "Charles John Kean, F.R.G.S.," whose epitaph occupies one side of this monument, it is difficult at first to recognize the famous actor, who, after playing well his varied parts in Shakespearean plays, and in melodrama, died in 1868, in his fifty-seventh year. His widow, Eleonora, survived him until 1880, when, at the age of seventy-three, she died, and "now lies with her loving husband."

The Admiral, after his eventful career, rests near at hand beneath an altar-tomb in an obscure corner of the graveyard, where ashes from the heating apparatus of the church are heaped, and defile, together with the miscellaneous dirt and foul rubbish of a neglected corner, his memorial, that sets forth his rank and a *précis* of his varied achievements. When the present writer visited the spot, a bottomless pail and the remains of an old boot placed on his tomb formed a hideous commentary upon the pride and enthusiasm of a grateful country, and preached a sermon, both painful and forcible, on the fleeting consideration of men for the distinguished dead. It is thirty-five years ago since "Charley Napier," as his contemporaries (brother-officers, or Tom, Dick, and Harry) called him, died, after having performed many services for his country in many parts of the world. It may seem, at the first blush, ungenerous to say so, but the fact remains that, had he quitted this scene but seven years earlier, his reputation had been brighter to-day, and this through no shortcoming of his own. He had achieved many important, if somewhat too theatrical, victories in his earlier days, when ordnance was comparatively light, and when the old line-of-battle ship was at its highest development; and so, when he was, in his old age, sent in command of the Baltic Fleet to reduce the heavily-armed sea-forts of Cronstadt and Bomarsund, the uninstructed but enthusiastic mob of his countrymen anticipated merely a naval promenade, ending with the capitulation of those fortresses of the North. When the Baltic Fleet cruised ingloriously for years in that icy sea, and the Russian strongholds yet remained unreduced, the disappointment of the million knew no bounds, and the Admiral's fame became tarnished. He was ridiculed, and he had himself to thank in some measure for this, because, in his characteristically reckless way, he had vowed to be either in Cronstadt or Heaven within a month, and Heaven had not claimed him nor Cronstadt submitted when the war was done.

But if, like General Trochu, of some sixteen years later, he had "a plan" and became the butt of witlings when that plan failed, he had the English-

man's infallible refuge and court of public appeal—
the "Times," and in the columns of that paper he
stormed and thundered from time to time, a great
deal more effectively than ever he had done in the
Baltic. He had nearly always possessed a pet grievance, and had, ere this, obtained election to Parliament
to air the injustice of the hour; and in the House he
was wont to hold forth in a fine old quarter-deck
manner that amused many, and let off the steam of
his wrath in an entirely harmless way. Between-
whiles he resided at Horndean, on a small estate he
had purchased years before, and in a house he had
re-christened "Merchistoun," from the place of that
name in Scotland where he was born. Here he,
a modern Cincinnatus, farmed his own land and
pottered about, a singular combination of sailor and
agriculturist, and one of the most extraordinary
figures of his time. "He is," said one who wrote
of his personal appearance, "stout and broad built;
stoops, from a wound in his neck; walks lame, from
another in his leg; turns out one of his feet, and has
a most slouching, slovenly gait; a large round face,
with black, bushy eyebrows, a double chin, scraggy,
grey, uncurled whiskers and thin hair, always be-
daubed with snuff, which he takes in immense
quantities; usually his trousers far too short, and
wears the ugliest pair of old shoes he can find." He
became quite an authority upon sheep and turnips,
and so died, after a busy life, on November 6, 1860.

Another great man lies at Catherington, within the
church; Sir Nicholas Hyde, Lord Chief Justice of
England, and uncle of the still greater Clarendon.

His splendid monument, with recumbent marble effigies of himself and his wife, occupies the east wall of the Hyde Chapel. Hinton House—the seat of the Hydes near here, and the scene of the marriage between James, Duke of York (afterwards James II.), and Anne Hyde, daughter of the Chancellor, Clarendon, in 1660—has long since been rebuilt.

From Catherington, one may either retrace one's steps to the Portsmouth Road above Horndean, or else continue on the by-lanes that bring the pedestrian to the highway below that wayside hamlet.

Horndean stands at the entrance to the Forest of Bere, and at the junction of roads that lead to Rowlands Castle and Havant. It is just a neat and comparatively recent place, like most of the wayside settlements that now begin to dot the highway between this and Portsmouth. An old house or two by way of nucleus, with some few decrepit cottages—the remainder of Horndean is made up of a great red-brick brewery and some rural-looking shops.

The Forest of Bere is at this day the most considerable remnant of that vast tract of woodland (computed at some ninety thousand acres) which formerly covered the face of southern Hants. It follows on either side of the roadway from this point to within a short distance of Purbrook, and extends for many miles across country, including Waltham Chase. Outlying woodlands still occur plentifully; among them the leafy coverts of Alice Holt (=*Axe-holt*, the Ash Wood), Liss Wood, Hawkley Hangers, and the green glades of Avington, Old Park, and Cheriton.

XXXIV

Presently the road becomes singularly suburban, and the beautiful glades of the old Forest of Bere, that have fringed the highway from Horndean, suddenly give place to rows of trim villas and recent shops. The highway, but just now as lonely as most of the old coach-roads are usually become in these days of steam and railways, is alive with wagons and tradesmen's carts, and neatly-kept footpaths are bordered with lamp-posts, furnished with oil-lamps.

This is the entirely modern neighbourhood of Waterlooville, a settlement nearly a mile in length, bordering the Portsmouth Road, and wearing not so much the appearance of an English village as that of some mushroom township in the hurried clearings of an American forest. The inns, past and present, of Waterlooville, have all been named allusively—the " Waterloo " Hotel, the " Wellington " Inn, the " Belle Alliance."

Waterlooville, as its ugly name would imply, is modern, but with a modernity much more recent than Wellington's great victory. The name, indeed, was only bestowed upon the parish in 1858, and is a dreadful example of that want of originality in recent place-names, seen both here and in America. Why some descriptive title, such as our Anglo-Saxon forebears gave to their settlements, could not have been conferred upon this place, is difficult to understand. Certainly " Waterlooville " is at once cumbrous and unmeaning, as here applied.

The history of Waterlooville is soon told. It was originally a portion of the Forest of Bere, and its site was sold by the Commissioners of Woods and Forests early in the present century. A tavern erected shortly afterwards was named the "Heroes of Waterloo," and became subsequently the halting-place for the coaches on this, the first stage out of Portsmouth and the last from London. Around the tavern sprang up four houses, and this settlement, some seven or eight miles from Portsmouth, was called Waterloo until 1830, when, a rage for building having set in, resulting in a church and some suburban villas, the "ville" was tacked on to the already unmeaning and sufficiently absurd name.

The church of Waterlooville is a building of so paltry and vulgar a design, and built of such poor materials, that a near sight of it would be sufficient to make the mildest architect swear loud and long. This plastered abomination is, of course, among the earliest buildings here; for no sooner are two or three houses gathered together than an unbeneficed clergyman—what we may on this sea-faring road most appropriately term a "sky-pilot"—comes along and solicits subscriptions towards the building of a church for the due satisfaction of the "spiritual needs" of a meagre flock. It would be ungenerous to assert that he always scents a living in this spiritual urgency, but the labourer is worthy of his hire, and if by dint of much canvassing for funds amongst pious old ladies and retired general officers (why is it that these men of war so frequently become pillars of the Church after their army days are done?) he succeeds in putting up some sort of a building called a church, who else so eligible as incumbent?

Where Waterlooville ends, the road runs for half-a-mile in mitigated rusticity, to become again, at the sixth milestone from Portsmouth, lively with the thriving, business-like village of Purbrook.

And at this point the traveller in coaching times came within sight of his destination. Painfully the old stages climbed up the steep ascent of Portsdown Hill before the road was lowered by cutting through the chalk at the summit, about 1820, and grumblingly the passengers obeyed the coachman and walked up the road to save the horses. But when they did reach the crest of the hill such a panorama met their gaze as nowhere else could be seen in England: Portsmouth, the Harbour, Gosport, the Isle of Wight, and the coast-line for miles on either hand lay spread out before their eyes as daintily as in a plan, and smiling like a Land of Promise. Unfortunately, however, our forebears were not yet educated to a proper appreciation and admiration of scenery. They, with that jovial bard of the Regency, Captain Morris, preferred the pavements of great cities to the pastorals of the country-side, and would with the greatest fervour have echoed him when he wrote—

> "In town let me live, then, in town let me die;
> For, in truth, I can't relish the country, not I.
> If one must have a villa in summer to dwell,
> Oh! give me the sweet shady side of Pall Mall."

Fortunately, however, the view remains unspoiled for a generation that takes its pleasures afield, and can find delight in country scenes which our great-grandfathers characterized as places of "horror and desolation."

This is the point of view from which Rowlandson has sketched his "Extraordinary Scene," and although we miss in the picture the "George Inn," that stands so four-square and stalwart, perched up above the road, yet the likeness to the place remains after these many years have flown.

The occasion that led to Rowlandson's producing the elaborate plate from which the accompanying illustration was made, is referred to at length in the title, which runs thus—

"An Extraordinary Scene on the Road from London to Portsmouth, Or an Instance of Unexampled speed used by a Body of Guards, consisting of 1920 Rank and File, besides Officers, who, on the 10th of June, 1798, left London in the Morning, and actually began to Embark for Ireland, at Portsmouth, at four o'Clock in the Afternoon; having travelled 74 Miles in 10 Hours."

Such a performance as this, at such a time, made a great impression, and Rowlandson has made a very spirited drawing of the scene, full of life and vigour. In the foreground is the "Portsmouth Fly," with officers inside, taking their ease, and a number of soldiers occupying a precarious perch on the roof, fifing and drumming, regardless of jolts and lurches. Flags are waving from the windows of the "Fly," soldiers on the box are "laying on" to the horses with a whip, while three others ride comfortably in the "rumble-tumble" behind. Other parties follow, in curricles and carts, hugging the shameless wenches

AN EXTRAORDINARY SCENE ON THE PORTSMOUTH ROAD. *By Rowlandson.*

who "doted on the military" in those times as demonstratively as Mary Jane does now. On the right hand stands an enthusiastic group at the door of the "Jolly Sailor": the landlord, in apron and shirt-sleeves, about to drink the soldiers' healths in a bumper of very respectable proportions, his womenkind looking on, while a young hopeful, who has donned a saucepan by way of helmet, is "presenting arms" with a besom. An ancient, with a wooden leg and a crutch, is fiddling away with vigour, and a dog runs forward, barking. The long cavalcade is seen disappearing down the hill, while away in the distance is Portsmouth Harbour with its crowded shipping.

XXXV

But the greater number of the travellers along the Portsmouth Road, whether they walked or rode, were sailors; and so salt of the sea are the records of this old turnpike that the romance of old-time travel upon it is chiefly concerned with them that went down to brave the elements on board ship; or with those happy mariners who, having entered port, came speeding up to home and beauty with all the ardour of men tossed and buffeted by winds and waves on a two or three years' cruise. Pepys, who happened to be on the road, on his way up from Portsmouth, June 12, 1667, met several of the crew of the "Cambridge," and describes them in a manner so unfavourable that I am inclined to suspect they showed too little consideration for the Secretary to the Admiralty. At any rate, he pictures them as being "the most debauched swearing rogues that ever were in the Navy, just like their prophane commander." My certes, sirs! just imagine Pepys playing the shocked Puritan, after having, perhaps, just committed some of those peccadilloes which he sets down so frankly in his ciphered "Diary."

That is one of the earliest glimpses we get of Jack ashore on this route, and by it we can well see that his spirits were as boisterous then as ever after. "Sailors earned their money like horses and spent it like asses," says an old writer, and certainly, once ashore, they were no niggards. It was the natural reaction from a long life of stern discipline, tempered by fighting, wounds, floggings, and marline-spikes, and for the most part cheerfully endured on a miserable diet of weevilly biscuit, "salt horse," and pork full of maggots. The Mutiny at Spithead, April 15, 1797, was due in part to the shameful quality of the provisions supplied, and partly to the open huckstering of the pursers, the unfair distribution of prize-money, to stoppages, and to insufficient pay. But these grievances were of old standing, and the Government actually felt and expressed indignation that sailors should object to be half starved and half poisoned with insufficient and rotten food. However indignant the Government may have been, redress was seen to be immediately advisable, and the demands of the mutineers were granted. Sailors rated as A.B.'s had their wages *raised* to a shilling a day, and were paid at more frequent intervals than once in ten years or so. It was stated (and names and dates were given)

THE SAILOR'S RETURN FROM PORTSMOUTH TO LONDON.

in the House of Commons that some ships' companies had not been paid for eight, ten, twelve, or fifteen years. Under such a system, or want of system, as this, it frequently happened in those days of much fighting and more disease that when the ships were paid off, the sailors to whom money was due had long been dead. In those cases it was very rarely that their heirs touched a penny, and certainly the Government reaped no advantage. The money went into the pockets of the Admiralty clerks and paymasters, who thrived on wholesale and shameless peculation. If by some strange chance, or by a singular strength of constitution, some hardy sailors remained to claim their due, they were paid it grudgingly, without interest, and whittled away by deductions amounting to as much as thirty or forty per cent.

But when a man *did* receive his pay, together with his prize-money, he was like a school-boy out at play. Nothing was too ridiculous or puerile for him to stoop to, and he was, as a class, so entirely innocent and unsophisticated that the land-sharks waiting hungrily for homeward-bound ships found him an easy prey. Stories innumerable have been told of his childlike innocence of landsmen's ways, and pictures and caricatures without end have been drawn and painted with the object of making men smile at his strange doings. Here is a caricature dated so far back as 1772, showing "The Sailor's Return from Portsmouth to London." The point of view chosen is, apparently, only a mile or two from Portsmouth, for in the background rise some ruins obviously intended to represent Porchester Castle. The sailor, after the manner so often dwelt upon, is keeping up a pleasing travesty of sea-faring life. His jaded nag is a ship, and the course is being steered by the nag's tail. The sailor himself has evidently "come aboard" by the rope-ladder, seen hanging down almost to the ground, and he keeps the fog-horn going to avoid collisions. A flag flies from his top-gallant—in plain English, his hat—while a Union Jack is fixed at the forepeak and an anchor is triced up at the bows, in readiness for "heaving-to." His log might well be that of "Jack Junk" on a similar journey:—"Hove out of Portsmouth on board the 'Britannia Fly'—a swift sailer—got an inside berth—rather drowsy the first watch or so—liked to have slipped off the stern—cast anchor at the 'George'—took a fresh quid and a supply of grog—comforted the upper works—spoke several homeward-bound frigates on the road—and after a tolerable smooth voyage entered the port of London at ten past five, post meridian."

Another, and a much more spirited, plate by Isaac Cruikshank, dated 1797, and entitled, "True Blue; or Britain's Jolly Tars Paid Off at Portsmouth," shows a coach-load going off to London without more ado, accompanied by Poll and Sue, Nancy, Kate, and Joan; all (nay, I will not say uproariously drunk) in the merriest of moods. The horses gallop, hats are waved in every direction, and those who have no hats flourish beer-bottles instead. Some jolly Jack-a-Dandy stands upon the roof, at the imminent risk of his neck, and scrapes a fiddle to what, considering the pace of the coach, must have been a tune of the most agonizing description; while an amorous fellow hugs

his girl behind. The Union Jack is, of course, in a prominent position, and a riotous, devil-me-care figure sits one of the horses backwards. I do not observe any one of this merry company "heaving the lead overboard," as became the pleasing fashion among sailor-men flush of money who rode outside the day coaches to town. These merry men would purchase long gold chains at Portsmouth, and on their journey would now and then hang them over the side of the coach with their watches suspended at the end by way of plummets, and would call out, in nautical style, so many fathoms. Some home-coming sailors would walk up the road, either because they had spent most of their money in drink and debauchery at Portsmouth, or else because the idea commended itself to their freakish natures; and the people of the inns and beerhouses on the way reaped a fine harvest from this class of customer. I have told you, on another page, how most of these sailor-men were accommodated, as to their sleeping arrangements, by being given a shake-down in the clean straw of some outhouse. They in many instances threw themselves down amid the straw, hopelessly drunk; and then entered unto them the honest innkeeper, who would not rob his guests, but saw no objection to taking them up by the heels and shaking them vigorously until the money fell out of their pockets among the straw. If they found the coin in the morning, why, it was bad luck from the publican's point of view; and if they reeled away, leaving their money behind them, it was a happy chance for mine host, who came and gleaned a golden hoard from his straw. But if some indignant sailor, full of horrid oaths and terrible threats, came and swore he had been robbed during the night, the virtuous publican could suggest that before he made such serious charges, it would be better if he made a search. He *might* have dropped his money!

Sometimes the Portsmouth Road was traversed by long processions of wagons containing treasure captured at sea and landed at Portsmouth for greater security in transmission to London. Such an occasion was that when Anson, returning in 1744 from his four years' cruise in South American waters, brought home a rich cargo of spoil in the "Centurion." This treasure was valued at no less than £500,000, and was stowed away in twelve wagons, which were sent up to London under an escort of sailors and marines. Eighteen years later, another splendid haul was made by the capture of the Spanish galleon "Hermione," from Lima, off Cadiz, and on this occasion the value was scarcely less than before. The prize-money distributed amounted to handsome fortunes for the officers, and conferred competencies upon every man and boy in the two ships' companies that took part in the capture. Such windfalls as these were not everyday occurrences, and many a man gave and took hard knocks all his life, to die in his old age in poverty and neglect. Very few, probably, of those fortunate prize-sharers from the "Hermione" treasure-chest retained their wealth.

The people who dwelt along the highway all shared to some degree in this marvellous good fortune, but they lived in fear of the murderous rascals who began to infest the roads in 1795, tramping or being sent down from London to join the navy at a time when every man was needed to help the nation through the vast wars we were continually engaged in. At that period of England's greatest struggle for existence the press-gang was in full tide of activity, but the pressed men were few in proportion to the number required to man the ships, and so Acts of Parliament were passed in order to provide a certain number of men from each county and from every seaport for the service of the navy. The men thus provided were induced to join by the extraordinarily large bounties offered, some of which were as much as £30; and many of these "quota-men," as they came to be called, belonged to the most depraved of the criminal classes. The *personnel* of the navy was lowered by these men, and the sailors were disgusted with them. The "quota-bounty," says an authority, " we conceive to have been the most ill-advised and fatal measure ever adopted by the Government for manning the fleet. The seamen who voluntarily entered in 1793 and fought some of the most glorious of our battles received the comparatively small bounty of £5. These brave fellows saw men totally ignorant of the profession, the very refuse and outcasts of society, flying from justice and the vengeance of the law, come on board with a bounty to the amount of £70. One of these objects, on coming on board a ship of war with £70 bounty, was seized by a boatswain's mate, who, holding him up with one hand by the waistband of his trousers, humorously exclaimed, 'Here's a fellow that cost a guinea a pound!'"

Criminals were allowed as an alternative to long terms of imprisonment, to volunteer for what was evidently regarded by the authorities as an equivalent to the gaol—a man-o'-war. "All the bad characters of a neighbourhood, loafers, poachers, footpads, possible murderers, men suspected of any crime, but against whom there was not sufficient evidence, were arrested and sent on board, with a note to the captain begging him to take measures to prevent their return; which, as such men were commonly stout-built fellows enough, he was no ways loath to do. The gaol-birds from the towns were unquestionably worse; worse physically, worse morally, and perhaps worse hygienically; they were not infrequently infected with gaol-fever, and brought the infection to the fleet; they were largely the cause of the severe, even brutal, discipline that ruled in the navy towards the end of last century." According to the sailors themselves—" Them was the chaps as played hell with the fleet: every grass-combing beggar as chose to bear up for the bounty had nothing to do but to dock the tails of his togs and take to the tender." They used to ship in shoals; they were drafted by forties and fifties to each ship in the fleet; they were hardly up the side, hardly mustered abaft, before there was "Send for the barber, shave their pates, and send 'em for'rd to the head, to be scrubbed and sluished from clue to ear-ring, afore you could venture to berth 'em below. Then, stand clear of their shore-going rigs—every finger was fairly a fish-hook; neither chest, nor bed, nor blanket, nor bag escaped their sleight-of-hand thievery; they pluck you, aye, as clean as a poulterer, and bone your very eyebrows whilst staring you full in the face."

These were the men who, instead of bringing prosperity to the innkeepers and country folk, robbed and plundered stray travellers and lonely houses by the way. Singly, they robbed hen-roosts and old market-women; in bands their courage rose to highway robbery on a larger scale, and even to murder. An official posting down to Portsmouth with money for a ship's company came within an ace of being relieved of several thousands of pounds; for on his coach being upset on Rake Hill a number of fellows appeared with offers of help, and would have carried off the gold had not the boxes in which it was contained been too heavy. As it was, while some of them were engaging every one's attention in attempting to raise the coach out of the slough in which it had become embedded, the remainder of the band had got hold of the specie-boxes, and were battering them in with great stones, when a party of marines opportunely arrived and caught them in the very act.

Men of this stamp were the curse of the navy. They were more often town-bred weaklings than robust countrymen, and to their constitutional disabilities they added the vices of the towns from which they came, and a sullen habit of mind that could leave no room for discipline. Those were the days of the press-gang, when likely fellows, whether seamen or landsmen, were taken by force from their occupations, shipped under guard upon men-o'-war in the harbours, and sent to fight, willy-nilly, for King and country. Merchantmen, coming home from long and tedious voyages, were seized and hurried off immediately upon their stepping ashore, and, in fact, any well-built young fellow, an apprentice or clerk, who could not prove himself to be a master-man became at one time the ordinary prey of the press-gangs that roamed about the seaboard towns in search of prey. Seamen only were their proper quarry, but when more, and still more, men were required as time went on, it mattered little whether pressed men were landlubbers or sailors; and as the members of the press-gang came to be paid so much a head for all the sturdy fellows they could seize, it may be seen that they were not apt to stand upon trifles or to weigh evidence very narrowly. There were exemptions from the press, and it was open to a man who considered himself to have been illegally seized to send a statement to the authorities. These became known as "state-the-case-men," but as, in many instances, the ship upon which they had been sent sailed almost immediately, this formality was simply a cruel farce. If their statements were ever forwarded to their destination, they only arrived by the time the ships were well out to sea; and if their complaints were ever investigated, the inquiries would most likely take place while the subjects of them were in the thick of an action with the enemy; perhaps wounded, possibly even already dead.

The forays of the press-gangs were battles in themselves, and many a man on either side was killed in these man-hunting expeditions. "Private mischief," said the Earl of Mansfield, "had better be submitted

THE LIBERTY OF THE SUBJECT, 1782. By James Gillray.

to than that public detriment and inconvenience should ensue;" but the men who fought with the press-gangs did not see matters in this light, and neither did their womenkind. The beautiful decorative drawing by Morland that forms the frontispiece to this book puts the sentiment of the time against impressment in a poetical way, but Gillray's more nervous and satirical pencil gives, in his "Liberty of the Subject," a realistic and satirical picture that shows how strenuously the press was resisted. It is a most graphic and humorous representation of a "hot press" in the streets of some seaport town, at a period immediately following upon the American War of Independence, when men were particularly scarce. A gang has seized a tailor, a poor, miserable-looking wretch with no fighting in him, almost literally as well as metaphorically the "ninth part of a man," and his captors are dragging him off, knock-kneed and incapable of resistance. But if he submits so easily, the women of the crowd have to be reckoned with, and are doing nearly all the fighting. The furious virago in the foreground is pulling at a midshipman's hair with all the strength of one hand, while with the other she is lugging his ear off, kicking him, at the same time, with her knee. A sailor in the rear, with an animated expression of countenance, has hold of her arm, and appears to be aiming a blow at her head with the butt-end of a pistol; while another woman with a heavy mop is preparing to fell him to the ground.

One of the "hottest presses," and at the same time the most successful, ever known, was that of March 8,

1803, at Portsmouth. Five hundred able seamen were obtained on that occasion by the strategy and cunning of a certain Captain Brown, who assembled a company of marines late at night with all the fuss and circumstance he could display, in order, as he gave out, to quell a mutiny at Fort Monckton. The news of this pretended mutiny spread rapidly, and great crowds came rushing down to see the affair. When they had all crossed Haslar Bridge they were cooped up like so many fowls, and that master of strategy, having posted his marines at the bridge end, seized every suitable man in the crowd.

But the pressed men, although they tried every dodge to escape this forced service, and though their unwillingness to serve his Majesty afloat has made a classic of the saying, " One volunteer is worth three pressed men," did good service when once they were trapped and trained. For one thing, they had no choice. 'Twas either a cheerful obedience to orders and readiness in action when once afloat, or else a flogging with the cat and a remand, heavily ironed, to the hold. Seeing how useless would be any malingering, the pressed men turned to with a will, and fought our battles with such spirit that the victories of Trafalgar, of " the glorious First of June," off Cape St. Vincent, and many of the other notable exploits of the British Fleet, are due to their courage and resolution.

When the pressed men came home (if ever they were so fortunate) they were as a rule so inured to sea-service and hard knocks, that, so soon as they had had a spree and spent their money, they were ready

REVELRY

for another cruise. But meanwhile they enjoyed themselves with the reckless prodigality possible only to such men. When the ships came home (and ships were always coming home then), Portsmouth ran with liquor, riot, and revelry; and on fine summer days the grassy slopes of Portsdown Hill were all alive with the jolly Jacks engaged with great earnestness in the business of pleasure. Here, in the taverns that overlook from this breezy height the harbour, the town, and the distant mud-flats, generations of soldiers and sailors, fresh from battle and the salt sea, have caroused. Here, opposite the "George" and the Belle Vue Gardens, where "the military" and the servant-girls, the sailors and their lasses, still disport on high-days and holidays, with swings, Aunt Sallies, cocoa-nut shies, and, in short, all the fun of the fair, have the look-out men of a hundred years ago shivered in the wind while scanning the distant horizon for signs of Bonaparte and his flotilla, the inglorious Armada that never left port.

XXXVI

WHEN workmen were engaged in lowering the road opposite the old "George" Inn, that stands so boldly and with such a fine last-century air on the hill brow, they opened a tumulus which was found to contain, at a depth of only eighteen inches, the well-preserved skeletons of sixteen men, the victims of some prehistoric fray. Their feet were all placed towards the east, and in the skull of one was found the iron head of a spear. Who were these vanquished soldiers in a forgotten fight? Were they Belgæ? Surely not. Were they Christianized Saxons, slain in battle with Pagan vikings, marauders from over sea? This seems more likely than any other theory. That they were Christians appears certain from the position of their skeletons, east and west; that they fell in battle is evident from the silent testimony of the spear-head.

Down goes the road in a long steady slope, flanked by the great forts of Purbrook and Widley, whose dingy red-brick walls and embrasures command the entrance to the harbour. Away, to right and left, for a distance of seven miles, runs a succession of these forts, from Fareham to Purbrook, cresting the ridge of the long hill, connected by telegraph, and furnished with extensive barrack accommodation.

Cosham village comes next, crouching at the foot of the ridge, with the great guns high overhead to the rearwards: Cosham, neither town nor village; busy enough for a town, sufficiently quaint for a village; with a railway-crossing barring the road; a station adjoining it; the tramp of soldiers re-echoing, and the blare of bugles familiar in the ears of the people all day and every day.

These are suburbs indeed, with the beginnings of pavements and the terminus of a tramway that runs from here, a distance of three miles, to Portsmouth itself. We cross over the bridges that span salty channels, oozy and redolent of ocean and sea-weed during the hours of ebb. Here we are immediately confronted with the ceinture of forts that embraces the towns and garrisons of Portsea Island in a ring of masonry, earthworks, and steel. The fortifications straddle across the road on brick arches containing Royal Engineers' stores, and ornamented with the device " 18 VR 61," done in red brick upon yellow; and obsolete cannon, buried up to their trunnions, guard the brickwork piers against the wear and tear of traffic.

Now come Hilsea Barracks, with Hilsea Post Office opposite, and further on, opposite the "Green Posts" Inn, an obelisk, marking the eighteenth-century bounds of the borough of Portsmouth, with the inscription, "Burgi de Portesmuth Limes MDCCXCIX. Rev. G. Cuthbert praetore." And so by stages through North End into Landport, past ever-growing settlements and suburban wildernesses where new-built rows of hutches miscalled villas look out upon market-gardens and those forlornest of fields already marked out for "building sites," but still innocent of houses; where builders' refuse cumbers the ground, and where muddy pools, islanded with piles of broken and slack-baked bricks, and wrinkled into furious wavelets by the blusterous winds, resemble miniature seas in which (to aid the resemblance) lie the discarded iron pots and kettles of Portsmouth households, their spouts and handles rising above the waters like the vestiges of so many wrecked ironclads.

Successive eras of suburb-rearing are most readily to be noted. First come the red-bricked suburbs still in the making; then those of the '60's and the '70's, brown-bricked and grey-stuccoed; and then the settlements of a period ranging from 1840 to 1860,

A A

contrived in a fashion fondly supposed to represent Italian villas, characteristically constructed of lath and plaster now very much the worse for wear, but at one time wearing a spick-and-span appearance that would have delighted Macaulay, to whom the sight of a row of "semi-detached suburban residences" gave visions of progress and prosperity that seem to us inexpressibly vulgar. The sight of wealthy tradesfolk and of plutocratic contractors seems to have warmed Macaulay into an enthusiasm which became eloquent in enlarging upon the rows of villas that encircle every great town. To him the ostentatious surroundings of the despicable rogues—the typical contractors of the early and mid-Victorian epoch—who contracted to supply hay and fodder for our armies in the Crimea, and forwarded in their consignments a large proportion of bricks and rotten straw—the vulgar display of men of this stamp recalled the most prosperous times of the ancient Romans, and was therefore to be approved. But these men have long since left their lath-and-plaster fripperies for a place where (let us hope) their bricks and their rotten straw will be remembered against them, and their descendants have mounted on the heaps of their inherited money to a very high social scale indeed. The eligible residences themselves, with their "grounds," are mostly to be let, and the firesides across which unctuous purveyors and middlemen and their wives grinned at one another and ate buttered toast at tea-time, and drank "sherry wine" at night, are cold.

Following upon this suburban stratum come the

egregious houses of the Regency period: pseudo-classic houses these, bay-windowed and approached by steep flights of stone steps surmounted by ridiculously skimpy little porches, with attenuated neo-classic pillars and pediments, done in wood. Some of these are gone—pulled down to make room for shops—and doubtless many more will shortly go the same way. Let us hope one or two will be preserved for all time, for, although by no means beautiful, they are interesting as tending to show the manners of a period now removed from us by nearly a century; the taste in domestic architecture of a time when the First Gentleman in Europe ruled the land.

Here, where we come into Landport, we also come into the less affected region of "streets." In the newer suburbs nothing less than "roads" will serve the turn of the jerry-builder; his ambitious phraseology soars far above what he thinks to be the more plebeian "street"; but perhaps, after all, he is wise in his generation, and is amply justified by the preferences of his clients; and if that is the situation, let us by all means condole with him as a much-maligned man, who does not what he would, but what he must.

Here, too, in these beginnings of the old town, shops jostle villas with "grounds," and they in turn elbow artisans' dwellings, where children swing with improvised swings of clothes-lines on the railings, and manufacture mud-pies in the "gardens"; sticking them afterwards upon the shutters of those ultimate shops of the suburbs which seem to be in a chronic state of bankruptcy, and hold out no hopes of a living for the pioneer butchers, bakers, and candlestick-makers who, having served the purpose and gone the way of all pioneers, leave them richer in experience but light of pocket.

It was in these purlieus that Charles Dickens was born, at 387 Mile End Terrace, Commercial Road, Landport, on February 7, 1812; the son of Mr. John Dickens, Navy pay-clerk, who is supposed to be portrayed in the character of Micawber—no flattering portraiture of a father by his son. Writers who have fallen under the spell of Dickens have tried to do some sort of poetic representation of his birthplace; and, truth to tell, they have failed, because there never was any poetry at all about the place,—and probably never will be any, so long as its scrubby brick front and paltry fore-court last: while as regards Dickens himself, he was a very excellent business man among authors, and as little poetic as can well be imagined.

XXXVII

LANDPORT left behind, one came, until within only a comparatively few years ago, upon Portsmouth town through a series of ditches, scarps, counterscarps, bastions, and defensible gates. They are all swept away now, as being obsolete, and where they stood are parks and barracks, military hospitals, and open spaces devoted to drilling. The surroundings of Portsmouth are, in fact, very modern, and probably the most ancient edifice here is the High Level railway station: a class of building which age has no power to render venerable. The latest effort of modernity is to be seen from this point in the Town Hall, of which every inhabitant of the allied towns of Portsmouth, Southsea, Gosport, and Landport is inordinately proud. And if size should count for anything, they have cause for pride in this municipal effort; for Portsmouth Town Hall is particularly immense. This is no place in which to enlarge upon its elephantine dimensions, nor to specify how many hundreds of feet its tower rises above the pavement; but it may be noted that it is a second-hand design, having been closely copied from the Town Hall of Bolton, in Lancashire. The architectural purist is at a loss how to describe its architecture; for it is neither good Classic nor passable Renaissance, although it partakes of the nature of both: it is, in view of the number of municipal buildings put up in this fashion over the country during the last forty years or so, perhaps best described as belonging to the Victorian Town Hall order of architectural design; and that seems to me a perspicuous definition of it. It has, however, an advantage that Bolton altogether lacks. The sooty atmosphere of that dingy manufacturing town has clothed the surface of its Town Hall with a mantle of grime, until the building, from topmost pinnacle to pavement level, is, to use a colloquialism, "as black as your hat." The fresh breezes that blow over Portsmouth at least spare its Town Hall this indignity, and the design, such as it is, seems as fresh to-day as when the building was first inaugurated.

In Leland's time Portsmouth was "mured from the est toure a forelonge's lengthe, with a mudde waulle armid with tymbre, whereon be great pieces both of yron and brassen ordinauns"; and in later ages these primitive defences had expanded into great bastions and massive walls, in which were no less than six gates. When the military authorities dismantled these town walls, with the gates and the fortifications, they did away at once with a great deal of inconvenience and annoyance experienced by the civil population of Portsmouth in being cooped up within bounds at night, and by their reforming zeal destroyed the greater part of the interest with which strangers viewed this old stronghold.

To-day one obtains too little historic colour in the streets of the old town. The "Blue Posts," where the midshipmen stayed and joked and quarrelled, was burned down in 1870, and the "Fountain" is now a Home for Sailors, conducted upon strictly non-alcoholic lines, and Broad Street, which was at one time so very, very lively a place, has declined from the riotous days of yore into a more or less sedate old age. The inns with which it abounded are still there, but how altered their custom, their use and wont, from the hard-drinking, hard-swearing, hard-fighting days of old!

One may look back upon those old days with regret for a vanished picturesqueness and yet not wish them back; may know that the sailor who drinks cocoa and banks his wages in the Post-office Savings Bank is better off and immeasurably happier than his ancestor who, if he survived to receive any pay at all, squandered it instantly upon all conceivable kinds of drink and debauchery, and yet can see that his was by far the most interesting figure. It is the same with the ships of the navy. No one will contend that life was healthier upon the old wooden line-of-battle ships than it is on the modern ironclads of the fleet; not a single voice could be raised in favour of the dim and dirty orlop-decks of the old men-o'-war, in comparison with the light, airy, and roomy quarters on board our battle-ships of to-day; and yet there is scarce an Englishman who does not heartily regret the old three-deckers that rode the waves so gallantly, whose tier over tier of guns rose high above the waves and made a braver show than ever the "iron pots" of modern times can do.

The old-time aspect of Portsmouth is gone for ever. An almost complete transformation has taken place in appearance, in thought, and manner in little over a century, and where the body of Jack the Painter hung, high as Haman, from a lofty gallows on Blockhouse Beach, no criminals swing to-day. Even the "cat," that instrument of discipline, too barbarous to be honoured even by immemorial usage, no longer flays the backs of A.B.'s, and is relegated to the cold shades of a museum, to rest beside such long-out-of-date instruments of torture as the branks and the thumb-screws.

But, tide what will betide, a fine martial-naval air clings about the old town, and will last while a bugle remains to be blown or a pennant is left to be hoisted. The salt sea-breezes still bluster through the narrow streets; the dockyard clangs louder, longer, busier than ever; the tramp of soldiers echoes; the boom of cannon peals across the waters, and God's Englishmen are ready as ever they have been, and ever will be; though out yonder at Spithead and in foreign waters their forebears have strewed the floor of the sea with their bones, and though, with treacherous iron and steel beneath their feet while afloat, they may at any moment, be it peace or war, be sent to the bottom to join the ill-fated ships' companies of the "Mary Rose," the "Royal George," the more recent "Captain," "Eurydice," "Atalanta," or "Victoria."

Here, where the stone stairs lead down into the water, is Portsmouth Point. Mark it well, for from this spot have embarked countless fine fellows to serve King and country afloat. What would we not give for a moment's glimpse of "Point" (as Portsmouth folk call it, with a brevity born of everyday use) just a hundred years ago? Fortunately the genius of Rowlandson has preserved for us something of the appearance of Portsmouth Point at that time, when war raged over nearly all the civilized world, when wooden ships rode the waves buoyantly, when battles were the rule and peace the exception.

The Point was in those days simply a collection of taverns giving upon the harbour and the stairs, whence departed a continuous stream of officers and men of the navy. It was a place throbbing with life and excitement—the sailors going out and returning home; the leave-takings, the greetings; the boozing and the fighting, are all shown in Rowlandson's drawing as on a stage, while the tall ships form an appropriate background, like the back-cloth of a theatrical scene. It is a scene full of humour. Sailors are leaning on their arms out of window; a gold-laced officer bids good-bye to his girl while his trunks are being carried down to the stairs; a drunken sailor and his equally drunken woman are belabouring one another with all the good-will in the world, and a wooden-legged sailor-man is scraping away for very life on a fiddle and dancing grotesquely to get a living. He is a funny figure, you say; but, by your leave, it seems to me that he is only a figure of a very great pathos. Belisarius, over whom historians have wept as they recounted his fall and his piteous appeals for the scanty charity of an obolus, was but a rascally Roman general who betrayed his trust and became a peculator of the first magnitude; and he deserved his fate. But here is a poor devil who has been maimed in battle and left to earn his bread by playing the fool before a crowd of careless folk, happy if he can excite their compassion to the extent of a stray sixpence or an occasional drink. No: his is not a funny figure.

DANCING SAILOR.

XXXVIII

THE old coach offices clustered about this spot. Several stood in Bath Square, and here, among others, was the Old Van Office, kept by Uriah Green. The vans were similar to the stage-coaches, but much larger and clumsier, and jogged along at a very easy pace. They took, in fact, from fifteen to sixteen hours to perform the journey under the most favourable circumstances, and in bad weather no one ventured to prophesy at what time they *would* arrive.

The fares were, consequently, very much lower than those of the swifter coaches, which stood at £1 1s. 0d. inside, and 12s. 6d. outside. One might, on the other hand, take a trip from Portsmouth to London on the outside of a van for 6s. 6d. The cheapness of these conveyances caused them to be largely patronized by blue-jackets. One van left Portsmouth at four p.m. every day for the "Eagle," City Road, London, arriving there at about seven or eight o'clock the next morning, and another left the "Eagle" for Portsmouth at the same time.

This was at the beginning of the present century, and was a vast improvement upon the still older, clumsier, and infinitely slower road-wagons. Thirty-five years earlier (*circa* 1770), even the quickest stages were no speedier than the vans. For instance, at that time the "Royal Mail" started daily from the "Blue Posts" at two p.m., and only arrived in London at six o'clock the next morning. Then came Clarke's "Flying Machine," which was so little like flying that it did the journey only in a day, leaving the "King's Arms" Inn, Portsmouth, every Monday, Wednesday, and Friday night at ten o'clock, and returning on alternate nights.

In 1805 the number and the speed of coaches were considerably augmented. Among them were the "Royal Mail," from the "George"; the "Nelson," from the "Blue Posts"; the "Hero," from the "Fountain"; the "Regulator," from the "George"; and Vicat and Co.'s speedy "Rocket," that started from the "Quebec" Tavern, and did the journey to town in nine hours. It was at this period that a local bard was moved to verse by the astonishing swiftness of the coaches, and this is how he sings their prowess:—

> "In olden times, two days were spent
> 'Twixt Portsmouth and the Monument;
> When Flying Diligences plied,
> When men in Roundabouts would ride,
> And at the surly driver's will,
> Get out and climb each tedious hill.
> But since the rapid Freeling's age,
> How much improved the *English Stage!*
> Now in ten hours the London Post
> Reaches from Lombard Street our coast."

Prodigious! But when the railway was opened from Portsmouth to Nine Elms in 1840, and did the journey in three hours, there were, alas! no votaries of the Muse to celebrate the event.

That year witnessed the last of the old coaching days upon the Portsmouth Road, so far, at least, as ordinary travellers were concerned. Some few, particularly conservative, still elected to travel by road; and, as may be seen from the appended copy of a Post-office Time-Bill, the Postmaster-General put no trust in new-fangled methods of conveyance:—

GENERAL POST OFFICE.

THE EARL OF LICHFIELD, HER MAJESTY'S POSTMASTER-GENERAL.

London and Portsmouth Time-Bill.

Contractors' Names.	In	Out	M.F.	Time Allowed. H.M.	
					Dispatched from the General Post Office, the of , 184 , at by time-piece, at by clock. Coach No. { With time-piece safe, sent out { No. to Arrived at the Gloucester Coffee-House at
			13.0	1.35	Arrived at Kingston at
			4.0		Esher
			3.4		Cobham
Chaplin and Gray			3.7	1.25	Arrived at Ripley at
			6.1		Guildford
			4.2	1.18	Arrived at Godalming at
			2.1		Mousehill
			10.1	1.32	Arrived at Liphook at
			8.3	1.3	Arrived at Petersfield at
Wise			7.4	57	Arrived at Horndean at
			5.6		Cosham
Guy			4.6	1.20	Arrived at the Post Office, Portsmouth, the of , 184 , at by time-piece, at by clock. Coach No. { Delivered time-piece safe, No. arrived { to

The time of working each stage, &c. Up-time allowed the same.

By Command of the Postmaster-General.

GEORGE STOW, Surveyor and Superintendent.

This time-bill, quoted by Mr. Stanley Harris in his "Coaching Age," is dated April 1841, and shows, by a side-light, the innate conservatism of all Government institutions. At that time the London and South-Western Railway—then called the London and Southampton—had been opened eleven months, with a station at Portsmouth and a London terminus at Nine Elms, yet her Majesty's mails still went by road, and at a pace scarcely equalled for slowness among all the coaches of England. Nine hours and ten minutes taken, at this late period, in journeying between London and Portsmouth! Why, the Jehus of the Bath and Exeter Roads, the drivers of the "Quicksilver" and the "Regulator," even, would have scorned this jog-trot.

The present generation, which knows less of coaching times than of the Wars of the Roses or any other equally far-removed period, will be puzzled over the references to clocks and time-pieces in the bill printed above. These time-pieces were served out at the General Post Office to all mail-coaches. They were wound up and set going in correct time, and, enclosed in a securely-fastened box to prevent its being tampered with, one was handed to the guard of each mail leaving London. By means of his time-piece the guard could check the progress of the mail, and could hurry up the driver on an occasion. It was the guard's duty to deliver up his time-piece on arrival at his destination, when the time shown by it was entered by the postmaster, and any late arrivals notified to the Postmaster-General.

That august public functionary finally yielded to the pressure of circumstances, and in 1842 her Majesty's mails went by rail instead of by road. The Queen's highway was then lonely indeed, and it was not until 1875, when the coaching revival was already some twelve or thirteen years old, that the revived "Rocket" coach was put on between London and Portsmouth. It ran from the "White Horse" Cellars every Tuesday, Thursday, and Saturday during the season, returning from the "George," Portsmouth, on Mondays, Wednesdays, and Fridays. In the earlier years of its running, the "Rocket" made good time, taking eight and a half hours, up or down; but its quickest time was made on the down journey during the season of 1881, when it left Piccadilly at 11.10 a.m., and reached Portsmouth at seven p.m. = seven hours fifty minutes, inclusive of seven changes, as against six changes in previous seasons. Captain Hargreaves was the bold projector of this long-distance coach, and since his retirement from the road none other has had the enterprise sufficient for so great an undertaking. The Portsmouth Road has known no through coach since his "Rocket" was discontinued. The Postmaster-General of this age of railways is, however, about to try an interesting and important revival of the old-time mail-coach along a portion of this route, as far as Guildford; and it is understood that, should his venture prove successful, this journey will be extended to Portsmouth. Meanwhile, night coaches will run, carrying the Parcel mails, from St. Martin's-le-Grand to Guildford, going by way of Epsom and Leatherhead. The reason for this reversion to old methods is that the railway companies demand rates for the carriage of the Parcel mails which, in the opinion of the Postal Department, are excessive, amounting as they do to about fifty-five per cent. of the gross receipts for the parcels carried. The coaches will leave London at ten p.m., arriving at Guildford at two a.m.; while, from Guildford, branch coaches will probably run, to serve the more remote country towns of Surrey.

HOME.

INDEX

ABBOT, George, Archbishop of Canterbury, 156—160, 235.
Abbot's Hospital, 59, 158, 235.
Abershawe, Jeremiah, 67—69.

BATTERSEA Rise, 63.
Bere, Forest of, 1, 326, 327, 328.
Bowling Green House, 78.
Buckingham, George Villiers, Duke of, 38.
Buriton, 20, 273, 285—294.
Butser Hill, 225, 295—297.
Byng, Admiral, 48—56.

CATHERINGTON, 320.
Chalton Downs, 225, 301, 320.
Charlotte, Princess of Wales, 127—134.
Charterhouse School, 188.
Clare, Earl of, 123.
Claremont, 120—134.
Clive, Lord, 124—127, 134.
Coaches—
    "Accommodation," the, 217.
    "Britannia Fly," the, 338.
    "Defiance," the, 217.
    "Flying Machine," the, 362.
    "Hero," the, 30, 363.
    "Independent," the, 217.
    "Light Post" Coach, the, 30.
    "Nelson," the, 215, 363.
    "New Times," the, 11, 94, 146, 147.
    "Night Post" Coach, the, 30.
    Perseverance," the, 104.
    Portsmouth Fly," the, 330.
    Portsmouth Machine," the, 29.

Coaches (*continued*)—
    "Portsmouth Regulator," the, 30.
    "Red Rover," the, 165.
    "Regulator," the, 363.
    "Rocket," the, 2, 10, 30, 216, 363.
    "Rocket," the new, 11, 81, 94, 259, 366.
    "Royal Mail," the, 30, 362, 363.
    "Star of Brunswick," the, 212, 216, 218.
    "Tally-ho," the, 104—118.
    "Tantivy," the, 218.
    "Telegraph," the, 30, 165, 166.
    "True Blue," the, 338.
    "Wanderer," the, 217.
Coaching Age, the, 2—11, 29, 118, 161—169, 175, 211—219, 362—367.
Coaching Notabilities—
    Balchin, William, 216.
    Brown, E., 194.
    Carter, James, 212, 218.
    Carter, Samuel, 215.
    Cotton, Sir St. Vincent, 8—10.
    Falconer, Francis, 216.
    Hargreaves, Capt., 11, 94, 259, 366.
    Jones, Capt. Tyrwhitt, 8.
    Nicholls, Robert, 217.
    "Nimrod," 108.
    Peers, John, 166.
    Rumney, P. J., 104, 107.
    Shoolbred, Walter, 11, 94.
    Stevenson, William, 8.
    Weller, Sam, 217.
    Worcester, Marquis of, 10.

INDEX

Cobbett, Richard, 202, 225—227, 282.
Cobham Street, 42, 135, 137, 239, 267.
Cold Ash Hill, 208, 219
Cortis, H. L., 146.
Cosham, 352.
Croft, Sir Richard, 128—131.
Croker, 98.
Cromwell, Oliver, 13.
Cromwell, Thomas, 15.
Cycling, 83, 140—146.

DEVIL'S Punch Bowl, 62, 197, 202, 218.
Dickens, Charles, Birthplace of, 356.
Ditton Marsh, 97.
Dorking, 104, 107, 114.
Duelling, 73, 78.
Duels—
    Lord Castlereagh and George Canning, 77.
    Lord Chandos and Col. Compton, 73.
    General Lorenzo Moore and Miles Stapylton, 77.
    Lord Paget and Capt. Cadogan, 77.
    William Pitt and George Tierney, 74.
    Duke of York and Col. Lennox, 73.

ESHER, 98, 118.

FAIRMILE Common, 135.
Farnborough, 218.
Felton, John, 38.
Fitzclarence, Lord Adolphus, 219.

GIBBON, Edward, 14, 17—20, 288—293.
Godalming, 41, 89, 170, 173—193, 216.
Godbold, Nathaniel, 184.
Gordon Riots, 29.
Guildford, 1, 59, 147—169, 217, 239, 366, 367.
Guildford Castle, 152—155.

HAMILTON, Hon. Charles, 137.
Hamilton, Lady Anne, 132.
Hampshire, 219, 224.
Hanway, Jonas, 42—47.
Harting Coombe, 268, 271, 315.
Highwaymen, 65, 67—72, 296, 301—305.
Hilsea, 218, 353.
Hindhead, 194, 197—203, 207, 211, 296, 305.
Hinton House, 326.
Hook, Theodore, 20—22, 98.
Horndean, 218, 301, 320, 325, 326 327.
Hungate, Sir Henry, 38.
Hyde, Sir Nicholas, 325.

INNS—
    "Anchor," the, Ripley, 140.
    "Angel," the, Ditton, 140.
    "Angel," the, Guildford, 161.
    "Angel," the, Strand, 30.
    "Bald-faced Stag," the, 67.
    "Bear," the, Esher, 101.
    "Belle'Alliance," the, 327.
    "Belle Sauvage," the, 30, 216.
    "Berkeley" Hotel, the, 94.
    "Blue Posts," the, Portsmouth, 30, 216, 301, 358, 362.
    "Burford Bridge" Hotel, the, 112.
    "Castle," the, Petersfield, 233, 278, 281.
    "Castle and Falcon," the, Aldersgate Street, 215.
    "Coach and Horses," the, Gravel Hill, 297.
    "Coach and Horses," the, Hilsea, 218.
    "Cock and Bottle," the, St. Martin's Lane, 37.
    "Cross Keys," the, Wood Street, 22, 217.
    "Crown," the, Guildford, 161.
    "Dog and Duck," the, 28.
    "Dolphin," the, Petersfield, 281—283.
    "Eagle," the, City Road, 362.

INDEX

Inns (*continued*)—
  "Elephant and Castle," the, 2, 11, 22—27, 29, 33, 34.
  "Flying Bull," the, Rake, 218, 268.
  "Fountain," the, Portsmouth, 30, 216, 217, 358, 363.
  "George," the, Portsdown Hill, 351.
  "George," the, Portsmouth, 30, 217, 363.
  "George and Gate," the, Gracechurch Street, 30.
  "Globe," the, Portsmouth, 215.
  "Golden Cross," the, Charing Cross, 22, 30.
  "Green Man," the, Putney Heath, 72.
  "Green Posts," the, Hilsea, 219.
  "Heroes of Waterloo," the, 328.
  "Huts" Hotel, the, 139.
  "Jolly Butchers," the, 93.
  "Jolly Drovers," the, 271.
  "King's Arms," the, Godalming, 175.
  "King's Arms," the, Portsmouth, 363.
  "Mitre," the, Hampton Court, 107.
  "New Inn," the, Old Change, 215.
  "Quebec," the, Portsmouth, 363.
  "Ram," the, Guildford, 217.
  "Red Lion," the, Dorking, 114.
  "Red Lion," the, Guildford, 161, 235, 239.
  "Red Lion," the, Petersfield, 281.
  "Robin Hood," the, Kingston Vale, 81, 267.
  "Royal Anchor," the, Liphook, 38, 218, 232—258, 296.
  "Royal Huts," the, Hindhead, 203, 207.
  "Royal Oak," the, Portsmouth, 217.
  "Seven Thorns," the, 208, 211, 218, 219, 220.

Inns (*continued*)—
  "Spotted Dog," the, 40.
  "Spread Eagle," the, Gracechurch Street, 30, 216, 217.
  "Sussex Bell," the, 219.
  "Talbot," the, Ripley, 135.
  "Telegraph," the, Putney Heath, 79.
  "White Bear," the, Piccadilly, 2, 30.
  "White Hart," the, Guildford, 161.
  "White Hart," the, Petersfield, 281.
  "White Horse," the, Dorking, 107, 114.
  "White Horse Cellars," the, 366.
  "White Lion," the, Cobham Street, 135.

JERROLD, Douglas, 104.
Johnson, Dr. Samuel, 43.

KEAN, Charles, 320—323.
Kean, Edmund, 323.
Kennington, 27, 63.
Kingston-on-Thames, 1, 81—94, 141, 201.

LADY Holt Park, 314, 316.
Landport, 353.
Leech, John, 189.
Leopold of Saxe-Coburg, Prince, 127—134.
Leopold, Prince, Duke of Albany, 134.
Louis Philippe, King of the French, 133.
Lussher, Richard, Epitaph, 14.
Liphook, 208, 216, 222, 225, 228, 230, 232—258, 260, 267, 296.

MILFORD, 193.
Milland, 231, 259, 272.
Mole, River, 108, 112.
Monmouth, James, Duke of, 59.
More, Sir Thomas, 16.

Murders by Smugglers, 310—318.

NAPIER, Admiral Sir Charles, 320—325.
Newington, 25, 267.
"Nicholas Nickleby," 61, 297.
Nine Elms, 218.

OGLETHORPE, General, 187.
Oxenbourne Downs, 297—301.

PAIN'S Hill, 42, 138.
Pepys, Samuel, 38, 160, 161, 202, 235—239, 281, 333.
Petersfield, 1, 216, 233, 235, 272—285.
Peter the Great, 192.
"Peter Simple," 34.
Pitt, William, 74, 78—80.
Porchester, 1.
Portsdown Hill, 274, 295, 329.
Portsea Island, 353.
Portsmouth, 41, 217, 218, 235, 329, 352, 357—367.
Portsmouth Point, 360.
Press-Gang, 345—350.
Purbrook, 301, 329, 352.
Putney, 2, 11, 13.
Putney Heath, 1, 11, 72.

RAKE, 218, 260, 267, 268, 315, 317, 318, 345.
"Recruiting Sergeant," the, 93.
Ripley, 135—146, 217.
Rogues and Vagabonds, 86—90, 342—345.

SAILOR-MEN, 334—351, 358—362.
St. Catherine's Chapel, 169.
Sandown Park, 98.
Selborne, 260, 267.
Sheet, 201, 272.
Shulbrede Priory, 220.

Smith, Henry, Alderman, 65, 66.
Smuggling, 305—319.
Stoke D'Abernon, 136.
Stone's End, 1, 22.
Sugden, Sir Edward, 98.
Sword House, 65.

TARTAR Hill, 139.
Thames Ditton, 98.
Thursley, 203—207.
Tibbet's Corner, 67.
Tofts, Mary, 176—182.
Toll-houses, 267.
Travellers, Old-time, 33, 56—63, 252—258, 330—345.
Turner, J. M. W., 169, 201.
Tyndall, Professor, 207, 230.

UP Park, 273.

VANBRUGH, Sir John, 120—123.
Vauxhall, 1.
Villiers, Lord Francis, 85.
Villiers, George, Duke of Buckingham, 38.

WANDLE, River, 63.
Wandsworth, 1, 22, 63—67.
Wandsworth Road, 15.
Warren, Samuel, Q.C., 101—104.
Waterloo, 1.
Waterlooville, 327—329.
Wellington, 327.
Wesley, Rev. John, 41, 188, 190.
White, Gilbert, 201, 230, 261—267.
"White Lady," the, 98.
Wilkes, John, 28, 38, 240—252.
Wimbledon Common, 72, 80.
Wisley, 139.
Witley Common, 203.
Wolfe, General, 60.
Wolsey, Cardinal, 15, 118, 120.
Woolmer Forest, 228, 232.

Richard Clay & Sons, Limited, London & Bungay.

www.ingramcontent.com/pod-product-compliance
Lightning Source LLC
Chambersburg PA
CBHW022334230426
43664CB00040B/481